# knit to flatter

*The only instructions you'll ever need to knit sweaters that make you look good and feel great!*

## AMY HERZOG

PHOTOGRAPHS BY KAREN PEARSON
PHOTOSTYLING BY KAREN SCHAUPETER

STC CRAFT | A MELANIE FALICK BOOK      NEW YORK

Published in 2013 by Stewart, Tabori & Chang

An imprint of ABRAMS

Text copyright © 2013 by Amy Herzog

Photographs copyright © 2013 by Karen Pearson

Library of Congress Cataloging-in-Publication Data

Herzog, Amy, 1975-

  Knit to flatter / by Amy Herzog.

     pages cm

  "STC Craft/A Melanie Falick Book."

  Includes bibliographical references and index.

  ISBN 978-1-61769-017-4 (alk. paper)

1.  Knitting—Patterns.  2.  Clothing and dress measurements.  I. Title.

  TT825.H475 2013

  746.43'2—dc23

                        2012022908

Editor: Liana Allday

Designer: Meg Mateo Ilasco

Production Manager: Tina Cameron

The text of this book was composed in Museo Slab, Ostrich Sans Rounded, and Sense.

Printed and bound in China

10 9 8 7 6 5 4 3

THE ART OF BOOKS SINCE 1949

115 West 18th Street

New York, NY 10011

www.abramsbooks.com

# CONTENTS

# INTRODUCTION

The seed for this book was planted when a friend and I were chatting about a sweater she had just finished knitting. She was unhappy with the result, and we talked for a while about all of the different ways this sweater disappointed her. The thing I found most striking in our discussion was her attitude of resignation toward the whole experience—as though she had had no control over the process. It shocked me to hear this from someone I knew to be a very experienced and accomplished knitter.

This theme is pervasive in the knitting community (both on- and offline). On Ravelry's project pages, sweater after sweater is shown off the body, laying lifeless on a table or on a dress form. "It's a nice sweater, and the pattern was great, but I'm not thrilled with how it looks on me." Why do we feel this way about a process we control from start to finish?

As knitters, we have the power to create a perfectly flattering sweater every single time. If we look *acceptingly* at our figures (instead of pining for unrealistic changes), we can use our power effectively and create wardrobe staples. Don't get me wrong: This takes a bit of a paradigm shift *and* a bit of skill! You need to look at your figure with kindness; you need to approach patterns as a partnership between you and the pattern designer; and you need to be confident in your ability to make modifications.

If that sounds daunting, don't worry! These pages will give you all of the tools you need to make sweaters that fit you perfectly and flatter your figure, too.

Before I get into the details, though, I'd like to set the record straight on flattering clothing. Beauty is in the eye of the wearer. Favorite sweaters, like all favorite clothing, are pieces that make you feel great when you wear them. For many knitters, feeling great means feeling attractive, and that might mean looking slender, curvaceous, or proportional. For other knitters, it does not. Both attitudes are fine! This book is **not** intended to be restrictive. It does **not** contain a rigid set of rules. It **is** intended to help you knit sweaters that you want to wear.

All of that being said, here is my philosophy on how to create flattering sweaters: Start by choosing patterns that will make your body's natural shape look more balanced. For instance, if you have a large bust and narrow hips, you might want to incorporate features that will strike a balance between your top and bottom; if you don't really have curves, you might want to play with features that will give you more of an hourglass shape. Of course, should you desire a different result, you can use the principles presented in each chapter to achieve whatever look you want—from playing up a larger bust to creating a long, straight shape, or anything else you fancy.

To that end, this book is part pattern collection and part guidebook, and you can read it cover to cover, from basic principles to tailored patterns to modification advice. Or, if you prefer, you can study each chapter as an individual unit. Here is an overview of each chapter:

Chapter 1: Discovering Your Body Type. In this chapter, you'll get ultrafamiliar with your own beautiful bod. Learn how clothing affects the appearance of your shape, and take the measurements you'll need to knit your next favorite sweater. Also learn why the pieces in this book are constructed with set-in sleeves, what "ease" means, and how to pick your perfect size.

Chapter 2: Top-Heavy Shapes. In this section, you'll learn how to flatter bodies with broader shoulders and/or larger busts with patterns designed to make these shapes shine.

Chapter 3: Bottom-Heavy Shapes. Here you'll learn how to flatter bodies with broader hips and/or thighs with patterns designed to balance the bottom-heavy figure.

Chapter 4: Proportional Shapes. In this chapter, you'll learn how to flatter bodies with balanced proportions, with designs meant to preserve your proportional figure.

Chapter 5: Other Figure Features. Big bust? Curvy waist? Ample tummy? This chapter shows you how to accommodate the things that make your body unique.

Chapter 6: Modifications. In this chapter, you'll learn the ins and outs of modifications: what's easy, what's not, and how to do it all.

As you read (and knit!) from this book, the skills you acquire will allow you to create sweaters that fit perfectly. But *please* don't get too hung up on knitting the "right" thing. This includes limiting yourself to the sweaters in your chapter. If you love a pattern, go for it! The sweaters in this book were designed so they can be easily modified and customized for many different bodies. (I've even given you some ideas on how to do that at the end of each pattern and in Chapter 6, so if there's a sweater you're dying to have, dive in!)

You are gorgeous, readers. Let's help you knit sweaters that make you feel that way, too.

# DISCOVERING YOUR BODY TYPE

All fired up to knit your new favorite sweater? Excellent! But before you pick up your needles, you need to gather some stats about your body. Grab your camera, a measuring tape, and (maybe) a glass of wine—it's time to discover your body's true shape!

**Proportional Figure**

Jenn has narrow hips that are proportional to her bust and shoulders.

**Top-Heavy Figure**

Jackie has broad shoulders that are slightly wider than her hips.

## Understanding Body Shapes

The concept of body shape has been around for a long time. The standard fruit-or-vegetable comparisons are familiar to us all but don't exactly tell us a lot of useful information (besides, who wants to be compared to a pear or an apple?). In order to knit sweaters that fit perfectly and flatter, it's important to have a clearer understanding of your form.

The first step is to fully accept that your body has a *shape*, quite apart from its size, and that clothing can manipulate the shape of your body—for better or worse. Most of us focus on our overall size, our weight (which is just a number), or some tiny aspect of our figure that we dislike. That's a shame—for more reasons than I can fit on this page. Neither those perceived figure "flaws" nor our overall size actually have much to do with whether or not a particular piece of clothing flatters our figure. It's our *shape*, which typically stays constant as we gain or lose weight, that is the crucial determining factor.

So, then, what *is* a shape? Simply put, it is the overall outline of a body's appearance (i.e., the proportions of your features, reduced to lines and curves). Believe it or not, this low-bandwidth impression forms a large part of our mental image of how people look. (Remember: Biologically speaking, we're trying to pick out animals from a distance and choose the ripe fruit, not figure out whether one tree is slightly larger than another!) We may spend hours nitpicking a side view of our *own* body in the mirror, but we certainly don't see others that way—and this is not how they think of *us*, either! Since we are reducing the complexity of a person's entire appearance to a few brush-strokes, it should come as no surprise that there are very few basic shapes.

But before we get into the specifics of the three shapes, let's discuss what is known as the "average" woman's shape. Of course this is a misnomer because there isn't really any one average shape. But since we no longer live in a time of custom-made clothing, the fashion industry—including hand-knit designers—has settled on one shape to facilitate standard manufacturing instructions, and this "average" shape tallies pretty closely with our culture's interpretation of beauty.

Ms. Average has narrow shoulders, a moderate-size bust that is the tiniest bit smaller than her hips, an hourglass waist, legs just a bit longer than her torso, and slender limbs. When other people look at her, she appears balanced from her shoulder/bust region to her hip/thigh region, and thus falls into the *Proportional* category.

But not all shapes in the Proportional category look just like Ms. Average: A proportional figure can have a thicker or curvier waist, larger or smaller bust, longer or shorter legs, or any other combination imaginable. The key characteristic of a proportional shape is that the shoulder/bust region and hip/thigh region visually balance each other.

Some figures appear wider in the shoulder/bust area than in the hip area when viewed from the front—these figures fall into the *Top-Heavy* category. Their bust may be very large or relatively small; their waist may or may not be curvy; and their legs may be long or short. The key characteristic of a top-heavy shape is narrower hips and thighs with a broader bust or shoulders.

Finally, some figures will appear wider in the hip/thigh area. These *Bottom-Heavy* figures appear unbalanced because their narrower shoulders or bust are paired with wider hips and/or thighs. As with any other category, a bottom-heavy shape can have a bust of any size, including a large bust. The key characteristic of a bottom-heavy figure is a narrower bust/shoulders to broader hips/thighs when viewed from the front.

Regardless of what category a shape falls into, there are a few other shape characteristics that you should take into consideration. The first is whether the waist appears, *from the front*, to be noticeably narrower than the hips or bust—a curvy waist is generally a beautiful figure feature to highlight. Another shape characteristic to consider is whether your bust is substantially larger (or smaller) than the "average" B or C cup. If so, there are special things to consider and modify in order to get a great fit. Finally, there are a host of smaller bumps and bulges you might need to accommodate when knitting sweaters, like rounded shoulders, a larger stomach without a defined waist, short legs, and so on.

Bottom-Heavy Figure

Jess has hips that are wider than her bust and narrow shoulders.

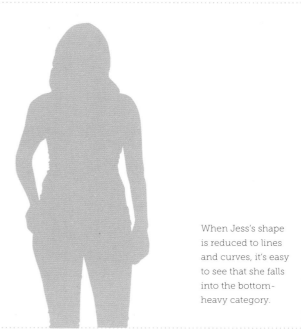

When Jess's shape is reduced to lines and curves, it's easy to see that she falls into the bottom-heavy category.

The Flutter sweater (page 57) brings Jess's bottom-heavy figure into alignment. A wide boatneck widens her shoulders and flared elbow-length sleeves draw attention to her waist.

## Flattering Features

Now that we've taken a moment to understand the different body shape categories, the next step is figuring out how to flatter those shapes. The secret to knitting sweaters that work for your shape is this: Alter the silhouette and certain design details of the sweater to create a visual effect that brings your body into balance. By changing the appearance of your proportions, you can produce the illusion of any shape you'd like. To do this, there are just a few principles to remember:

- To *widen* the appearance of some portion of your body, place a horizontal visual element over that portion.

- To *narrow* the appearance of some portion of your body, place a vertical visual element over that portion.

- To *lengthen* the appearance of some portion of your body, cover that portion in a vertical block of color and texture.

- To *shorten* the appearance of some portion of your body, break up that portion into different vertical blocks of color and texture.

- To create the illusion of *curves* on some portion of your body, wear clothes with diagonal or curved lines on or near that area.

- When working the *sleeves*, pay attention to where you place the cuffs because they draw attention to (and broaden) the coordinating spot on the body. Long sleeves typically draw the eye to the leg; three-quarter-length sleeves, to the hip; elbow sleeves, to the waist; short sleeves, to the bust.

## What's Your Shape?

A picture is worth . . . if not a thousand words, then certainly a thousand dollars of fancy yarn used to knit sweaters that make you feel great. So, get out your camera! It's time to discover your shape.

When I first wrote the tutorial series that led to this book, a bunch of girlfriends and I got together and spent several hours taking pictures, trying on sweaters, and noshing on great food and wine. While I fully endorse the strategy of making a party out of the shape pictures, it's easy to do them by yourself, too. Here's a foolproof method:

1   Remove all busy visual distractions from the place where you'll be shooting (a white wall works best).

2   Use a tripod, stack of books, or an end table to create an even surface for the camera to rest. The camera should be level with your chest and your whole body should be in frame.

3   Get yourself into something formfitting, and be sure to wear your usual foundation garments! You want these pictures to be an accurate representation of your underlying shape on a normal sweater-wearing day.

4   Stand with your feet hip-width apart, let your arms hang naturally, and face the camera squarely. If you're working alone, take a picture using the camera's timer or a remote control.

5   Now, turn so your body is perpendicular to the camera. Put your arms down at your sides and stand up straight. If you're working alone, take a picture using the camera's timer or a remote control.

6   Take a deep breath, and download the pictures to your computer.

Front view

From the front, DeeDee's bust and hips look proportional.

Profile

From the side, we see that DeeDee has a generous bosom and round backside.

Once you've taken your photos, print them out and grab a marker. Draw the following four lines across the front-view picture of yourself and then compare them:

- LINE 1: Draw the first line from just above one side of your armpit across to the other side. This line signifies the width of your upper torso. Err on the narrow side—we're trying to measure the breadth of your shoulders *without* including any of your arm.

- LINE 2: Draw a second line at the widest point of your bust. This line may or may not differ in width from your torso/shoulder line.

- LINE 3: Draw a third line at the narrowest point of your waist. Note that your narrowest point can be anywhere from just below your bust all the way down to your hips! If you're straight up and down from bust to hips, draw the line at your belly button.

- LINE 4: Draw a fourth line at the widest point of your hip region.

- LINE 5 (OPTIONAL): If your widest "bottom" point *differs from your hips*, draw an optional fifth line at. This fifth line is only necessary for women whose legs are the widest part of their hip/thigh region.

Next, compare the *widest* of the shoulder and bust lines to the hip line. Do this by drawing vertical lines straight down the photo, originating at either end of your widest bust/shoulder line and going past the widest hip/thigh line. This identifies which sets of lines are wider and by how much.

Now, look at where the vertical line crosses the hip line. If you have a proportional figure, the "bottom" lines will be just a tiny bit wider than the widest "top" line. If you have a top-heavy figure, the "top" line will be exactly the same as or larger than the largest "bottom" line. If you have a bottom-heavy figure, the "bottom" line(s) will be substantially larger than the largest "top" line.

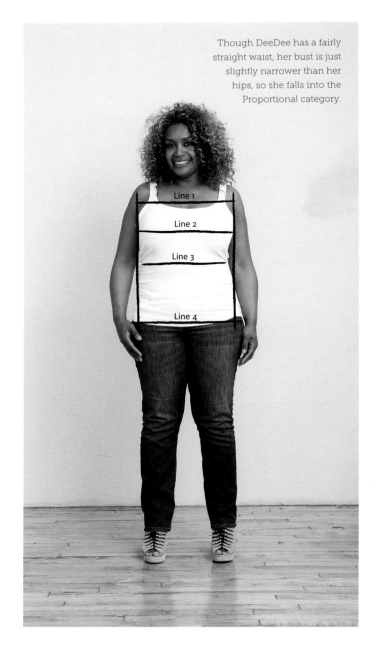

Though DeeDee has a fairly straight waist, her bust is just slightly narrower than her hips, so she falls into the Proportional category.

Line 1

Line 2

Line 3

Line 4

From this front-view picture, you can also tell if you have a curvy waist by noting whether your waist line is substantially shorter than the bust/hip lines. Finally, you can get a visual sense of your torso-to-leg proportions from this picture. Note that these characteristics, while important for fit, have nothing to do with which category your shape falls into; only the comparison of bust/shoulder to hip region will determine that.

Now, consider the second side-view picture. It is not necessary to draw lines on this photo to get a large amount of information from it. Here are some figure characteristics that will reveal themselves in a side-view photo:

- A generous bosom
- Whether you carry weight in your stomach
- Rounded shoulders
- A deep back curve
- A flat or round backside

For now, simply note these for future reference. In chapters 5 and 6, we will cover how to account for these curves (or lack thereof) in your knitting with short rows and shaping.

Thanks to these two photos, you've gained an enormous amount of data about your own shape. Keep in mind: It's just data! It's tempting to look at these photos and nitpick, but I encourage you to resist that urge. When others look at you, they focus most of their attention on your face, your attitude, and what you're saying. Your overall demeanor combined with the way your clothing flatters your underlying shape is a far more accurate view of how you look than this clinical set of pictures.

Now that you've done this exercise, you should be comfortable in your knowledge of:

- Whether you're top-heavy, proportional, or bottom-heavy.
- Whether you're curvy or straight and how sharp those curves are.
- Whether you have a long or short torso.
- Whether you're busty.
- Any special needs you'll want to accommodate.

## Learning to Love the Camera (and Yourself)

I rarely meet a woman who is happy to have her picture taken. More often than not, when a camera comes out, most of us leave the room or dive behind a nearby piece of furniture! Until recently, I was one of those people. In fact, it seemed that the only photos I ever saw of myself were taken furtively, when I was least expecting it, and when I was inevitably doing something unflattering like eating pie with my mouth open. But when I was pregnant with my second son, many of my online friends were participating in a project called "365." The idea was to share one self-portrait per day, for an entire year, on the photo site Flickr. Hopped up on hormones of one kind or another, I decided that the first year of this baby's life would be a great time to do my own 365. I'd start on the day he was born, finish on his first birthday, and have a wonderful memento of that very special slice of motherhood.

So, that's just what I did. I got very (*very*) familiar with my camera's remote option, learned the ins and outs of a tripod, and quickly discovered that you need to take at least ten shots (and often more) to ensure one of them is well lit, in focus, contains all relevant parts of your body, and involves no blinking. I kept it up, more or less, for that whole first year. And while it is a lovely collection of photos, the best part about the project was that I learned to see myself with kindness, which is how I think others see me. By the second month, I'd taken hundreds of pictures of myself. *Hundreds.* And while I wasn't exactly in the best shape of my life (see also: two months postpartum, ten-pound baby), I wasn't noticing all of the bumps and bulges and short legs anymore. I was seeing *me*—my smile, my hair, how much I was obviously enjoying (or not) whatever was happening each day.

It's a wonderful perspective to have. It's hands-down the best gift I have ever, ever given myself, and it has made me a happier person by far.

While these "shape photos" may not make you less critical of yourself, if you try hopping in *front* of the camera more often, you might be surprised by how great you really look!

## Taking Your Measurements

Of course, there's one last ingredient to making those wardrobe-staple sweaters: your measurements. Along with an understanding of your shape, they are the key to making sweaters that fit you perfectly.

The following instructions will take you through gathering your own measurements (which you should write down on page 19 or on a photocopy of that page). You'll need to work with a friend for some of them, as bending to read a tape measure can cause inaccuracies. With all measurements, except where noted, pull the tape measure snug, but not tight, and ensure that it is straight all the way around.

### BUST, WAIST, AND HIP

Most knitters are already pretty familiar with these three measurements, but here is a refresher on how to take them: Hold the tape measure at the fullest part of your bust and the smallest part of your waist, regardless of where on your torso they are located. Measure your hips at "mid-hip," which is in line with your hip bones. This will typically be somewhat smaller than your full hip measurement, which is okay, since this book isn't about knitting pants.

### UPPER TORSO

Your upper torso circumference is the single most important measurement you can take when knitting sweaters because it can and should be used as your "full bust size" when selecting a "base" pattern size to knit for yourself. When you choose a size based on your upper torso circumference, all of your sweaters will fit nicely in the hardest area of the sweater to modify: the shoulders.

To measure your upper torso circumference, run a tape measure around your upper torso, the way you did for the bust measurement, but way up in the armpit, above most of your bust tissue.

Pull the tape measure quite snug. When selecting a base size in a knitting pattern, act as though *this measurement* is your bust size and then add the amount of ease you would like to include. For more information on ease, read the box on page 16.

### NECKLINE DEPTH

Ms. Average's bust is a certain distance below her shoulder seams, and like everything else, your measurements may differ from Ms. Average's in this regard. It's important to ensure that any neckline *meant* to be deep actually opens deep enough on the wearer to visually "group" the bust with the shoulders and face (rather than with the waist and hips). Thus, it's important to know how deep a given pattern's neckline will appear on your own body. We measure this depth down from the shoulder, since that is how it will appear in a pattern schematic.

To take this measurement, place a ruler or other flat object horizontally across the fullest part of your bust so that the top of the ruler is approximately ½ to 1'' / 1.5 to 2.5 cm above the fullest part of your bust (or wherever your own personal comfort dictates a deep neckline should begin). Measure from your shoulder seam down to the ruler.

### SLEEVE LENGTHS

Your sleeves may need to be longer or shorter than specified in a pattern. It is easiest to measure sleeve length on the outside of your arm from the top of your shoulder, but many knitting patterns do not include sleeve cap height in their schematic. Thus, we need to measure the length of our arms to the sleeve cap shaping. To find the right spot, hold your arm comfortably at your side and locate a spot roughly 1 ½'' / 4 cm down from the deepest part of your armpit. Measure from this spot down your (relatively straight) arm to short-sleeve, elbow-sleeve, three-quarter sleeve, and full-sleeve lengths.

### BICEP AND WRIST

Like the bust, waist, and hip measurements, these are simple circumferences: The bicep measurement should be taken at the widest point and the wrist measurement at the narrowest point. All sweaters should have positive ease in the bicep and wrist; the amount is up to personal preference but the wrist should have *more* ease than the bicep because an extremely tapered sleeve will make the bicep appear wider than it actually is (remember, our eye sees proportion much more readily than size). A sleeve with a less-exaggerated taper will result in a more slender-looking arm.

## HIP-TO-ARMHOLE LENGTH

We'll now measure the length of your torso from hip to armhole shaping and determine where in that area your actual waistline falls.

Regardless of which shape category you belong to, you do not want your sweater to end exactly at the "low hip" point. This sweater length will typically break up a person's entire height into two equal halves, which looks innately less interesting to us than if the person's height were broken up into obviously unequal parts.

That said, proportional and top-heavy shapes tend to look best in sweaters that reach their true mid-hip (or just a smidge lower), and bottom-heavy shapes tend to look best in sweaters that end above their widest point (often at the mid-hip or just a bit higher). To find this spot, put on a shirt and pin the hem so it hits the appropriate hip point for you, then get a friend to measure both the total distance from hem (shirt hem) to armhole shaping (that same spot roughly 2'' / 5 cm down from the depth of the armpit) and note the distance from hem to narrowest waist point on that same tape measure. Then subtract to get the waist-to-armhole shaping distance, and write down all three numbers.

## BUST SHAPING MEASUREMENTS

Many knitters, when choosing a size based on their upper torso circumference, will choose a sweater size that (if unmodified) will be far too snug in the bust. Of course, a larger bust doesn't go away simply because we're knitting smaller sweaters! Unless it is accommodated, a larger bust will pull the front of the sweater out of shape, making it appear shorter in front than in back.

The knitter has two options for dealing with the bust: Either make just the front of the sweater

Take your measurements as shown on the diagram below and jot them down on page 19.

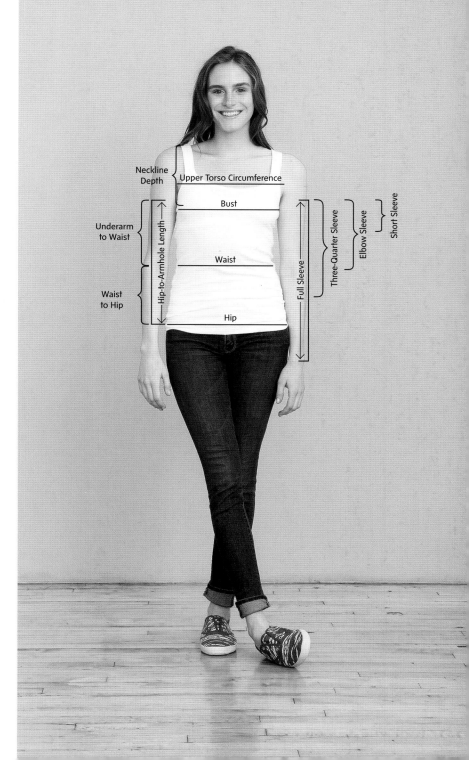

Ease is the difference between the circumference of a garment in one particular spot and the circumference of your body at the same spot. Positive ease means the garment is larger than you in that particular spot; negative ease means the garment is smaller than you in that spot; and zero ease is when the two measurements are exactly the same.

Ease recommendations in hand-knitting patterns typically refer to ease in the bust. Traditional guidelines suggest that everyone should wear sweaters with 2 to 4" / 5 to 10 cm of positive ease in the bust. But if you combine these old-timey recommendations with a busty knitter choosing a size 46" / 117 cm sweater for her 43" / 109 cm bust, you have a recipe for unhappiness! The shoulder seams will be entirely off her shoulders. Instead, I recommend adding ease to your *torso* measurement rather than your full bust measurement. I also recommend dialing back the ease recommendations a bit from a few decades ago: Tightly fitted sweaters can definitely work with zero ease in the upper torso; average-fitting sweaters with 1 to 2" / 2.5 to 5 cm of positive ease in the upper torso; oversize sweaters with 3 to 4" / 7.5 to 10 cm of positive ease in the upper torso. So, if you are a knitter with a 43"/109 cm bust and an upper torso of 39"/99 cm, you would choose a size 39"/99 cm for an extremely tailored sweater, a size 40 to 41"/101.5 to 104 cm for an average-fit sweater, and go up to a 43"/109 cm sweater only if you wanted something oversized.

Also note that if you're wearing your sweater with negative ease, it will become shorter as it stretches horizontally. If this is the case for the main body of your sweater (say, because you're allowing for an inch or two of negative ease in the fullest part of your bust), you'll need to make the body of the sweater longer than the measurements you've written down. You can use a roughly two-thirds substitution as a base rule of thumb and adjust as necessary—that is, if you're aiming for an inch of negative ease in the bust and zero ease in the hips, knit the sweater $2/3$" / 1.7 cm longer to the armholes than you planned.

The same principle applies to the sleeve lengths if you're knitting sleeves with negative ease. If you're knitting sleeves with zero or positive ease in the bicep, however, you can knit your sleeves to the exact lengths as written.

wider with vertical darts (see page 152), or make only the front of the sweater longer via short rows of bust darts (see page 155). In a few cases, both might be needed.

To find out how many inches of short rows you will need, measure the difference in length from hem to shoulder over your front and over your back. Place one measuring tape around your hips (it should be an equal distance from the floor all around your body). Have a friend measure from the top of your shoulder down your back to the top of the measuring tape around your hips, and then again on the front to the same spot, measuring over the fullest part of your bust. Take the difference, then subtract approximately 2" / 5 cm to account for the stretchability of knitwear. This is how many inches of short rows you'll need in an "average" sweater. (Tighter sweaters require more short rows; looser sweaters require fewer.)

Alternatively, if your side-view photo showed a flatter stomach combined with a larger bust, you can use vertical darts to add width just to the front of your sweater: To determine how many darts you will need, subtract your upper torso measurement from your full bust measurement; subtract approximately 1 to 2" / 2.5 to 5 cm from this difference. (Again, tighter sweaters will need more shaping and looser sweaters will need less.)

If your side-view photo showed both a large bust and a large belly, take your vertical dart measurement both at the hips and at the bust. Measure from side seam to side seam at mid-hip level across the front and back. Take the difference and this time subtract just 1" / 2.5 cm. This will give you a new cast on width for the front; see page 154 for instructions on what to do with these measurements.

## Construction

There are plenty of ways to knit a sweater. And in the long run, I don't want to steer you away from any of them. But in the short run (as in, the patterns you'll knit from this book), I'd like you to focus on garments that are knit in pieces and sewn together and that have set-in sleeves.

In my classes, this statement is almost always met with a chorus of groans and several knitters asking *"Why?! I hate seaming!"* I can almost hear you doing the same right now.

There are several reasons, actually, but first and foremost among them are those dreaded seams. Knit fabric does a great job of stretching over all of our bulges and bumps. On one hand, this is great because we don't need to take as much care in fitting our sweaters as a seamstress working with stiff cotton would. (A book on sewing perfectly fitted shirts would require a lot more detail!) However, this can also be bad news for the long-term stability and wearability of a garment. Without seams, knit sweaters tend to droop under their own weight, particularly over the shoulders, in the back, and down the sleeves. Seams provide a firm anchor point for the weight of the garment, ensuring that the sweater stays where it's supposed to.

That being said, all seams are not created equal: Shoulder seams are the most important, followed by sleeve seams, both of which are typically the weight-bearing points of the sweater. Side seams play an important role, too—without them, the fabric of the sweater will tend to cling more tightly to the body and can bias if you inadvertently add twist to your yarn while knitting. With seams, a sweater will keep its shape, nicely define yours, and appear well fitted without being clingy.

Well . . . that's *almost* true. The sweater will nicely define your shape if the *sweater* has a nice shape. The fact is, the fabric we produce as hand-knitters will never form itself to our bodies in quite the same way as a Lycra-enhanced store-bought knit will. Whether we're knitting in lace-weight or bulky yarn, our body's shape tends to appear like the sweater's shape instead of the other way around.

This is why adding waist shaping to your sweaters is the single most important thing you can do if you want to avoid looking like a box. With few exceptions, our sweaters fit best when vertical waist darts are placed *in the middle* of our sweater fronts and backs rather than at the edges. All of the sweaters in this book use this method of waist shaping, and many other sweaters are easy to modify this way, too.

You might be intrigued by this talk of seams and shaping, but doubtful that a bottom-up, in-pieces sweater could ever fit properly because it cannot be tried on like a top-down style. But oftentimes, "trying on" the sweater-in-progress involves either shoving point protectors on the needles and wriggling into the sweater with the stitches bunched in back, or slipping the sweater onto waste yarn and trying it on. In both cases, the stitches are not likely to be laying as they will in your finished garment, nor will they be pulled down by the weight of the finished garment, so you won't necessarily get an accurate read on how the sweater will eventually look when it's done.

I *promise* you that if you start with a pieced sweater and your measurements, you will get a perfect fit.

## Pre-Knitting Checklist

To help your confidence, let's go through a checklist for making sure the fit of your next sweater will be spot-on.

- Begin by choosing a base size for your sweater by comparing the pattern's finished full bust circumference to your upper torso measurement, plus ease (see page 16).

- Examine the pattern's schematic and identify all of the measurements for your size. Then compare them to your own measurements. Make a note of any measurements that differ (e.g., sweater length to underarm shaping, neckline depth, sleeve length, etc.).

- It's entirely likely that some part of your body won't match up perfectly with the pattern's schematics, in which case you'll need to make some modifications. Take a good look at Chapter 6 and determine what needs to change.

- Now, photocopy the pattern and note where you'll make any changes you've identified.

Where do measurements in knitting patterns come from? For hand-knitting designers, Ms. Average (remember her?) has been reduced to a convenient and comprehensive set of measurements based on bust size. That means that for any given bust size, all other measurements (the arm length, shoulder breadth, torso length, neck width, bicep circumference, bust height, and so on) assume that you share Ms. Average's proportional shape. If you share Ms. Average's shape, these measurements will work well for you—and they will not work so well for you if you don't. Plus-size knitters, knitters with larger busts, and many, many more women will need to make modifications from the as-written pattern instructions.

But that's okay! (In fact, it couldn't possibly be any other way. Can you imagine a knitting pattern written in 100+ sizes?) The good news is: If your shape differs from the standard measurement table (like the one shown below), it will always differ in the same way, so you'll make the same modifications to nearly every sweater pattern you knit. Once you know how to select the appropriate size for your body and make these modifications, the world of well-fit sweaters will be yours.

| WOMAN'S SIZE | X-SMALL | SMALL | MEDIUM | LARGE | 1X | 2X | 3X | 4X | 5X |
|---|---|---|---|---|---|---|---|---|---|
| Bust (in) | 28–30 | 32–34 | 36–38 | 40–42 | 44–46 | 48–50 | 52–54 | 56–58 | 60–62 |
| (cm) | 71–76 | 81.5–86.5 | 91.5–96.5 | 101.5–106.5 | 112–117 | 122–127 | 132–137 | 142–147 | 152–157.5 |
| Waist | 23–24 | 25–26½ | 28–30 | 32–34 | 36–38 | 40–42 | 44–45 | 46–47 | 49–50 |
| | 58.5–61 | 63.5–67.5 | 71–76 | 81.5–86.5 | 91.5–96.5 | 101.5–106.5 | 112–114.5 | 117–119 | 124.5–127 |
| Hips | 33–34 | 35–36 | 38–40 | 42–44 | 46–48 | 52–53 | 54–55 | 56–57 | 61–62 |
| | 83.5–86.5 | 89–91.5 | 96.5–101.5 | 106.5–112 | 117–122 | 132–134.5 | 137–139.5 | 142–144.5 | 155–157.5 |
| Bicep Circumference | 9¾ | 10¼ | 11 | 12 | 13½ | 15½ | 17 | 18½ | 19½ |
| | 25 | 26 | 28 | 30.5 | 34.5 | 39.5 | 43 | 47 | 49.5 |

Measurements based on those provided by the Craft Yarn Council.

## Ready, Set, Knit!

And there you have it! You now know into which shape category you fall and the ways in which you differ from Ms. Average. You know your measurements and the general ways in which clothing manipulates your shape's appearance. You know about sweater construction and why I recommend choosing a size based on your upper torso measurement. In short: You're ready to make your new sweater!

Now, I encourage you to seek out your "own" chapter—Top-Heavy Shapes (page 20), Bottom-Heavy Shapes (page 46), and Proportional Shapes (page 72)—for specific advice and designs created just for you. Once you've finished your first incredibly fantastic sweater, I suggest you glance through the other chapters. Let yourself fall in love and then modify the design so that it fits just the way you like. (Remember, all the details you need for modifications are in Chapter 6.)

## Your Measurements

Use this worksheet to jot down your measurement as you take them, as well as any ease you would like to add. All of the measurements included here are used on the pattern schematics in this book.

| MEASUREMENT | INCHES/CM | EASE | YOUR MEASUREMENTS + EASE |
|---|---|---|---|
| Bust | | | |
| Waist | | (I recommend adding 1–2" / 2.5–5 cm for comfort) | |
| Hip | | (I recommend subtracting 1" / 2.5 cm to avoid "floating" sweater hem) | |
| Upper Torso | | (Close fit: 0–1" / 0–2.5 cm of ease; Average fit: 1–2" / 2.5–5 cm; Roomy fit: 2–3" / 7.5–10 cm) | |
| Neckline Depth | | | |
| Short-Sleeve Length | | | |
| Elbow-Sleeve Length | | | |
| Three-Quarter-Sleeve Length | | | |
| Full-Sleeve Length | | | |
| Bicep Circumference | | (I recommend 0–2" / 0–5 cm of ease) | |
| Wrist Circumference | | (I recommend 2–3" / 5–7.5 cm of ease at the narrowest part of the wrist) | |
| Hip-to-Waist Length | | | |
| Waist-to-Armhole Length | | | |
| Hip-to-Armhole Length | | | |
| Vertical Bust Darts | | | |
| Short Row Shaping | | | |

# TOP-HEAVY SHAPES

Are you the proud owner of a powerful set of shoulders? A bodacious bust? Some of both? Are they paired with narrower hips? Welcome to the top-heavy club! You're in good company—athletes and models also tend to be top heavy, and many (like you) struggle to find perfectly fitted tops. Of course, that's not an issue for the savvy hand-knitter.

Top-heavy shapes in three different ways (left to right): Morgan has a large bust and narrow shoulders; Jackie has broad shoulders and a large bust; Ann has broad shoulders with a smaller bust.

## Welcome to the Top-Heavy Club

If the photo you took of yourself from the front (see page 11) revealed that your shoulder or bust lines are wider than or equal to your hip line, then your top half will appear wider than your bottom half when viewed from the front. This means you fall into the top-heavy category! It's possible for a person's shape to appear top-heavy because their narrower hips are paired with a large bust, broad shoulders, or both. Nothing is ever universal when we're talking about all of humanity, but it's typically the case that top-heavy shapes have a hip circumference equal to or smaller than their upper torso (in the case of broad-shouldered shapes) or bust (in the case of bustier shapes). But again, don't get too hung up on the measurements! It's really your outline as viewed from the front that matters.

In addition to the hallmark broader-top-with-narrower-hips combination, you'll typically find a few other characteristics in top-heavy shapes, such as:

- Longer legs
- Slimmer upper arms
- A tendency to carry weight in the tummy (especially for large-busted top-heavy women)

## Perfect Top-Heavy Sweaters

When selecting a sweater pattern, remember this: Our eye registers shape much more easily than size, so you will want to find a pattern that creates the illusion of a more balanced figure, then modify that pattern as needed. Top-heavy shapes are generally most flattered by clothing that broadens the appearance of the hips while minimizing the shoulder/bust region, which brings the proportions into alignment.

Since horizontal visual elements broaden a region of the wearer's body and vertical visual elements narrow it, top-heavy shapes are flattered by sweaters that, when laid flat on a table, appear broader at the hem than at the neckline.

This can be achieved in many ways: To broaden the appearance of the hips, you can use wide bands of ribbing, colorwork, or other texture at the hem, or you can make three-quarter-length or longer sleeves, which typically end in line with the hem of

the sweater, widening the lower region of the body. Pair these features with narrowing elements at the neckline/torso region, like a deep, narrow V neckline, an open cardigan front, or vertical stripes. Together, these visual elements will balance out the top-heavy figure.

## Less Ideal Choices

As for all shapes, there are sweater elements that throw a top-heavy shape further out of proportion. The following elements tend to be less flattering for a top-heavy figure and should be used with caution (and lots of balancing elements!):

- Broad, shallow necklines that widen the shoulders and lengthen the appearance of the bust can be difficult for a top-heavy wearer. Boatnecks, colorful Fair Isle yokes, and wide cowls all fall into this category.

- Top-heavy shapes tend to look wider overall in sleeve constructions that result in excess fabric at the underarms. These include drop-shoulder construction, dolman sleeves, oversize set-in sleeves, and (for very busty shapes) raglan constructions.

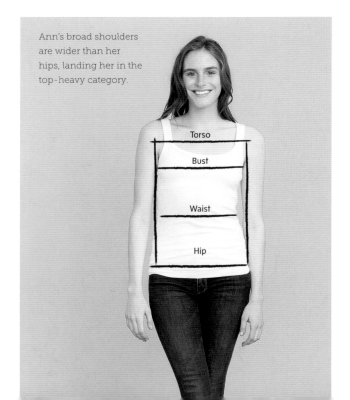

Ann's broad shoulders are wider than her hips, landing her in the top-heavy category.

- Cropped or shorter sweater lengths tend to fall directly in the middle of a top-heavy shape's most pudge-prone region, drawing the eye toward narrower hips. This tends to give top-heavy figures an unbalanced look.

- Short sleeves tend to draw the eye upward to the bust/shoulder region and have a broadening effect, which can be tricky to pull off with a top-heavy shape.

## Common Modifications

Have a pattern in hand? All set to knit your favorite sweater? Before you get started, consider the following common modifications for top-heavy shapes and check out Chapter 6 for instructions that might apply to you.

- Sweaters for top-heavy shapes often require less waist shaping on the front of the sweater than the back because more weight is usually carried in the front (see page 147).

- Bust darts are a frequent requirement for busty top-heavy shapes (see page 152).

- Top-heavy shapes typically need to lengthen the body of the sweater to ensure it maximizes the hip width (see page 148).

- Sometimes it can help to narrow the neckline of a sweater to ensure it rests close to the neck and presents a vertical visual impression. (See page 150 for more on changing necklines.)

## Flattering Features For Top-Heavy Sweaters

To flatter a top-heavy figure, look for sweater patterns with the following features:

### STYLES

Cardigans (particularly great when worn open) with deep, prominent hem treatments, and garments with longer lengths. If you include cables, stripes, and lace patterns, make sure they are used in vertical panels.

### NECKLINES

Deep V-necks, narrow scoopnecks, turtlenecks, or crewnecks.

### SLEEVES

Belled or triangular sleeves, which widen the entire length of the belled portion. Sleeves that are three-quarter length (or longer) draw the eye to the leg and widen the hips.

The long lapels draw the eye down toward the legs and broaden the appearance of the hips.

Deep 1x1 ribs and the long, open cardigan both have a slimming effect.

Ann is wearing the vest in size 32–33" (81.5–84 cm) with approximately 2" (5 cm) positive ease in the upper torso.

# DRAPER VEST/CARDIGAN

Top-heavy shapes look great in long, clean vertical lines, and this "multiple choice" vest/cardigan pattern is all about them. (Ann is wearing the vest, at left, and Jackie is wearing the cardigan on page 29.) While the texture of the collar panels allow the sweater to fall smoothly over the body and minimize a thicker middle, the vertical waist shaping keeps the sweater from looking boxy.

• • • • • • • • • • • • • • • • • • • • • • • • •

## SIZES

To fit upper torso sizes 28–29 (30–31, 32–33, 34–35, 36–37, 38–39, 40–41, 44–45, 48–49, 52–53)" [71–73.5 (76–78.5, 81.5–84, 86.5–89, 91.5–94, 96.5–99, 101.5–104, 112–114.5, 122–124.5, 132–134.5) cm]

## FINISHED MEASUREMENTS

30 (32, 34, 36, 38, 40, 42, 46, 50, 54)" [76 (81.5, 86.5, 91.5, 96.5, 101.5, 106.5, 117, 127, 137) cm] chest

*Note: Vest/Cardigan is intended to be worn with 1–2" (2.5–5 cm) positive ease in the upper torso.*

## YARN

Lorna's Laces Sportmate [70% superwash merino wool / 30% outlast viscose; 270 yards (247 meters) / 100 grams]: **Vest:** 4 (4, 4, 5, 5, 5, 6, 7, 7, 8) hanks Pewter; **Cardigan:** 4 (5, 5, 6, 6, 6, 7, 8, 8, 9) hanks Brick

## NEEDLES

One pair straight needles size US 4 (3.5 mm)

One pair double-pointed needles (dpn) size US 4 (3.5 mm)

Change needle size if necessary to obtain correct gauge.

## NOTIONS

Stitch markers

## GAUGE

24 sts and 32 rows = 4" (10 cm) in Stockinette stitch (St st)

32 sts and 32 rows = 4" (10 cm) in 1x1 Rib

## NOTES

Unless otherwise specified, decreases should be worked to match the slant of the edge being shaped, as follows: For left-slanting edges: On RS rows, k1, ssk, work to end; on WS rows, work to last 3 sts, ssp, p1. For right-slanting edges: On RS rows, work to last 3 sts, k2tog, k1; on WS rows, p1, p2tog, work to end. Increases should also be worked to match the slant of the edge being shaped, as follows: For right-slanting edges: On RS rows, work 1 st, M1-r, work to end; on WS rows, work to last st, M1-p, work 1 st. For left-slanting edges: On RS rows, work to last st, M1-l, work 1 st; on WS rows, work 1 st, M1-p-l, work to end.

## STITCH PATTERN

### 1x1 Rib

(even number of sts; 1-row repeat)

**Row 1 (RS):** *K1, p1; repeat from * to end.

**Row 2:** Knit the knit sts and purl the purl sts as they face you.

Repeat Row 2 for 1 x 1 Rib.

## BACK

CO 90 (96, 102, 108, 114, 120, 126, 138, 150, 162) sts. Begin 1x1 Rib; work even for 1" (2.5 cm).

**Next Row (RS):** Change to St st; work even until piece measures 2 ½" (6.5 cm) from the beginning, ending with a RS row.

**Next Row (WS):** P30 (32, 34, 36, 38, 40, 42, 46, 50, 54), pm, p30 (32, 34, 36, 38, 40, 42, 46, 50, 54), pm, purl to end.

### Shape Waist

**Decrease Row (RS):** Decrease 2 sts this row, then every 8 rows 4 times, as follows: Knit to 2 sts before first marker, ssk, sm, knit to next marker, sm, k2tog, knit to end—80 (86, 92, 98, 104, 110, 116, 128, 140, 152) sts remain. Work even until piece measures 8" (20.5 cm) from the beginning, ending with a WS row.

## Shape Bust

**Increase Row (RS):** Increase 2 sts this row, then every 8 rows 4 times, as follows: Work to first marker, M1-r, sm, work to next marker, sm, M1-l, work to end—90 (96, 102, 108, 114, 120, 126, 138, 150, 162) sts. Work even, removing markers on first row, until piece measures 13 ½ (13 ¾, 14, 14 ¼, 14 ½, 14 ¾, 15, 15 ½, 16, 16)" [34.5 (35, 35.5, 36, 37, 37.5, 38, 39.5, 40.5, 40.5) cm] from the beginning, ending with a WS row

## Shape Armholes

**Next Row (RS):** BO 6 (6, 6, 6, 6, 6, 8, 10, 12, 14) sts at beginning of next 2 rows, 2 (2, 2, 2, 2, 4, 4, 6, 8, 10) sts at beginning of next 2 rows, then decrease 1 st each side every other row 2 (4, 5, 7, 7, 6, 6, 6, 7, 6) times—70 (72, 76, 78, 84, 88, 90, 94, 96, 102) sts remain. Work even until armhole measures 5 ½ (6, 6 ¼, 6 ½, 7, 7 ¼, 7 ½, 7 ¾, 8, 8 ½)" [14 (15, 16, 16.5, 18, 18.5, 19, 19.5, 20.5, 21.5) cm], ending with a WS row.

## Shape Neck

**Next Row (RS):** K22 (22, 23, 24, 26, 27, 27, 28, 29, 31), join a second ball of yarn, BO center 26 (28, 30, 30, 32, 34, 36, 38, 38, 40) sts, knit to end. Working both sides at the same time, purl 1 row. Decrease 1 st at each neck edge every other row twice—20 (20, 21, 22, 24, 25, 25, 26, 27, 29) sts remain each side for shoulders. Work even until armhole measures 6 ½ (7, 7 ¼, 7 ½, 8, 8 ¼, 8 ½, 8 ¾, 9, 9 ½)" [16.5 (18, 18.5, 19, 20.5, 21, 21.5, 22, 23, 24) cm], ending with a WS row.

## Shape Shoulders

**Next Row (RS):** BO 10 (10, 11, 11, 12, 13, 13, 13, 14, 15) sts at each armhole edge once, then 10 (10, 10, 11, 12, 12, 12, 13, 13, 14) sts once.

## LEFT FRONT

CO 46 (48, 52, 54, 58, 60, 64, 70, 76, 82) sts. Begin 1x1 Rib; work even for 1" (2.5 cm).

**Next Row (RS):** Change to St st; work even until piece measures 2 ½" (6.5 cm) from the beginning, ending with a RS row.

**Next Row (WS):** P23 (24, 26, 27, 29, 30, 32, 35, 38, 41), pm, purl to end.

## Shape Waist

**Decrease Row (RS):** Decrease 1 st this row, then every 8 rows 4 times, as follows: Knit to 2 sts before marker, ssk, sm, knit to end—41 (43, 47, 49, 53, 55, 59, 65, 71, 77) sts remain. Work even until piece measures 8" (20.5 cm) from the beginning, ending with a WS row.

## Shape Bust

**Increase Row (RS):** Increase 1 st this row, then every 8 rows 4 times, as follows: Work to marker, M1-r, sm, work to end—46 (48, 52, 54, 58, 60, 64, 70, 76, 82) sts. Work even, removing marker on first row, until piece measures 13 ½ (13 ¾, 14, 14 ¼, 14 ½, 14 ¾, 15, 15 ½, 16, 16)" [34.5 (35, 35.5, 36, 37, 37.5, 38, 39.5, 40.5, 40.5) cm] from the beginning, ending with a WS row.

## Shape Armhole and Neck

*Note: Armhole and neck shaping are worked at the same time; please read entire section through before beginning.*

**Next Row (RS):** BO 6 (6, 6, 6, 6, 6, 8, 10, 12, 14) sts at armhole edge once, 2 (2, 2, 2, 2, 4, 4, 6, 8, 10) sts once, then decrease 1 st at armhole edge every other row 2 (4, 5, 7, 7, 6, 6, 6, 7, 6) times. AT THE SAME TIME, beginning on the fifth shaping row, work neck shaping as follows:

**Next Row (RS):** Decrease 1 st at neck edge every other row 16 (16, 18, 17, 19, 19, 21, 22, 22, 23) times—20 (20, 21, 22, 24, 25, 25, 26, 27, 29) sts remain. Work even until armhole measures 6 ½ (7, 7 ¼, 7 ½, 8, 8 ¼, 8 ½, 8 ¾, 9, 9 ½)" [16.5 (18, 18.5, 19, 20.5, 21, 21.5, 22, 23, 24) cm], ending with a WS row.

### Shape Shoulder

**Next Row (RS):** BO 10 (10, 11, 11, 12, 13, 13, 13, 14, 15) sts at armhole edge once, then 10 (10, 10, 11, 12, 12, 12, 13, 13, 14) sts once.

## RIGHT FRONT

Work as for Left Front, reversing st pattern and all shaping.

## LEFT COLLAR

CO 5 sts.

### Shape Lower Edge

**Increase Row 1 (RS):** K1, M1, p1, work in 1x1 Rib to end—6 sts.

**Increase Row 2:** Slip 1, work in 1x1 Rib as established to last st, M1, p1—7 sts.

Repeat Increase Rows 1 and 2 nine times—25 sts. Place marker at end of last row. Work even in 1x1 Rib, slipping first st of every WS row, until piece measures 14 (14 ¼, 14 ½, 14 ¾, 15, 15 ¼, 15 ½, 16, 16 ½, 16 ½)" / 35.5 (36, 37, 37.5, 38, 38.5, 39.5, 40.5, 42, 42) cm] from marker, ending with a RS row.

### Shape Neck Edge

**Next Row (WS):** Repeat Increase Row 2 every other row 16 (16, 18, 17, 19, 19, 21, 22, 22, 23) times—41 (41, 43, 42, 44, 44, 46, 47, 47, 48) sts. Work even until piece measures 20 (20 ¾, 21 ¼, 21 ¾, 22 ½, 23, 23 ½, 24 ¼, 25, 25 ½)" [51 (52.5, 54, 55, 57, 58.5, 59.5, 61.5, 63.5, 65) cm] from first marker. Place second marker. Work even until piece measures 3 ¼ (3 ¼, 3 ¼, 3 ¼, 3 ½, 3 ½, 3 ¾, 4 ¼, 4, 4 ¼)" [8.5 (8.5, 8.5, 8.5, 9, 9, 9.5, 11, 10, 11) cm] from second marker. BO all sts in pattern.

## RIGHT COLLAR

Work as for Left Collar, reversing st pattern and shaping.

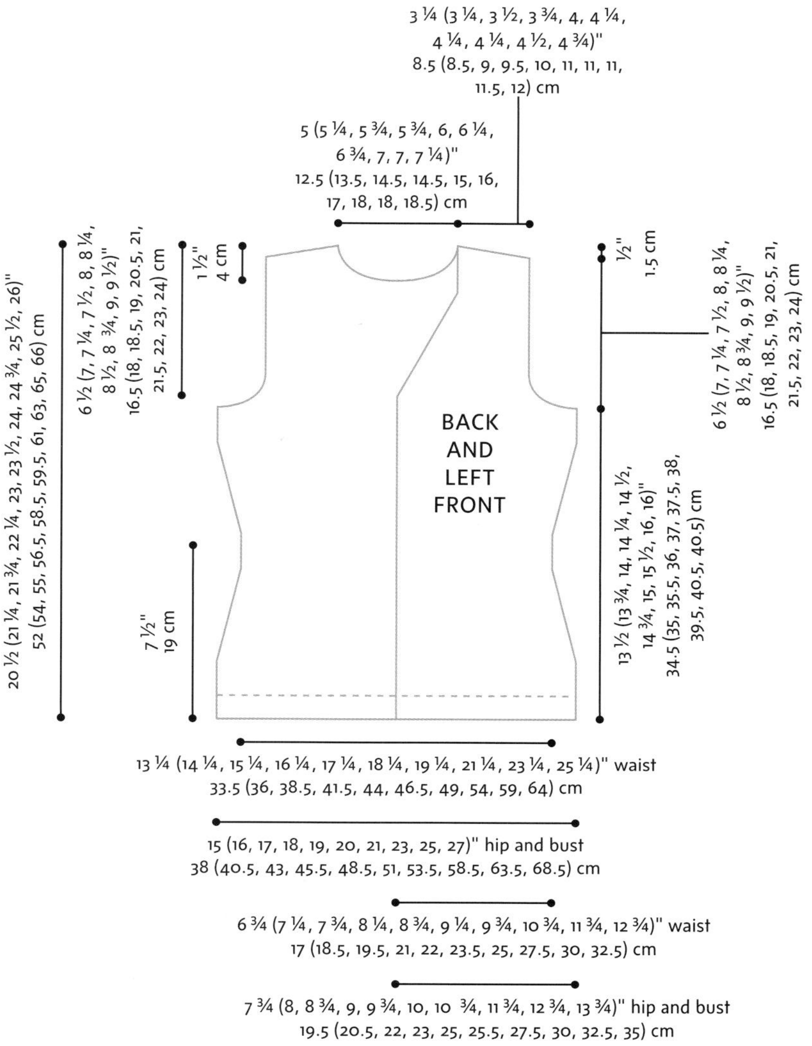

3 ¼ (3 ¼, 3 ½, 3 ¾, 4, 4 ¼, 4 ¼, 4 ¼, 4 ½, 4 ¾)"
8.5 (8.5, 9, 9.5, 10, 11, 11, 11, 11.5, 12) cm
5 (5 ¼, 5 ¾, 5 ¾, 6, 6 ¼, 6 ¾, 7, 7, 7 ¼)"
12.5 (13.5, 14.5, 14.5, 15, 16, 17, 18, 18, 18.5) cm
20 ½ (21 ¼, 21 ¾, 22 ¼, 23, 23 ½, 24, 24 ¾, 25 ½, 26)"
52 (54, 55, 56.5, 58.5, 59.5, 61, 63, 65, 66) cm
6 ½ (7, 7 ¼, 7 ½, 8, 8 ¼, 8 ½, 8 ¾, 9, 9 ½)"
16.5 (18, 18.5, 19, 20.5, 21, 21.5, 22, 23, 24) cm
1 ½"
4 cm
7 ½"
19 cm
BACK AND LEFT FRONT
½"
1.5 cm
6 ½ (7, 7 ¼, 7 ½, 8, 8 ¼, 8 ½, 8 ¾, 9, 9 ½)"
16.5 (18, 18.5, 19, 20.5, 21, 21.5, 22, 23, 24) cm
13 ½ (13 ¾, 14, 14 ¼, 14 ½, 14 ¾, 15, 15 ½, 16, 16)"
34.5 (35, 35.5, 36, 37, 37.5, 38, 39.5, 40.5, 40.5) cm
13 ¼ (14 ¼, 15 ¼, 16 ¼, 17 ¼, 18 ¼, 19 ¼, 21 ¼, 23 ¼, 25 ¼)" waist
33.5 (36, 38.5, 41.5, 44, 46.5, 49, 54, 59, 64) cm
15 (16, 17, 18, 19, 20, 21, 23, 25, 27)" hip and bust
38 (40.5, 43, 45.5, 48.5, 51, 53.5, 58.5, 63.5, 68.5) cm
6 ¾ (7 ¼, 7 ¾, 8 ¼, 8 ¾, 9 ¼, 9 ¾, 10 ¾, 11 ¾, 12 ¾)" waist
17 (18.5, 19.5, 21, 22, 23.5, 25, 27.5, 30, 32.5) cm
7 ¾ (8, 8 ¾, 9, 9 ¾, 10, 10 ¾, 11 ¾, 12 ¾, 13 ¾)" hip and bust
19.5 (20.5, 22, 23, 25, 25.5, 27.5, 30, 32.5, 35) cm


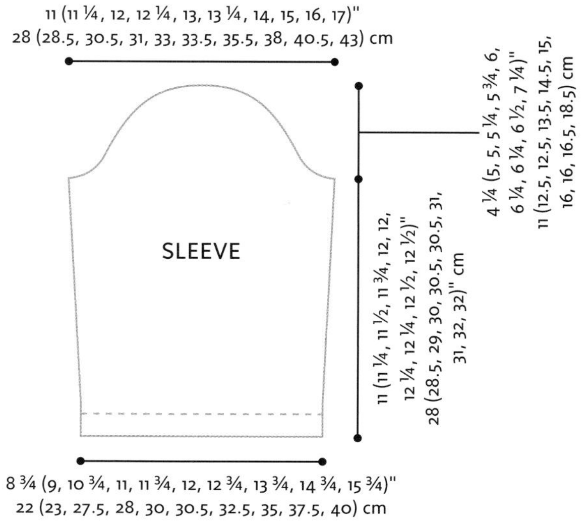

11 (11 ¼, 12, 12 ¼, 13, 13 ¼, 14, 15, 16, 17)"
28 (28.5, 30.5, 31, 33, 33.5, 35.5, 38, 40.5, 43) cm
4 ¼ (5, 5, 5 ¼, 5 ¾, 6, 6 ¼, 6 ¼, 6 ½, 7 ¼)"
11 (12.5, 12.5, 13.5, 14.5, 15, 16, 16, 16.5, 18.5) cm
SLEEVE
11 (11 ¼, 11 ½, 11 ¾, 12, 12, 12 ¼, 12 ¼, 12 ½, 12 ½)"
28 (28.5, 29, 30, 30.5, 30.5, 31, 31, 32, 32)" cm
8 ¾ (9, 10 ¾, 11, 11 ¾, 12, 12 ¾, 13 ¾, 14 ¾, 15 ¾)"
22 (23, 27.5, 28, 30, 30.5, 32.5, 35, 37.5, 40) cm

## BUST DARTS

The Cardigan sample shown has bust darts added to each Front. The pattern calls for you to increase 1 stitch at the bust every 8 rows 5 times (see Increase Row under Shape Bust for Left and Right Fronts). In order to add bust darts to the sample, Increase Rows were worked at the bust every other row instead of every 8, until a total of 10 bust Increase Rows were worked, instead of 5; this resulted in an extra 5 stitches at the bust. In order to get rid of those 5 extra stitches and end the neck shaping with the number of stitches required for the shoulders, the extra stitches were decreased along the neck edge by working 5 additional right-side Decrease Rows (see Shape Armhole and Neck for Left and Right Fronts).

## CARDIGAN SLEEVES

CO 52 (54, 64, 66, 70, 72, 76, 82, 88, 94) sts. Begin 1x1 Rib; work even for 1" (2.5 cm).

**Next Row (RS):** Change to St st; work even for 4 rows.

### Shape Sleeve

**Increase Row (RS):** Increase 2 sts this row, then every 10 (10, 20, 22, 22, 22, 22, 24, 24, 24) rows 6 (6, 3, 3, 3, 3, 3, 3, 3, 3) times—66 (68, 72, 74, 78, 80, 84, 90, 96, 102) sts. Work even until piece measures 11 (11 ¼, 11 ½, 11 ¾, 12, 12, 12 ¼, 12 ¼, 12 ½, 12 ½)" [28 (28.5, 29, 30, 30.5, 30.5, 31, 31, 32, 32) cm] from the beginning, ending with a WS row.

### Shape Cap

**Next Row (RS):** BO 6 (6, 6, 6, 6, 8, 10, 12, 14) sts at beginning of next 2 rows, 2 (2, 2, 2, 2, 4, 4, 6, 8, 9) sts at beginning of next 2 rows, decrease 1 st each side every 6 rows 1 (2, 1, 1, 1, 2, 2, 5, 6, 8) time(s), every 4 rows 0 (0, 0, 0, 0, 0, 1, 1, 1, 0) time(s), then every other row 10 (10, 13, 14, 16, 14, 13, 4, 2, 1) time(s), then BO 3 (3, 3, 3, 3, 3, 4, 4, 4) sts at beginning of next 4 rows. BO remaining 16 (16, 16, 16, 16, 16, 16, 22, 22, 22) sts.

## FINISHING

Block pieces as desired. Sew shoulder seams. With RSs of Right Front and Right Collar facing, sew shorter, shaped side edge of Right Collar to Right Front, sewing Collar along Front edge from first marker to beginning of neck edge shaping, along Front neck edge to second marker, then along Back neck edge to end. Repeat for Left Collar. With WSs of Collars facing, sew BO edges of Collars together at center Back neck. *Note: Back Collar seam will be on RS, but will be covered when Collar is folded over.*

## CARDIGAN ONLY

Set in Sleeves; sew side and Sleeve seams.

## VEST ONLY

Sew side seams.

### I-Cord Armhole Edging

With RS facing, using DPNs, and beginning at center underarm, pick up and knit 1 st for each bound-off st, and 1 st for each row around armhole opening. CO 3 sts. *Do not turn; slide sts to opposite end of dpn. Using a second dpn and bringing yarn around behind dpn to right-hand side, k2, skp (1 st from I-Cord together with 1 st from circ needle). Repeat from * until all sts on circ needle have been worked. Thread tail through remaining sts, pull tight, and fasten off.

Jackie is wearing the cardigan in size 36–37" (91.5–94 cm) with approximately 1½" (4 cm) of bust darts added and approximately zero ease in the upper torso.

## MODIFICATION IDEAS

Want to knit this sweater even though you're not top-heavy? No problem! Proportional knitters might consider making the bottom of the lapels even with the main body of the sweater by casting on the entire bottom at once rather than working the specified increases. Bottom-heavy knitters might consider shortening the lapels and also widening the neckline a bit to broaden the shoulders—for details on how to make these changes, see page 144. Shortening the sleeves is another great option for bottom-heavy knitters or knitters either wanting to draw the eye to a curvy waist (elbow sleeves) or wanting to emphasize the appearance of the bust (short sleeves). Busty knitters can add bust darts as described in the pattern, altering the number of darts worked to suit specific needs.

The narrow, deep scoopneck visually groups a large bust with the head and neck region (rather than down with the waist).

The deep ribbed hem on both the sweater and the sleeves broadens the appearance of the hips.

The vertical lace panels narrow the torso.

Morgan is wearing size 40" (101.5 cm) with 3" (7.5 cm) of bust darts added and approximately 1" (2.5 cm) of positive ease in the upper torso.

# CYPRESS CARDIGAN

The lush green color and leaf lace pattern of this cardigan make me think of a walk through a beautiful grove of cypress trees. The vertical lace panels on the front and back of the cardigan are fun to knit, and the waist shaping keeps everything shapely and tidy.

. . . . . . . . . . . . . . . . . . . . . . . . . . . . . . . . . . . . . . . . .

## SIZES

To fit upper torso sizes 30 (32, 34, 36, 38, 40, 42, 46, 50, 54)" [76 (81.5, 86.5, 91.5, 96.5, 101.5, 106.5, 117, 127, 137) cm]

## FINISHED MEASUREMENTS

31 ½ (33 ¼, 36, 37 ¾, 39 ½, 41 ¼, 43 ¾, 47 ¼, 51 ¾, 55 ¼)" [83 (84.5, 91.5, 96, 100.5, 105, 111, 120, 131.5, 140.5) cm] chest

*Note: Cardigan is intended to be worn with 1" (2.5 cm) positive ease in the upper torso.*

## YARN

Fibre Company Canopy Worsted [50% baby alpaca / 30% merino wool / 20% bamboo; 100 yards (91 meters) / 50 grams]: 7 (8, 9, 10, 10, 12, 12, 13, 15, 16) hanks Laguna

## NEEDLES

One pair straight needles size US 7 (4.5 mm)

One pair straight needles size US 8 (5 mm)

One 24" (60 cm) long circular (circ) needle size US 7 (4.5 mm)

Change needle size if necessary to obtain correct gauge.

## NOTIONS

Stitch markers; 7 (8, 8, 8, 8, 8, 8, 8, 8, 8) ¾" (19 mm) buttons

## GAUGE

20 sts and 26 rows = 4" (10 cm) in Stockinette stitch (St st), using smaller needles

## NOTES

Unless otherwise specified, decreases should be worked to match the slant of the edge being shaped, as follows: For left-slanting edges: On RS rows, k1, ssk, work to end; on WS rows, work to last 3 sts, ssp, p1. For right-slanting edges: On RS rows, work to last 3 sts, k2tog, k1; on WS rows, p1, p2tog, work to end. Increases should also be worked to match the slant of the edge being shaped, as follows: For right-slanting edges: On RS rows, work 1 st, M1-r, work to end; on WS rows, work to last st, M1-p, work 1 st. For left-slanting edges: On RS rows, work to last st, M1-l, work 1 st; on WS rows, work 1 st, M1-p-l, work to end.

## STITCH PATTERNS

**Twisted Rib**

(even number of sts; 2-row repeat)

**Row 1 (RS):** *K1-tbl, p1; repeat from * to end.

**Row 2:** *K1, p1-tbl; repeat from * to end.

Repeat Rows 1 and 2 for Twisted Rib.

**Twisted Rib for Bands**

(multiple of 2 sts + 1; 2-row repeat)

**Row 1 (WS):** P1-tbl, *k1, p1-tbl; repeat from * to end.

**Row 2:** K1-tbl, *p1, k1-tbl; repeat from * to end.

Repeat Rows 1 and 2 for Twisted Rib for Bands.

**Shell Lace for Back (see Chart)**

(multiple of 11 sts + 12; 12-row repeat)

**Row 1 (RS):** K2tog, *k5, yo, k1, yo, k2, sk2p; repeat from * to last 11 sts, k5, yo, k1, yo, k2, ssk.

**Row 2 and all WS Rows:** Purl.

**Row 3:** K2tog, *k4, yo, k3, yo, k1, sk2p; repeat from * to last 11 sts, k4, yo, k3, yo, k1, ssk.

**Row 5:** K2tog, *k3, yo, k5, yo, sk2p; repeat from * to last 11 sts, k3, yo, k5, yo, ssk.

**Row 7:** K2tog, *k2, yo, k1, yo, k5, sk2p; repeat from * to last 11 sts, k2, yo, k1, yo, k5, ssk.

**Row 9:** K2tog, *k1, yo, k3, yo, k4, sk2p; repeat from * to last 11 sts, k1, yo, k3, yo, k4, ssk.

**Row 11:** K2tog, *yo, k5, yo, k3, sk2p; repeat from * to last 11 sts, yo, k5, yo, k3, ssk.

**Row 12:** Purl.

Repeat Rows 1–12 for Shell Lace for Back.

## Shell Lace for Back

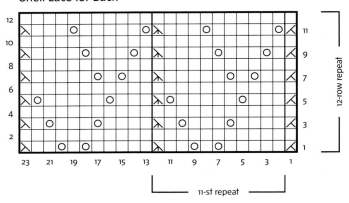

## Shell Lace for Front (see Chart)

(panel of 12 sts; 12-row repeat)

**Row 1 (RS):** K2tog, k5, yo, k1, yo, k2, ssk.

**Row 2 and all WS Row:** Purl.

**Row 3:** K2tog, k4, yo, k3, yo, k1, ssk.

**Row 5:** K2tog, k3, yo, k5, yo, ssk.

**Row 7:** K2tog, k2, yo, k1, yo, k5, ssk.

**Row 9:** K2tog, k1, yo, k3, yo, k4, ssk.

**Row 11:** K2tog, yo, k5, yo, k3, ssk.

**Row 12:** Purl.

Repeat Rows 1–12 for Shell Lace for Front.

## Shell Lace for Front

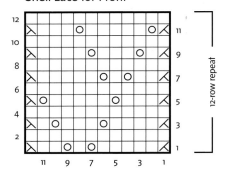

## KEY

| | |
|---|---|
| ☐ | Knit on RS, purl on WS. |
| Ⓞ | Yo |
| ╱ | K2tog |
| ╲ | Ssk |
| ╱╲ | Sk2p |

## BACK

Using larger needles and Tubular CO (see Special Techniques, page 159), CO 76 (80, 86, 90, 96, 100, 106, 116, 126, 136) sts. Begin Twisted Rib; work even until piece measures 2" (5 cm) from the beginning, ending with a WS row.

**Next Row (RS):** *Slip 1, k1; repeat from * to end.

**Next Row:** P1, M1-p 1 (1, 1, 1, 1, 1, 0, 0, 0, 0) time(s), p25 (27, 30, 32, 35, 37, 35, 40, 45, 50), pm, p23 (23, 23, 23, 23, 23, 34, 34, 34, 34), pm, purl to end—77 (81, 87, 91, 97, 101, 106, 116, 126, 136) sts.

**Next Row:** Knit to first marker, sm, work Shell Lace for Back (from text or Chart) to next marker, sm, knit to end. Work even until piece measures 3" (7.5 cm) from the beginning, ending with a RS row.

**Next Row (WS):** P24 (26, 29, 30, 32, 33, 35, 39, 42, 45), pm, work 29 (29, 29, 31, 33, 35, 36, 38, 42, 46) sts, pm, purl to end.

### Shape Waist

**Decrease Row (RS):** Decrease 2 sts this row, then every 4 rows 3 times, as follows: Knit to 2 sts before first marker, ssk, sm, knit to last marker, sm, k2tog, knit to end—69 (73, 79, 83, 89, 93, 98, 108, 118, 128) sts remain. Work even until piece measures 7" (18 cm) from the beginning, ending with a WS row.

## Shape Bust

**Increase Row (RS):** Increase 2 sts this row, then every 8 rows 3 times, as follows: Knit to first marker, M1-r, sm, work to last marker, sm, M1-l, knit to end—77 (81, 87, 91, 97, 101, 106, 116, 126, 136) sts. Work even until piece measures 13 ½ (13 ¾, 14, 14 ¼, 14 ½, 14 ¾, 15, 15, 15 ¼, 15 ½)" [34.5 (35, 35.5, 36, 37, 37.5, 38, 38, 38.5, 39.5) cm] from the beginning, ending with a WS row.

## Shape Armholes

**Next Row (RS):** BO 6 (6, 6, 6, 6, 6, 6, 8, 10, 12) sts at beginning of next 2 rows, 0 (2, 2, 2, 2, 2, 4, 6, 8, 8) sts at beginning of next 2 rows, then decrease 1 st each side every other row 3 (2, 3, 4, 4, 5, 5, 5, 5, 5) times—59 (61, 65, 67, 73, 75, 76, 78, 80, 86) sts remain. Work even until armhole measures 5 ½ (6, 6 ¼, 6 ½, 7, 8 ¼, 8 ¼, 8 ½, 8 ½, 8 ½)" [14 (15, 16, 16.5, 18, 21, 21, 21.5, 21.5, 21.5) cm], ending with a WS row.

## Shape Neck

**Next Row (RS):** Work 18 (19, 20, 21, 22, 23, 23, 24, 24, 26) sts, join a second ball of yarn, BO center 23 (23, 25, 25, 29, 29, 30, 30, 32, 34) sts, work to end. Working both sides at the same time, work even for 1 row. Decrease 1 st at each neck edge every other row twice—16 (17, 18, 19, 20, 21, 21, 22, 22, 24) sts remain each side for shoulders. Work even until armhole measures 6 ½ (7, 7 ¼, 7 ½, 8, 9 ¼, 9 ¼, 9 ½, 9 ½, 9 ½)" [16.5 (18, 18.5, 19, 20.5, 23.5, 23.5, 24, 24, 24) cm], ending with a WS row.

## Shape Shoulders

**Next Row (RS):** BO 8 (9, 9, 10, 10, 11, 11, 11, 11, 12) sts at each armhole edge once, then 8 (8, 9, 9, 10, 10, 10, 11, 11, 12) sts once.

## LEFT FRONT

Using larger needles and Tubular CO, CO 38 (40, 44, 46, 48, 50, 54, 58, 64, 68) sts. Begin Twisted Rib;

work even until piece measures 2" (5 cm) from the beginning, ending with a WS row.

**Next Row (RS):** *Slip 1, k1; repeat from * to end.

**Next Row:** P2, pm, p12 (12, 12, 12, 12, 12, 12, 12, 24, 24), pm, purl to end.

**Next Row:** Knit to first marker, sm, work Shell Lace for Front (from text or Chart) to next marker, sm, knit to end.

Work even until piece measures 3" (7.5 cm) from the beginning, ending with a RS row.

**Next Row (WS):** Work 19 (20, 22, 23, 24, 25, 27, 29, 32, 34) sts, pm, work to end.

## Shape Waist

**Decrease Row (RS):** Decrease 1 st this row, then every 4 rows 3 times, as follows: Knit to 2 sts before first marker, ssk, sm, work to end—34 (36, 40, 42, 44, 46, 50, 54, 60, 64) sts remain. Work even until piece measures 7" (18 cm) from the beginning, ending with a WS row.

## Shape Bust

**Next Row (RS):** Increase 1 st this row, then every

---

3 ¼ (3 ½, 3 ½, 3 ¾, 4, 4 ¼, 4 ¼,
4 ½, 4 ½, 4 ¾)"
8.5 (9, 9, 9.5, 10, 11, 11, 11.5, 11.5,
12) cm

5 ½ (5 ½, 5 ¾, 5 ¾, 6 ½, 6 ½,
6 ¾, 6 ¾, 7 ¼, 7 ½)"
14 (14, 14.5, 14.5, 16.5, 16.5, 17, 17,
18.5, 19) cm

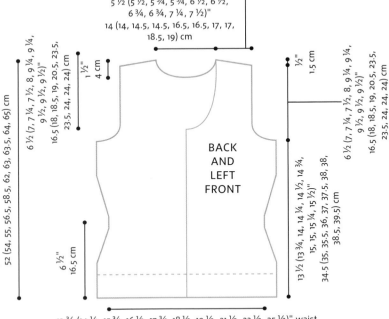

6 ½ (7, 7 ¼, 7 ½, 8, 9 ¼, 9 ¼,
9 ½, 9 ½, 9 ½)"
16.5 (18, 18.5, 19, 20.5, 23.5, 23.5,
24, 24, 24) cm

1 ½"
4 cm

BACK
AND
LEFT
FRONT

½"
1.5 cm

6 ½ (7, 7 ¼, 7 ½, 8, 9 ¼, 9 ¼,
9 ½, 9 ½, 9 ½)"
16.5 (18, 18.5, 19, 20.5, 23.5, 23.5,
24, 24, 24) cm

20 ½ (21 ¼, 21 ¾, 22 ¼, 23, 24 ½, 24 ¾, 25, 25 ¼, 25 ½)"
52 (54, 55, 56.5, 58.5, 62, 63, 63.5, 64, 65) cm

6 ½ (7, 7 ¼, 7 ½, 8, 9 ¼, 9 ¼, 9 ½, 9 ½, 9 ½)"
16.5 (18, 18.5, 19, 20.5, 23.5, 23.5, 24, 24, 24) cm

6 ½"
16.5 cm

13 ½ (13 ¾, 14, 14 ¼, 14 ½, 14 ¾,
15, 15, 15 ¼, 15 ½)"
34.5 (35, 35.5, 36, 37, 37.5, 38, 38,
38.5, 39.5) cm

13 ¾ (14 ½, 15 ¾, 16 ½, 17 ¾, 18 ½, 19 ½, 21 ½, 23 ½, 25 ½)" waist
35 (37, 40, 42, 45, 47, 49.5, 54.5, 59.5, 65) cm

15 ½ (16 ¼, 17 ½, 18 ¼, 19 ½, 20 ¼, 21 ¼, 23 ¼, 25 ¼, 27 ¼)" hip and bust
39.5 (41.5, 44.5, 46.5, 49.5, 51.5, 54, 59, 64, 69) cm

6 ¾ (7 ¼, 8, 8 ½, 8 ¾, 9 ¼, 10, 10 ¾, 12, 12 ¾)" waist
17 (18.5, 20.5, 21.5, 22, 23.5, 25.5, 27.5, 30.5, 32.5) cm

7 ½ (8, 8 ¾, 9 ¼, 9 ½, 10, 10 ¾, 11 ½, 12 ¾, 13 ½)" hip and bust
19 (20.5, 22, 23.5, 24, 25.5, 27.5, 29, 32.5, 34.5) cm

10 ¾ (11 ½, 12, 12 ½, 12 ¾, 13 ½, 14, 14 ¾, 16, 16 ¾)"
27.5 (29, 30.5, 32, 32.5, 34.5, 35.5, 37.5, 40.5, 42.5) cm

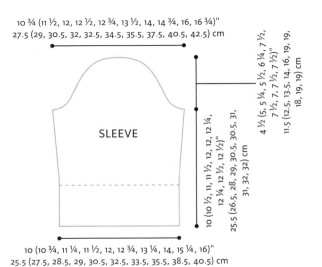

4 ½ (5, 5 ¼, 5 ½, 6 ¼, 7, 7 ½,
7 ½, 7, 7 ½, 7 ½)"
11.5 (12.5, 13.5, 14, 16, 19, 19,
18, 19, 19) cm

SLEEVE

10 (10 ½, 11, 11 ½, 12, 12, 12 ¼,
12 ¼, 12 ½, 12 ½)"
25.5 (26.5, 28, 29, 30.5, 30.5, 31,
31, 32, 32) cm

10 (10 ¾, 11 ¼, 11 ½, 12, 12 ¾, 13 ¼, 14, 15 ¼, 16)"
25.5 (27.5, 28.5, 29, 30.5, 32.5, 33.5, 35.5, 38.5, 40.5) cm

8 rows 3 times, as follows: Work to first marker, M1-r, sm, work to end—38 (40, 44, 46, 48, 50, 54, 58, 64, 68) sts. Work even until piece measures 13 ½ (13 ¾, 14, 14 ¼, 14 ½, 14 ¾, 15, 15, 15 ¼, 15 ½)" [34.5 (35, 35.5, 36, 37, 37.5, 38, 38, 38.5, 39.5) cm] from the beginning, ending with a WS row.

### Shape Armhole and Neck

*Note: Armhole and neck shaping are worked at the same time; please read entire section through before beginning.*

**Next Row (RS):** BO 6 (6, 6, 6, 6, 6, 6, 8, 10, 12) sts at armhole edge once, 0 (2, 2, 2, 2, 2, 4, 6, 8, 8) sts once, then decrease 1 st at armhole edge every other row 3 (2, 3, 4, 4, 5, 5, 5, 5, 5) times. AT THE SAME TIME, beginning on the fourth armhole shaping row, shape neck as follows:

**Next Row (WS):** BO 6 (6, 7, 7, 8, 8, 9, 8, 9, 9) sts at neck edge once, 2 (2, 2, 2, 2, 3, 2, 3, 3) sts once, decrease 1 st at neck edge every row 2 (2, 3, 3, 3, 3, 3, 3, 3) times, every other row twice, then every 4 rows 1 (1, 1, 1, 1, 1, 2, 2, 2) time(s)—16 (17, 18, 19, 20, 21, 21, 22, 22, 24) sts remain when all shaping is complete. Work even until armhole measures 6 ½ (7, 7 ¼, 7 ½, 8, 9 ¼, 9 ¼, 9 ½, 9 ½, 9 ½)" [16.5 (18, 18.5, 19, 20.5, 23.5, 23.5, 24, 24, 24) cm], ending with a WS row.

### Shape Shoulders

**Next Row (RS):** BO 8 (9, 9, 10, 10, 11, 11, 11, 11, 12) sts at armhole edge once, then 8 (8, 9, 9, 10, 10, 10, 11, 11, 12) sts once.

### RIGHT FRONT

Work as for Left Front until piece measures 2" (5 cm) from the beginning, ending with a WS row.

**Next Row (RS):** *Slip 1, k1; repeat from * to end.

**Next Row:** P24 (26, 30, 32, 34, 36, 40, 44, 38, 42), pm, purl to last 2 sts, pm, p2.

Complete as for Left Front, reversing all shaping.

### SLEEVES

Using larger needles and Tubular CO, CO 50 (54, 56, 58, 60, 64, 66, 70, 76, 80) sts. Begin Twisted Rib; work even until piece measures 3 ½" (9 cm) from the beginning, ending with a WS row.

**Next Row (RS):** *Slip 1, k1; repeat from * to end. Purl 1 row.

#### Shape Sleeve

**Next Row (RS):** Continuing in St st, increase 1 st each side this row, then every 12 rows once—54 (58, 60, 62, 64, 68, 70, 74, 80, 84) sts remain. Work even until piece measures 10 (10 ½, 11, 11 ½, 12, 12, 12 ¼, 12 ¼, 12 ½, 12 ½)" [25.5 (26.5, 28, 29, 30.5, 30.5, 31, 31, 32, 32) cm] from the beginning, ending with a WS row.

#### Shape Cap

**Next Row (RS):** BO 6 (6, 6, 6, 6, 6, 8, 10, 12) sts at beginning of next 2 rows, 0 (2, 2, 2, 2, 2, 4, 6, 7, 7) sts at beginning of next 2 rows, decrease 1 st each side every 6 rows 0 (1, 1, 1, 2, 3, 5, 6, 6) time(s), every 4 rows 1 (0, 0, 0, 1, 1, 0, 1, 0, 0) time(s), then every other row 9 (9, 10, 11, 11, 12, 11, 2, 2, 2) times, then BO 2 (2, 2, 2, 2, 2, 3, 3, 3) sts at beginning of next 4 rows. BO remaining 14 (14, 14, 14, 14, 14, 14, 18, 18, 18) sts.

### FINISHING

Block pieces as desired. Sew shoulder seams. Set in Sleeves; sew side and Sleeve seams.

#### Button Band

With RS facing, using smaller needles, and beginning at base of Left Front neck edge, pick up and knit 71 (73, 75, 75, 77, 77, 77, 79, 79, 79) sts along Left Front edge. Begin Twisted Rib for Bands; work even

until piece measures 1" (2.5 cm) from pick-up row, ending with a RS row. BO all sts in pattern.

#### Buttonhole Band

With RS facing, using smaller needles, and beginning at lower Right Front edge, pick up and knit 71 (73, 75, 75, 77, 77, 77, 79, 79, 79) sts along Right Front edge. Work as for Button Band until piece measures ½" (1.5 cm) from pick-up row, ending with a WS row. Place markers for 7 (8, 8, 8, 8, 8, 8, 8, 8, 8) buttons, the first ¼" (.5 cm) below neck edge, the last ¾" (2 cm) from bottom edge, and the remaining buttons evenly spaced between.

**Buttonhole Row (RS):** Work to first marker, *yo, work 2 sts together (k2tog-tbl if next st to be worked is a purl st, p2tog if next st to be worked is a knit st); repeat from * through last marker, work to end. Complete as for Button Band.

#### Neckband

With RS facing, using circ needle, and beginning at edge of Buttonhole Band, pick up and knit 41 (44, 47, 50, 53, 55, 57, 56, 58, 58) sts along Right Front neck edge, 35 (35, 37, 37, 41, 41, 41, 41, 43, 45) sts along Back neck edge, then 41 (44, 47, 50, 53, 55, 57, 56, 58, 58) sts along Left Front neck edge—117 (123, 131, 137, 147, 151, 155, 153, 159, 161) sts. Begin Twisted Rib for Bands; work even until piece measures ¾" (2 cm) from pick-up edge, ending with a RS row. BO all sts in pattern.

The wide cable panel and turtleneck slim the shoulders and the entire torso.

Waist shaping keeps the sweater from looking boxy.

Long, belled sleeves combine with thick, tall ribbing to maximize the visual width of the hips.

Ann is wearing size 32–33" (81.5–84 cm) with approximately 1" (2.5 cm) of positive ease in the upper torso.

# ELORIA TURTLENECK

The cable on this classic pullover distracts the eye from a smaller bust (and hides a belly, should the wearer have one). At the hem, the long, belled sleeves combine with thick, tall ribbing to maximize the visual width of the hips and bring them into balance with the shoulders.

• • • • • • • • • • • • • • • • • • • • • • • • • •

## SIZES

To fit upper torso sizes 28–29 (30–31, 32–33, 34–35, 36–37, 38–39, 40–41, 44–45, 48–49, 52–53)" [71–73.5 (76–78.5, 81.5–84, 86.5–89, 91.5–94, 96.5–99, 101.5–104, 112–114.5, 122–124.5, 132–134.5) cm]

## FINISHED MEASUREMENTS

30 ½ (32, 34 ½, 36, 38 ½, 40, 42 ½, 46 ½, 50 ½, 54 ½)" [77.5 (81.5, 87.5, 91.5, 98, 101.5, 108, 118, 128.5, 138.5) cm] chest

*Note: Sweater is intended to be worn with 1-2" (2.5-5 cm) positive ease in the upper torso.*

## YARN

Louet Gems Light Worsted [100% merino wool; 175 yards (160 meters) / 100 grams]: 6 (7, 7, 7, 8, 8, 9, 10, 11, 12) skeins #01 Champagne

## NEEDLES

One pair straight needles size US 5 (3.75 mm)

One pair straight needles size US 6 (4 mm)

One 16" (40 cm) long circular (circ) needle size US 5 (3.75 mm)

One 16" (40 cm) long circular needle size US 6 (4 mm)

One 16" (40 cm) long circular needle size US 7 (4.5 mm)

Change needle size if necessary to obtain correct gauge.

## NOTIONS

Stitch markers; cable needle (cn)

## GAUGE

20 sts and 28 rows = 4" (10 cm) in Stockinette stitch (St st), using larger needles

## NOTES

Unless otherwise specified, decreases should be worked to match the slant of the edge being shaped, as follows: For left-slanting edges: On RS rows, k1, ssk, work to end; on WS rows, work to last 3 sts, ssp, p1. For right-slanting edges: On RS rows, work to last 3 sts, k2tog, k1; on WS rows, p1, p2tog, work to end. Increases should also be worked to match the slant of the edge being shaped, as follows: For right-slanting edges: On RS rows, work 1 st, M1-r, work to end; on WS rows, work to last st, M1-p, work 1 st. For left-slanting edges: On RS rows, work to last st, M1-l, work 1 st; on WS rows, work 1 st, M1-p-l, work to end.

## STITCH PATTERNS

### 2x2 Rib Flat

(multiple of 4 sts + 2; 1-row repeat)

**Row 1 (WS):** P2, *k2, p2; repeat from * to end.

**Row 2:** Knit the knit sts and purl the purl sts as they face you.

Repeat Row 2 for 2x2 Rib Flat.

### 2x2 Rib in the Rnd

(multiple of 4 sts; 1-rnd repeat)

**All Rnds:** *K2, p2; repeat from * to end.

## BACK

Using larger needles, CO 78 (82, 86, 90, 98, 102, 106, 118, 126, 138) sts. Begin 2x2 Rib Flat; work even until piece measures 2 1/2" (6.5 cm) from the beginning, ending with a WS row.

**Next Row (RS):** Change to St st across all sts, decrease 2 (2, 0, 0, 2, 2, 0, 2, 0, 2) sts evenly on first row—76 (80, 86, 90, 96, 100, 106, 116, 126, 136) sts remain. Work even until piece measures 3 ½" (9 cm), ending with a RS row

**Next Row (WS):** P25 (27, 29, 30, 32, 33, 35, 39, 42, 45), pm, p26 (26, 28, 30, 32, 34, 36, 38, 42, 46), pm, purl to end.

## Shape Waist

**Decrease Row (RS):** Decrease 2 sts this row, then every 6 rows 3 times, as follows: Knit to 2 sts before first marker, ssk, sm, knit to next marker, sm, k2tog, knit to end—68 (72, 78, 82, 88, 92, 98, 108, 118, 128) sts remain. Work even until piece measures 8" (20.5 cm) from the beginning, ending with a WS row.

## Shape Bust

**Increase Row (RS):** Increase 2 sts this row, then every 8 rows 3 times, as follows: Purl to first marker, M1-r, sm, purl to next marker, sm, M1-l, purl to end—76 (80, 86, 90, 96, 100, 106, 116, 126, 136) sts. Work even, removing markers on first row, until piece measures 13 ½ (13 ¾, 14, 14 ¼, 14 ½, 14 ¾, 15, 15 ½, 16, 16)" [34.5 (35, 35.5, 36, 37, 37.5, 38, 39.5, 40.5, 40.5) cm] from the beginning, ending with a WS row.

## Shape Armholes

**Next Row (RS):** BO 6 (6, 6, 6, 6, 6, 6, 8, 10, 12) sts at beginning of next 2 rows, 0 (2, 2, 2, 2, 2, 4, 6, 8, 8) sts at beginning of next 2 rows, then decrease 1 st at each side every other row 3 (2, 3, 4, 4, 5, 5, 5, 5) times—58 (60, 64, 66, 72, 74, 76, 78, 80, 86) sts remain. Work even until armhole measures 5 ½ (6, 6 ¼, 6 ½, 7, 7 ¼, 7 ½, 7 ¾, 8, 8 ½)" [14 (15, 16, 16.5, 18, 18.5, 19, 19.5, 20.5, 21.5) cm], ending with a WS row.

## Shape Neck

**Next Row (RS):** K18 (19, 20, 21, 22, 23, 23, 24, 24, 26), join a second ball of yarn, BO center 22 (22, 24, 24, 28, 28, 30, 30, 32, 34) sts, knit to end. Working both sides at the same time, work even for 1 row. Decrease 1 st at each neck edge every other row twice—16 (17, 18, 19, 20, 21, 21, 22, 22, 24) sts remain each side for shoulders. Work even until armhole measures 6 ½ (7, 7 ¼, 7 ½, 8, 8 ¼, 8 ½, 8 ¾, 9, 9 ½)" [16.5 (18, 18.5, 19, 20.5, 21, 21.5, 22, 23, 24) cm], ending with a WS row.

## Body Cable

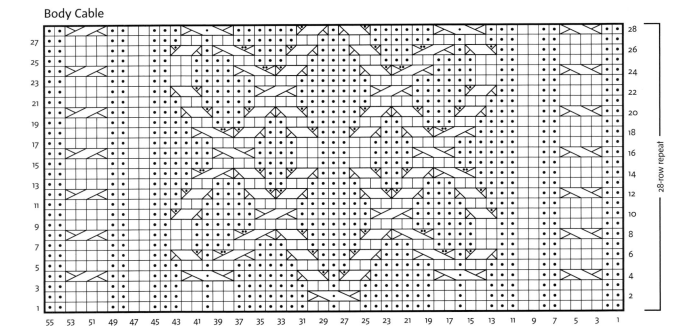

Note: Body Cable Chart begins with a WS row; work first row from left to right.

## Shape Shoulders

**Next Row (RS):** BO 8 (9, 9, 10, 10, 11, 11, 11, 12) sts at each armhole edge once, then 8 (8, 9, 9, 10, 10, 10, 11, 11, 12) sts once.

## FRONT

Using larger needles, CO 91 (91, 99, 99, 107, 115, 123, 131, 139, 147) sts.

**Next Row (WS):** Work 2x2 Rib Flat over next 18 (18, 22, 22, 26, 30, 34, 38, 42, 46) sts, pm, work Body Cable from Chart over next 55 sts, pm, work 2x2 Rib Flat to end. Work even, working sts between markers in Body Cable, and remaining sts in rib as established, until piece measures 2 ½" (6.5 cm) from the beginning, ending with a WS row.

**Next Row (RS):** Work in St st to first marker, decreasing 1 (0, 0, 0, 0, 1, 2, 1, 0, 0) or increasing 0 (1, 0, 2, 1, 0, 0, 0, 0, 1) st(s) to marker, sm, work as established to next marker, sm, work in St st, decreasing 1 (0, 0, 0, 0, 1, 2, 1, 0, 0) or increasing 0 (1, 0, 2, 1, 0, 0, 0, 0, 1) st(s) to end—89 (93, 99, 103, 109, 113, 119, 129, 139, 149) sts. Work even until piece measures 3 ½" (9 cm) from the beginning, ending with a WS row. Place markers 0 (0, 0, 0, 0, 0, 27, 29, 32, 34) sts in from each side. *Note: Markers for cable pattern will serve as shaping markers for first 6 sizes.*

## Shape Waist

**Decrease Row (RS):** Decrease 2 sts this row, then every 6 rows 3 times, as follows: Knit to 3 sts before first marker, ssk, k1, sm, work to last marker, sm, k1, k2tog, knit to end—81 (85, 91, 95, 101, 105, 111, 121, 131, 141) sts remain. Work even until piece measures 8" (20.5 cm) from the beginning, ending with a WS row.

## Shape Bust

**Increase Row (RS):** Increase 2 sts this row, then every 8 rows 3 times, as follows: Knit to 1 st before first marker, M1-r, sm, work to last marker, sm, k1, M1-l, knit to end—89 (93, 99, 103, 109, 113, 119, 129, 139, 149) sts. Work even until piece measures 13 ½ (13 ¾, 14,

Sleeve Cable

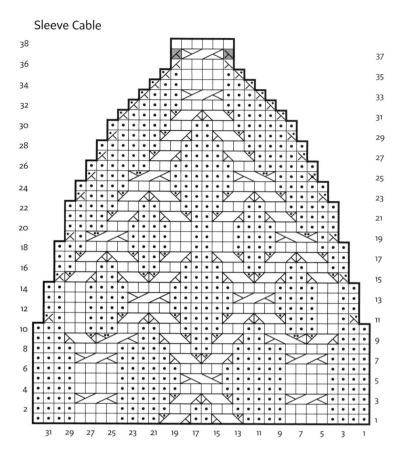

## KEY

| | |
|---|---|
| ☐ | Knit on RS, purl on WS. |
| ⦁ | Purl on RS, knit on WS. |
| ⊠ | P2tog on RS, k2tog on WS. |
| ⊠ | Ssp on RS, ssk on WS. |
| ◩ | P2tog on WS. |
| ◩ | Ssp on WS. |
| ◼ | Ssk (last st before marker together with first st of Chart). |
| ◼ | K2tog (last st of Chart together with first st after marker). |

Slip next st to cn, hold to back, k2, p1 from cn.

Slip 2 sts to cn, hold to front, p1, k2 from cn.

Slip 2 sts to cn, hold to back, k2, k2 from cn.

Slip 2 sts to cn, hold to front, k2, k2 from cn.

Slip 2 sts to cn, hold to back, k2, p2 from cn.

Slip 2 sts to cn, hold to front, p2, k2 from cn.

Slip 3 sts to cn, hold to front, k2, slip last from cn back to left-hand needle, p1, k2 from cn.

14 ¼, 14 ½, 14 ¾, 15, 15 ½, 16, 16)" [34.5 (35, 35.5, 36, 37, 37.5, 38, 39.5, 40.5, 40.5) cm] from the beginning, ending with a WS row.

### Shape Armholes

**Next Row (RS):** BO 6 (6, 6, 6, 6, 6, 6, 8, 10, 12) sts at beginning of next 2 rows, 0 (2, 2, 2, 2, 2, 4, 6, 8, 8) sts at beginning of next 2 rows, then decrease 1 st each side every other row 3 (2, 3, 4, 4, 5, 5, 5, 5, 5) times—71 (73, 77, 79, 85, 87, 89, 91, 93, 99) sts remain. Work even until armhole measures 5 ½ (6, 6 ¼, 6 ½, 7, 7 ¼, 7 ½, 7 ¾, 8, 8 ½)" [14 (15, 16, 16.5, 18, 18.5, 19, 19.5, 20.5, 21.5) cm], ending with a WS row.

### Shape Neck

**Next Row (RS):** Work 23 (24, 26, 27, 29, 30, 30, 31, 31, 34) sts, join a second ball of yarn, BO center 25 (25, 25, 25, 27, 27, 29, 29, 31, 31) sts, work to end. Working both sides at the same time, decrease 1 st at each neck edge every row 5 (5, 6, 6, 7, 7, 7, 7, 7, 7) times, then every other row 2 (2, 2, 2, 2, 2, 2, 2, 2, 3) times—16 (17, 18, 19, 20, 21, 21, 22, 22, 24) sts remain. Work even until armhole measures 6 ½ (7, 7 ¼, 7 ½, 8, 8 ¼, 8 ½, 8 ¾, 9, 9 ½)" [16.5 (18, 18.5, 19, 20.5, 21, 21.5, 22, 23, 24) cm], ending with a WS row.

### Shape Shoulders

**Next Row (RS):** BO 8 (9, 9, 10, 10, 11, 11, 11, 11, 12) sts at each armhole twice, then 8 (8, 9, 9, 10, 10, 10, 11, 11, 12) sts once.

## SLEEVES

Using smaller needles, CO 66 (68, 70, 70, 70, 74, 76, 76, 80, 84) sts. Begin St st; work even until piece measures 1 ½" (4 cm) from the beginning, ending with a RS row, increasing 6 sts evenly spaced on last row—72 (74, 76, 76, 76, 80, 82, 82, 86, 90) sts. Change to larger needles; knit 1 row (Turning Row).

**Next Row:** K20 (21, 22, 22, 22, 24, 25, 25, 27, 29), pm, work Sleeve Cable from Chart over next 32 sts, pm, knit to end. Continuing to work Sleeve Cable between markers, and remaining sts in St st, and working decreases as indicated in Chart, work until Chart is complete—44 (46, 48, 48, 48, 52, 54, 54, 58, 62) sts remain. Work even in St st across all sts until piece measures 6" (15 cm) from Turning Row, ending with a WS row.

### Shape Sleeve

**Next Row (RS):** Increase 1 st each side this row, then every 10 (10, 12, 10, 8, 8, 8, 6, 6, 6) rows 5 (6, 5, 6, 7, 7,

7, 10, 10, 11) times—56 (58, 60, 62, 64, 68, 70, 76, 80, 86) sts. Work even until piece measures 15 ½ (15 ¾, 16, 16 ¼, 16 ½, 16 ¾, 17, 17, 17, 17 ½)" [39.5 (40, 40.5, 41.5, 42, 42.5, 43, 43, 43, 44.5) cm] from Turning Row, ending with a WS row.

### Shape Cap

**Next Row (RS):** BO 6 (6, 6, 6, 6, 6, 6, 8, 10, 12) sts at beginning of next 2 rows, 0 (2, 2, 2, 2, 2, 4, 6, 7, 7) sts at beginning of next 2 rows, decrease 1 st each side every 6 rows 0 (2, 1, 1, 2, 1, 2, 4, 6, 6) time(s), every 4 rows 0 (0, 1, 1, 0, 0, 1, 1, 0, 1) time(s), then every other row 11 (8, 9, 10, 11, 14, 11, 4, 2, 2) times, then BO 2 (2, 2, 2, 2, 2, 2, 3, 3, 3) sts at beginning of next 4 rows. BO remaining 14 (14, 14, 14, 14, 14, 14, 18, 18, 18) sts.

## FINISHING

Block pieces as desired. Sew shoulder seams. Set in Sleeves; sew side and Sleeve seams.

### Turtleneck

With RS facing, using smallest circ needle, and beginning at right shoulder, pick up and knit 44 (44, 48, 48, 52, 52, 54, 54, 56, 58) sts along Back neck, then 52 (52, 52, 52, 56, 56, 58, 58, 60, 62) sts along Front neck—96 (96, 100, 100, 108, 108, 112, 112, 116, 120) sts. Join to work in the rnd; pm for beginning of rnd. Begin 2x2 Rib in the Rnd; work even until piece measures 7" (18 cm) from pick-up rnd, changing to progressively larger needles at 3" (7.5 cm) and 6" (15 cm). BO all sts in pattern.

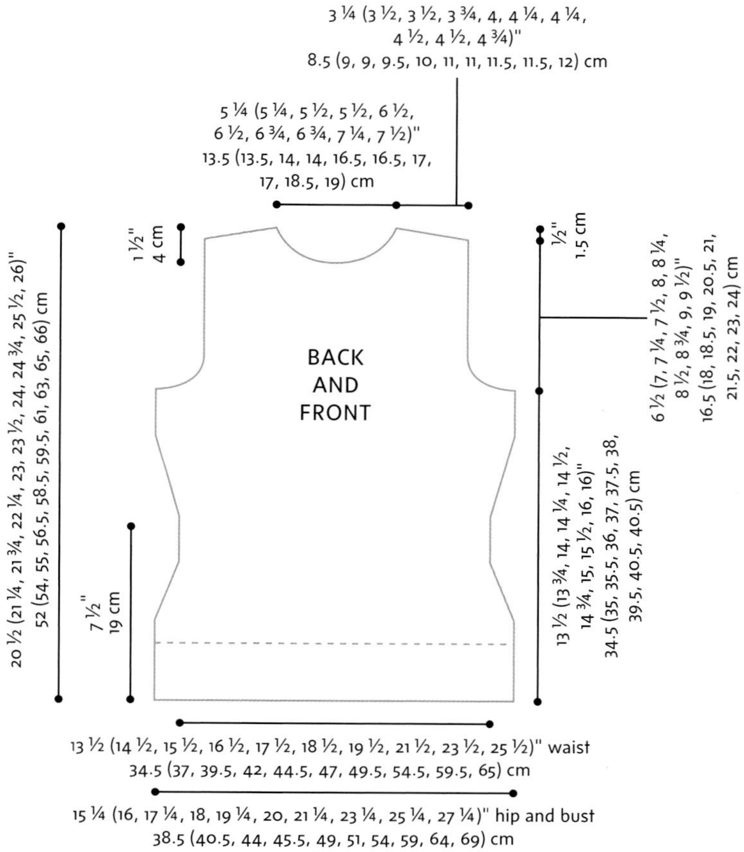
3 ¼ (3 ½, 3 ½, 3 ¾, 4, 4 ¼, 4 ¼, 4 ½, 4 ½, 4 ¾)"
8.5 (9, 9, 9.5, 10, 11, 11, 11.5, 11.5, 12) cm
5 ¼ (5 ¼, 5 ½, 5 ½, 6 ½, 6 ½, 6 ¾, 6 ¾, 7 ¼, 7 ½)"
13.5 (13.5, 14, 14, 16.5, 16.5, 17, 17, 18.5, 19) cm
1 ½"
4 cm
½"
1.5 cm
BACK AND FRONT
6 ½ (7, 7 ¼, 7 ½, 8, 8 ¼, 8 ½, 8 ¾, 9, 9 ½)"
16.5 (18, 18.5, 19, 20.5, 21, 21.5, 22, 23, 24) cm
20 ½ (21 ¼, 21 ¾, 22 ¼, 23, 23 ½, 24, 24 ¾, 25 ½, 26)"
52 (54, 55, 56.5, 58.5, 59.5, 61, 63, 65, 66) cm
7 ½"
19 cm
13 ½ (13 ¾, 14, 14 ¼, 14 ½, 14 ¾, 15, 15 ½, 16, 16)"
34.5 (35, 35.5, 36, 37, 37.5, 38, 39.5, 40.5, 40.5) cm
13 ½ (14 ½, 15 ½, 16 ½, 17 ½, 18 ½, 19 ½, 21 ½, 23 ½, 25 ½)" waist
34.5 (37, 39.5, 42, 44.5, 47, 49.5, 54.5, 59.5, 65) cm
15 ¼ (16, 17 ¼, 18, 19 ¼, 20, 21 ¼, 23 ¼, 25 ¼, 27 ¼)" hip and bust
38.5 (40.5, 44, 45.5, 49, 51, 54, 59, 64, 69) cm

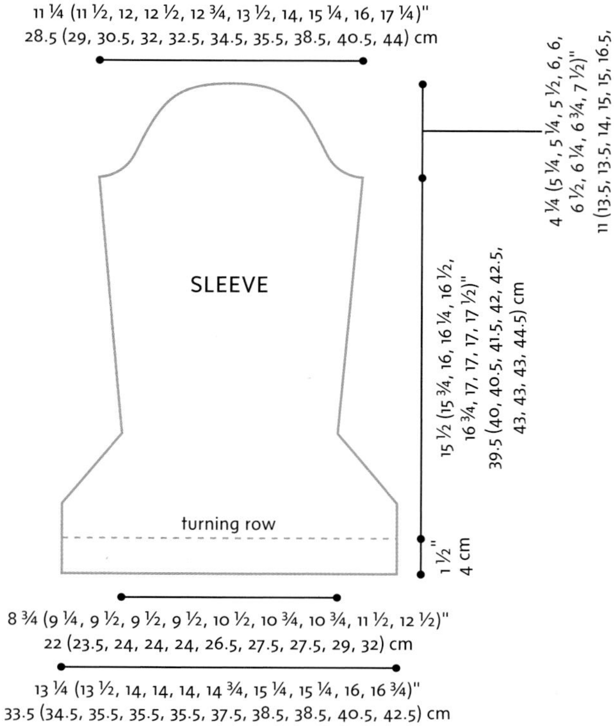
11 ¼ (11 ½, 12, 12 ½, 12 ¾, 13 ½, 14, 15 ¼, 16, 17 ¼)"
28.5 (29, 30.5, 32, 32.5, 34.5, 35.5, 38.5, 40.5, 44) cm
4 ¼ (5 ¼, 5 ¼, 5 ½, 6, 6, 6 ½, 6 ¼, 6 ¾, 7 ½)"
11 (13.5, 13.5, 14, 15, 15, 16.5, 16, 17, 19) cm
SLEEVE
15 ½ (15 ¾, 16, 16 ¼, 16 ½, 16 ¾, 17, 17, 17, 17 ½)"
39.5 (40, 40.5, 41.5, 42, 42.5, 43, 43, 43, 44.5) cm
turning row
1 ½"
4 cm
8 ¾ (9 ¼, 9 ½, 9 ½, 9 ½, 10 ½, 10 ¾, 10 ¾, 11 ½, 12 ½)"
22 (23.5, 24, 24, 24, 26.5, 27.5, 27.5, 29, 32) cm
13 ¼ (13 ½, 14, 14, 14, 14 ¾, 15 ¼, 15 ¼, 16, 16 ¾)"
33.5 (34.5, 35.5, 35.5, 35.5, 37.5, 38.5, 38.5, 40.5, 42.5) cm

Knitted fabric widens the appearance of the hips, drawing the eyes to the legs.

The flared hem brings the shoulders and bust into balance.

Jackie is wearing size 38" (96.5 cm) with approximately 2" (5 cm) of negative ease in the hips.

# OCEANIC SKIRT
## BY KIRSTEN KAPUR

No woman can pull off the knitted skirt quite as well as one who falls into the top-heavy category. Knitted fabric tends to enlarge the appearance of the wearer, but in the form of a skirt, that works in the top-heavy shape's favor, widening the appearance of the hips and drawing the eye to the legs.

● ● ● ● ● ● ● ● ● ● ● ● ● ● ● ● ● ● ● ● ● ● ● ● ● ● ● ● ● ● ● ● ● ● ●

### SIZES

To fit hip sizes 30 (32, 34, 36, 38, 40, 42, 44, 46, 48, 50, 52, 54)" [76 (81.5, 86.5, 91.5, 96.5, 101.5, 106.5, 112, 117, 122, 127, 132, 137) cm]

### FINISHED MEASUREMENTS

30 (32, 34, 36, 38, 40, 42, 44, 46, 48, 50, 52, 54)" [76 (81.5, 86.5, 91.5, 96.5, 101.5, 106.5, 112, 117, 122, 127, 132, 137) cm] hip circumference

### YARN

Lion Brand LB Collection Organic Wool [100% organic wool; 185 yards (170 meters) / 100 grams]: 5 (5, 5, 6, 6, 6, 7, 7, 7, 8, 8, 8, 9) skeins #178 Dark Teal

### NEEDLES

One 24" (60 cm) long or longer circular (circ) needle size US 7 (4.5 mm)

Change needle size if necessary to obtain correct gauge.

### NOTIONS

Crochet hook size US H/8 (5 mm); stitch marker; waste yarn; 1" (2.5 cm) wide elastic, 1" (2.5 cm) longer than desired finished waist measurement; large safety pin; sewing needle and thread; tapestry needle

### GAUGE

20 sts and 29 rows = 4" (10 cm) in Rib Pattern A or B

### NOTE

Skirt is worked from the top down.

### SPECIAL TECHNIQUE

**Kitchener Stitch:** Using a blunt tapestry needle, thread a length of yarn approximately 4 times the length of the section to be joined. Hold the pieces to be joined WSs together, with the needles holding the sts parallel, both ends pointing to the right. Working from right to left, insert tapestry needle into first st on front needle as if to purl, pull yarn through, leaving st on needle; insert tapestry needle into first st on back needle as if to knit, pull yarn through, leaving st on needle; *insert tapestry needle into first st on front needle as if to knit, pull yarn through, remove st from needle; insert tapestry needle into next st on front needle as if to purl, pull yarn through, leave st on needle; insert tapestry needle into first st on back needle as if to purl, pull yarn through, remove st from needle; insert tapestry needle into next st on back needle as if to knit, pull yarn through, leave st on needle. Repeat from *, working 3 or 4 sts at a time, then go back and adjust tension to match the pieces being joined. When 1 st remains on each needle, cut yarn and pass through last 2 sts to fasten off.

### STITCH PATTERNS

#### Rib Pattern A

(multiple of 4 sts; 1-rnd repeat)

**All Rnds:** *K3, p1; repeat from * to end.

#### Rib Pattern B

(multiple of 9 sts; 1-rnd repeat)

**All Rnds:** *K3, p1, k4, p1; repeat from * to end.

#### Lace Border (see Chart)

(st count varies; 14-row repeat)

*Note: On final k2tog of every WS row, work last st of Lace Border together with 1 st from Body.*

**Row 1 (WS):** K4, p10, k2, yo, k2tog, k2tog (last st of Lace Border together with 1 st from Body).

**Row 2:** Slip 1, k2, yo, k2tog, k3, yo, k5, yo, k2tog, yo, k4.

## Lace Border

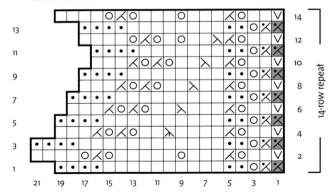

Note: Chart begins with a WS row; work first row from left to right.

### KEY

| | |
|---|---|
| ☐ | Knit on RS, purl on WS. |
| ▪ | Purl on RS, knit on WS. |
| Ⅴ | Slip st purlwise. |
| O | Yo |
| ⟋ | K2tog |
| ⟍ | Ssk |
| ⊠ | K2tog on WS (1 st from Lace Border together with 1 st from Body). |
| ⟋ | K2tog on WS. |
| ⟑ | Sk2p |

**Row 3:** K4, p12, k2, yo, [k2tog] twice.

**Row 4:** Slip 1, k2, yo, k2tog, k4, sk2p, k2, [yo, k2tog] twice, k3.

**Row 5:** K4, p10, k2, yo, [k2tog] twice.

**Row 6:** Slip 1, k2, yo, k2tog, k3, ssk, k2, [yo, k2tog] twice, k3.

**Row 7:** K4, p9, k2, yo, [k2tog] twice.

**Row 8:** Slip 1, k2, yo, k2tog, k2, ssk, k2, [yo, k2tog] twice, k3.

**Row 9:** K4, p8, k2, yo, [k2tog] twice.

**Row 10:** Slip 1, k2, yo, k2tog, k1, ssk, k2, [yo, k2tog] twice, k3.

**Row 11:** K4, p7, k2, yo, [k2tog] twice.

**Row 12:** Slip 1, k2, yo, k2tog, ssk, k2, yo, k1, yo, k2tog, yo, k4.

**Row 13:** K4, p8, k2, yo, [k2tog] twice.

**Row 14:** Slip 1, k2, yo, k2tog, k3, yo, k3, yo, k2tog, yo, k4.

Repeat Rows 1-14 for Lace Border.

### SKIRT

CO 120 (128, 136, 144, 152, 160, 189, 198, 207, 216, 225, 234, 243) sts. Join for working in the rnd, being careful not to twist sts; pm for beginning of rnd. Begin Rib Pattern A (A, A, A, A, A, B, B, B, B, B, B, B): work even for 7 rnds. Purl 1 rnd (Turning Rnd). Work even in Rib Pattern until piece measures 4 ½" (11.5 cm) from Turning Rnd.

#### Shape Skirt

##### SIZES 30-40 ONLY

**Increase Rnd 1:** *K1, M1, k2, p1; repeat from * to end—150 (160, 170, 180, 190, 200, -, -, -, -, -, -, -) sts.

##### SIZES 42-54 ONLY

**Increase Rnd 1:** *K1, M1, k2, p1, k4, p1; repeat from * to end— - (-, -, -, -, -, 210, 220, 230, 240, 250, 260, 270) sts.

## ALL SIZES

**Next Rnd:** *K4, p1; repeat from * to end. Work even until piece measures 10" (25.5 cm) from Turning Rnd.

**Increase Rnd 2:** *K2, M1, k2, p1; repeat from * to end—180 (192, 204, 216, 228, 240, 252, 264, 276, 288, 300, 312, 324) sts.

**Next Rnd:** *K5, p1; repeat from * to end. Work even until piece measures 17 (17, 18, 18, 19, 19, 20, 20, 20, 20, 20, 20, 20)" [43 (43, 45.5, 45.5, 48.5, 48.5, 51, 51, 51, 51, 51, 51, 51) cm], or to 4" (10 cm) less than desired finished length from Turning Rnd.

**Increase Rnd 3:** *K3, M1, k2, p1; repeat from * to end—210 (224, 238, 252, 266, 280, 294, 308, 322, 336, 350, 364, 378) sts.

## LACE BORDER

Using crochet hook, waste yarn, and Provisional CO (see page 159), CO 19 sts. Begin Lace Border (from text or Chart); work even, working 1 st from Lace Border together with 1 st from Body at end of WS rows as indicated, until all sts from Body have been worked, end with Row 14 of Lace Border—19 sts remain. Carefully unravel Provisional CO and place sts on needle. Using Kitchener st (see page 43), join ends of Lace Border.

## FINISHING

Block piece as desired.

### Waist Casing

Fold CO edge to WS at Turning Rnd and sew to WS, being careful not to let sts show on RS, and leaving 3" (7.5 cm) unsewn. Measure your waist. Cut length of elastic 1" (2.5 cm) longer than waist measurement. Attach safety pin to one end of elastic and pull elastic through Casing. Being careful not to twist elastic, overlap ends by 1" (2.5 cm) and sew together. Sew opening in Waist Casing closed.

42 (44 ¾, 47 ½, 50 ½, 53 ¼, 56, 58 ¾, 61 ½, 64 ½, 67 ¼, 70, 72 ¾, 75 ½)"
106.5 (113.5, 120.5, 128.5, 135.5, 142, 149, 156, 164, 171, 178, 185, 192) cm

30 (32, 34, 36, 38, 40, 42, 44, 46, 48, 50, 52, 54)" hip
76 (81.5, 86.5, 91.5, 96.5, 101.5, 106.5, 112, 117, 122, 127, 132, 137) cm

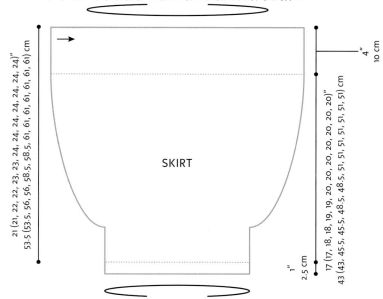

SKIRT

4" / 10 cm

21 (21, 22, 22, 23, 23, 24, 24, 24, 24, 24, 24, 24)"
53.5 (53.5, 56, 56, 58.5, 58.5, 61, 61, 61, 61, 61, 61, 61) cm

17 (17, 18, 18, 19, 19, 20, 20, 20, 20, 20, 20, 20)"
43 (43, 45.5, 45.5, 48.5, 48.5, 51, 51, 51, 51, 51, 51, 51) cm

1" / 2.5 cm

24 (25 ½, 27 ¼, 28 ¾, 30 ½, 32, 37 ¾, 39 ½, 41 ½, 43 ¼, 45, 46 ¾, 48 ½)" waist
61 (65, 69, 73, 77.5, 81.5, 96, 100.5, 105.5, 110, 114.5, 118.5, 123) cm

# 3

# BOTTOM-HEAVY SHAPES

Do you have gorgeously full hips? Strong, powerful legs? A bodacious booty? All of the above? Are they combined with delicate shoulders? A collarbone to die for? A slimmer torso? Welcome to the bottom-heavy group! Your generous curves have been the epitome of female beauty to countless artists for centuries. Pants shopping might be a bit of a chore sometimes, but your shape is flattered by many sweaters and can handle lots of fun colors and textures. Rejoice in your shape, and read on!

Ali (left) has broad shoulders; Tessa (middle) has narrow shoulders; and Jessica (right) has narrow shoulders and a larger bust, but all three have hips that are broader than their busts or upper torsos.

# Welcome to the Bottom-Heavy Club

If the photo you took of yourself from the front (see page 11) revealed that your hip and/or thigh region is substantially wider than your bust and/or shoulder region, you possess a bottom-heavy shape. This category can encompass both women with wider hips (that "classic pear") and women who carry their weight in their legs—provided that these features are combined with a more delicate torso and top. While bottom-heavy shapes can absolutely be busty, as our models show, it is typically the case that a bottom-heavy shape's full hip circumference is larger than the bust.

While broader hips/thighs and narrower shoulders are the hallmarks of bottom-heavy figures, other common characteristics include:

- Slender arms and neck
- A bustline that is narrower than the hips/legs
- A tendency to carry weight in the backside or legs

## Perfect Bottom-Heavy Sweaters

When selecting a sweater pattern, remember this: Our eye registers shape much more easily than size, so you will want to find a pattern that creates the illusion of a more balanced figure, then modify that pattern as needed. Bottom-heavy shapes are generally most flattered by clothing that draws the eye to the neck/bust area and broadens the appearance of the shoulders and bust. The hips can be minimized by wearing slightly shorter sweater lengths and plain hem treatments, which bring the proportions of bottom-heavy shapes into alignment.

Since horizontal visual elements broaden a region of the wearer's body and vertical visual elements narrow it, bottom-heavy shapes are flattered by sweaters that, when laid flat on a table, appear broader at the neck and shoulders than at the hem.

By adding colorwork, wide necklines, large collars, and shorter sleeves to a sweater, you can broaden the appearance of the shoulders and bust, drawing the eye upward. Most bottom-heavy shapes are also flattered by sweaters with shorter sleeves, which bring the focus up, highlighting the waist

or bust. Long sleeves can achieve this same effect through visual elements that draw the eye away from the cuff, such as extremely deep ribbing or colorwork that reaches far up the sleeve. When these sweater elements are paired with plain hems and shorter sweater lengths, the bottom-heavy figure becomes balanced and fundamentally flattered.

## Less Ideal Choices

As for all shapes, there are sweater elements that throw a bottom-heavy shape further out of proportion. The following styles tend to be less flattering for a bottom-heavy figure and should be used with caution (and lots of balancing elements!):

- Deep necklines that rest close to the neck will narrow the shoulders and slim the appearance of the torso and bust, which can be unflattering on a bottom-heavy figure. Cardigans worn open with a narrow slice of torso showing, narrow turtlenecks, and narrow, deep V-necks fall into this category.

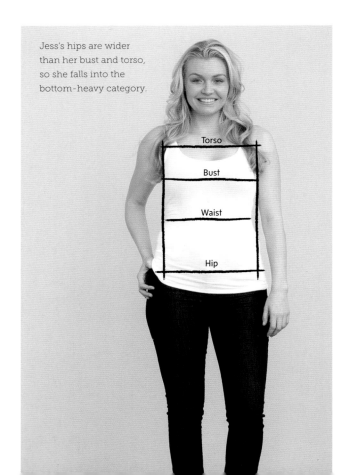

Jess's hips are wider than her bust and torso, so she falls into the bottom-heavy category.

Bottom-heavy shapes tend not to be flattered by sweaters that draw the eye directly to the legs. Long, belled sleeves, deep, intricate hem treatments, and bright bands of color at the hem of a sweater can be difficult for bottom-heavy knitters to wear.

Bottom-heavy shapes tend to look thicker in sweaters that reach to (or past) their widest hip point, as this broadens the hips further and tends to throw this shape out of balance. This is particularly true if the knitter doesn't build in enough positive ease in the hips and the sweater looks stretched.

## Common Modifications

Have a pattern in hand? All set to knit your favorite sweater? Before you get started, consider the following common modifications for bottom-heavy shapes and check out Chapter 6 for instructions that might apply to you.

- The bottom-heavy category tends to have the highest concentration of curvy figures, and the sweaters often require additional waist shaping (see page 147). Bottom-heavy shapes often need to move the waist shaping to a higher location, closer to the bust.

- Bottom-heavy shapes frequently need to shorten their sweater bodies to ensure the hem falls above the widest point of their hips (see page 148).

- Bust darts can be a necessary modification for busty bottom-heavy shapes (see page 152).

- Sometimes bottom-heavy shapes need to widen a neckline to ensure that it falls away from the neck, broadening the shoulders (see page 150).

## Flattering Features for Bottom-Heavy Shapes

To flatter a bottom-heavy shape, look for sweater patterns with the following features:

### STYLES

Sweaters with interesting visual elements at the top, like textured stitches at the neckline or cables that stretch all the way up the front. Balance these textures with a plain, thin hem treatment.

### NECKLINES

Deep, wide V-necks, scoop necks, and boatnecks; large, eye-catching collars, cowls, or hoods; and yoked sweater construction.

### SLEEVES

Cap sleeves, short sleeves, and elbow-length sleeves, all of which draw the eye upward. For long sleeves, use colorwork or textural details that reach up the forearm to the elbow.

Wide neckline and colorwork at the shoulders broaden the upper torso.

The tied waist allows for a nice, close fit.

Gradually brightening stripes draw the eye upward from the hem to the waist.

Ali is wearing size 37" (94 cm) with 1 ½" (4 cm) of bust darts added and approximately 2" (5 cm) of positive ease in the upper torso.

# STRIPER WRAP

The deep line of this wrap flatters busty and non-busty knitters alike (just make sure the tie falls at your natural waistline). The Fair Isle is worked in gradations of color in the round on the sleeves, but note that it is worked flat on the shoulders—a little more work, but definitely worth it for the effect!

. . . . . . . . . . . . . . . . . . . . . . . . . . . . . . . . . . . . . . . .

## SIZES

To fit upper torso sizes 29 (31, 33, 35, 37, 39, 41, 45, 49, 53)" [73.5 (78.5, 84, 89, 94, 99, 104, 114.5, 124.5, 134.5) cm]

## FINISHED MEASUREMENTS

30 ½ (32, 34, 36 ½, 38 ½, 40, 42, 46 ½, 50, 54 ½)" [77.5 (81.5, 86.5, 92.5, 98, 101.5, 106.5, 118, 127, 138.5) cm] chest

*Note: Wrap is intended to be worn with 1-2" (2.5-5 cm) positive ease in the upper torso.*

## YARN

Blue Sky Alpacas Melange [100% alpaca; 110 yards (100 meters) / 50 grams]: 9 (10, 11, 11, 12, 13, 14, 15, 17, 19) hanks #813 Pomegranate (MC); 1 hank each #808 Relish (B) and #800 Cornflower (C)

Blue Sky Alpacas Sport Weight [100% alpaca; 110 yards (100 meters) / 50 grams]: 1 hank each #508 Medium Gray (A) and #507 Light Gray (D)

## NEEDLES

One pair straight needles size US 5 (3.75 mm)

One 36" (90 cm) long circular (circ) needle size US 5 (3.75 mm)

Change needle size if necessary to obtain correct gauge.

## NOTIONS

Stitch markers; 1 ½ yards (1.5 meters) 1" (2.5 cm) wide grosgrain ribbon (optional)

## GAUGE

22 sts and 28 rows = 4" (10 cm) in Stockinette stitch (St st)

## NOTES

Unless otherwise specified, decreases should be worked to match the slant of the edge being shaped, as follows: For left-slanting edges: On RS rows, k1, ssk, work to end; on WS rows, work to last 3 sts, ssp, p1. For right-slanting edges: On RS rows, work to last 3 sts, k2tog, k1; on WS rows, p1, p2tog, work to end. Increases should also be worked to match the slant of the edge being shaped, as follows: For right-slanting edges: On RS rows, work 1 st, M1-r, work to end; on WS rows, work to last st, M1-p, work 1 st. For left-slanting edges: On RS rows, work to last st, M1-l, work 1 st; on WS rows, work 1 st, M1-p-l, work to end.

## BACK

Using MC, CO 84 (88, 94, 100, 106, 110, 116, 128, 138, 150) sts. Begin Garter st (knit every row); work even for 7 rows.

**Next Row (RS):** Change to St st; work even until piece measures 3" (7.5 cm) from the beginning, ending with a RS row.

**Next Row (WS):** P28 (29, 31, 33, 35, 37, 39, 43, 46, 50), pm, p28 (30, 32, 34, 36, 36, 38, 42, 46, 50), pm, purl to end.

### Shape Waist

**Decrease Row (RS):** Decrease 2 sts this row, then every 6 rows 4 times, as follows: Knit to 2 sts before first marker, ssk, sm, knit to next marker, sm, k2tog, knit to end—74 (78, 84, 90, 96, 100, 106, 118, 128, 140) sts remain. Work even until piece measures 7" (18 cm) from the beginning, ending with a WS row.

### Shape Bust

**Increase Row (RS):** Increase 2 sts this row, then every 8 rows 4 times, as follows: Knit to first marker, M1-r, sm, knit to next marker, sm, M1-l, work to end—84 (88, 94, 100, 106, 110, 116, 128, 138, 150) sts. Work even, removing markers on first row, until piece measures 12 ½ (12 ¾, 13, 13 ¼, 13 ½, 13 ¾, 14, 14 ½, 15, 15)" [32

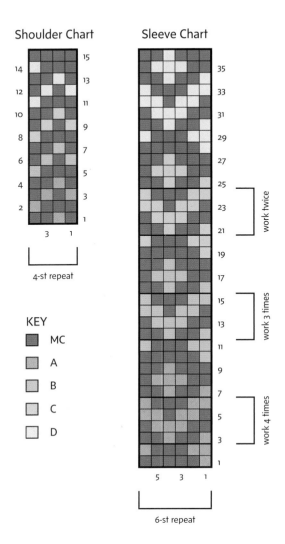

Shoulder Chart

Sleeve Chart

work twice

work 3 times

work 4 times

4-st repeat

6-st repeat

KEY

▪ MC

▪ A

▪ B

▪ C

▫ D

(32.5, 33, 33.5, 34.5, 35, 35.5, 37, 38, 38) cm] from the beginning, ending with a WS row.

## Shape Armholes

**Next Row (RS):** BO 6 (6, 6, 6, 6, 6, 6, 10, 10, 12) sts at beginning of next 2 rows, 2 (2, 2, 2, 2, 4, 4, 6, 8, 10) sts at beginning of next 2 rows, then decrease 1 st each side every other row 2 (3, 4, 6, 6, 5, 6, 5, 6, 6) times—64 (66, 70, 72, 78, 80, 84, 86, 90, 94) sts remain. Work even until armhole measures 4 ½ (5, 5 ¼, 5 ½, 6, 6 ¼, 6 ½, 6 ¾, 7, 7 ½)" [11.5 (12.5, 13.5, 14, 15, 16, 16.5, 17, 18, 19) cm], ending with a WS row.

**Next Row (RS):** Work Shoulder Chart to end. *Note: You may not work a complete final repeat at end of row.* Work even until armhole measures 5 ½ (6, 6 ¼, 6 ½, 7, 7 ¼, 7 ½, 7 ¾, 8, 8 ½)" [14 (15, 16, 16.5, 18, 18.5, 19, 19.5, 20.5, 21.5) cm], ending with a WS row.

## Shape Neck

**Next Row (RS):** K18 (19, 20, 20, 22, 22, 23, 24, 25, 26), join a second ball of yarn, BO center 28 (28, 30, 32, 34, 36, 38, 38, 40, 42) sts, knit to end. Working both sides at the same time, decrease 1 st each side every other row twice—16 (17, 18, 18, 20, 20, 21, 22, 23, 24) sts remain each side for shoulders. Work even until armhole measures 6 ½ (7, 7 ¼, 7 ½, 8, 8 ¼, 8 ½, 8 ¾, 9, 9 ½)" [16.5 (18, 18.5, 19, 20.5, 21, 21.5, 22, 23, 24) cm], ending with a WS row.

## Shape Shoulders

**Next Row (RS):** BO 8 (9, 9, 9, 10, 10, 11, 11, 12, 12) sts at each armhole edge once, then 8 (8, 9, 9, 10, 10, 10, 11, 11, 12) sts once.

## LEFT FRONT

Using MC, CO 76 (80, 86, 92, 98, 102, 108, 120, 130, 142) sts. Begin Garter st; work even for 7 rows.

**Next Row (RS):** Change to St st; work even until piece measures 3" (7.5 cm) from the beginning, ending with a RS row.

**Next Row (WS):** P13 (14, 16, 17, 19, 20, 21, 24, 27, 30), pm, p42 (44, 46, 50, 52, 54, 58, 64, 68, 74), pm, purl to end.

## Shape Waist

**Decrease Row (RS):** Decrease 2 sts this row, then every 6 rows 4 times, as follows: Knit to 2 sts before first marker, ssk, sm, knit to next marker, sm, k2tog, knit to end—66 (70, 76, 82, 88, 92, 98, 110, 120, 132) sts remain. Work even until piece measures 6 ½" (16.5 cm) from the beginning, ending with a WS row.

## Shape Neck Edge and Bust

*Note: Neck edge and bust shaping are worked at the same time; please read entire section through before beginning. Neck edge shaping will not be completed until approximately 1 ¼" (3 cm) before beginning of shoulder shaping.*

**Decrease Row (RS):** Decrease 1 st at neck edge this row, every row 11 (11, 15, 19, 23, 25, 29, 37, 43, 53) times, then every other row 33 (35, 35, 35, 35, 36, 36, 34, 34, 31) times. AT THE SAME TIME, when piece measures 7" (18 cm) from the beginning, ending with a WS row, shape bust as follows:

**Increase Row (RS):** Continuing with neck edge shaping, increase 1 st this row, then every 8 rows 4 times, as follows: Work to marker, M1-r, sm, work to end. AT THE SAME TIME, continue with neck edge shaping until piece measures 12 ½ (12 ¾, 13, 13 ¼, 13 ½, 13 ¾, 14, 14 ½, 15, 15)" [32 (32.5, 33, 33.5, 34.5, 35, 35.5, 37, 38, 38) cm] from the beginning, ending with a WS row. *Note: If your row gauge matches the given gauge, and you have worked to the exact measurements given, you should have 66 (70, 76, 82, 88, 92, 98, 110, 120, 132) sts remaining. However, due to differences in gauge and measuring, you may find that you have a few sts more or less than these st counts; this will not be a problem because the shaping was written with 1 ½" (4 cm) of work-even space between the end of the neck edge shaping and the end of the shoulders, to accommodate differences in row gauge.*

## Shape Neck Edge and Armhole, and Begin Shoulder Chart

*Note: Neck edge, armhole shaping, and Shoulder Chart are worked at the same time; please read entire section through before beginning.*

**Next Row (RS):** Continuing with neck edge shaping, BO 6 (6, 6, 6, 6, 6, 6, 10, 10, 12) sts at armhole edge once, 2 (2, 2, 2, 2, 4, 4, 6, 8, 10) sts once, then decrease 1 st at armhole edge every other row 2 (3, 4, 6, 6, 5, 6, 5, 6, 6) times—16 (17, 18, 18, 20, 20, 21, 22, 23, 24) sts remain. AT THE SAME TIME, when armhole measures 4 ½ (5, 5 ¼, 5 ½, 6, 6 ¼, 6 ½, 6 ¾, 7, 7 ½)" [11.5 (12.5, 13.5, 14, 15, 16, 16.5, 17, 18, 19) cm], ending with a WS row, begin Shoulder Chart as follows:

**Next Row (RS):** Continuing with neck edge shaping, work Shoulder Chart to end. *Note: You may not work a complete final repeat at end of row. Make note of st on which you end at neck edge; you will begin with that st for Right Front. Continue with neck edge shaping until armhole measures 6 ½ (7,*

## BUST DARTS

The sample shown has bust darts added to each Front. The pattern calls for you to increase 1 stitch at the bust every 8 rows 5 times (see Increase Row under Shape Neck Edge and Bust for Left and Right Fronts). In order to add bust darts to the sample, Increase Rows were worked at the bust every 4 rows instead of every 8, until a total of 9 bust Increase Rows were worked, instead of 5; this resulted in an extra 4 sts at the bust. In order to get rid of those 4 extra sts and end the neck shaping with the number of stitches required for the shoulders, the extra stitches were decreased along the neck edge, by working 4 additional wrong-side Decrease Rows than what the pattern called for (see Decrease Row under Shape Neck Edge and Bust for Left and Right Fronts), evenly distributed among the right-side Decrease Rows.

7 ¼, 7 ½, 8, 8 ¼, 8 ½, 8 ¾, 9, 9 ½)" [16.5 (18, 18.5, 19, 20.5, 21, 21.5, 22, 23, 24) cm], ending with a WS row.

### Shape Shoulder

**Next Row (RS):** BO 8 (9, 9, 9, 10, 10, 11, 11, 12, 12) sts at armhole edge once, then 8 (8, 9, 9, 10, 10, 10, 11, 11, 12) sts once.

### RIGHT FRONT

Work as for Left Front until piece measures 3" (7.5 cm) from the beginning, ending with a RS row.

**Next Row (WS):** P21 (22, 24, 25, 27, 28, 29, 32, 35, 38), pm, work 42 (44, 46, 50, 52, 54, 58, 64, 68, 74) sts, pm, purl to end.

Complete as for Left Front, reversing all shaping and Shoulder Chart.

### SLEEVES

Using MC, CO 48 (54, 56, 58, 62, 64, 66, 72, 78, 84) sts. Join for working in the rnd, being careful not to twist sts; pm for beginning of rnd. Begin Garter st (purl 1 rnd, knit 1 rnd); work even for 7 rnds.

### Begin Sleeve Chart and Shape Sleeve

*Note: Sleeve Chart and Sleeve shaping will be worked at the same time; please read entire section through before beginning.*

**Next Rnd:** Work Sleeve Chart to end. Continue, working Chart row repeats as indicated, until entire Chart is complete. AT THE SAME TIME, when piece measures 7" (18 cm) from the beginning, shape Sleeve as follows:

**Increase Rnd:** Continuing with Sleeve Chart, increase 2 sts this rnd, then every 10 (12, 12, 12, 12, 14, 14, 14, 14, 14) rnds 5 (4, 4, 4, 4, 4, 4, 4, 4, 4) times, as follows: Work 1 st, M1-r with MC, work to last st, M1-l with MC, work 1 st—60 (64, 66, 68, 72, 74, 76, 82, 88, 94) sts. *Note: Work increased sts into Chart pattern as they become available.* Once Chart is complete, change to MC and work even until piece measures 15 ½ (15 ¾, 16, 16 ¼, 16 ½, 16 ¾, 17, 17, 17, 17 ½)" [39.5 (40, 40.5, 41.5, 42, 42.5, 43, 43, 43, 44.5) cm] from the beginning.

### Shape Cap

**Next Row (RS):** Change to working back and forth. BO 6 (6, 6, 6, 6, 6, 6, 10, 10, 12) sts at beginning of next 2 rows, 2 (2, 2, 2, 2, 4, 4, 6, 8, 10) sts at beginning of next 2 rows, decrease 1 st each side every 6 rows 0 (0, 0, 0, 0, 1, 1, 5, 5, 6) time(s), every 4 rows 1 (1, 1, 1, 0, 0, 0, 1, 0, 1) time(s), then every other row 10 (12, 13, 14, 17, 15, 16, 1, 3, 0) times, then BO 2 (2, 2, 2, 2, 2, 2, 4, 4, 4) sts at beginning of next 4 rows. BO remaining 14 (14, 14, 14, 14, 14, 14, 20, 20, 20) sts.

## FINISHING

Block pieces as desired. Sew shoulder seams. Set in Sleeves. Sew side seams, leaving 1" (2.5 cm) hole in left side seam at your natural waist for Tie.

### Neckband/Ties

Using circ needle, CO 154 (159, 166, 171, 176, 181, 188, 198, 210, 220) sts, with RS facing, beginning at base of Right Front neck edge (opposite hole in left side seam), pick up and knit 80 (85, 90, 95, 100, 105, 110, 117, 125, 133) sts along Right Front neck edge, 44 (44, 46, 48, 50, 52, 54, 54, 56, 58) sts along Back neck, 80 (85, 90, 95, 100, 105, 110, 117, 125, 133) sts along Left Front neck edge, CO 71 sts—429 (444, 463, 480, 497, 514, 533, 557, 587, 615) sts. *Note: The total number of sts does not have to be exact.* Begin Garter st; work even for 7 rows. BO all sts firmly.

Cut 2 lengths of ribbon (optional), one to match length of each Tie. Sew to WS of Tie, being careful not to let sts show on WS.

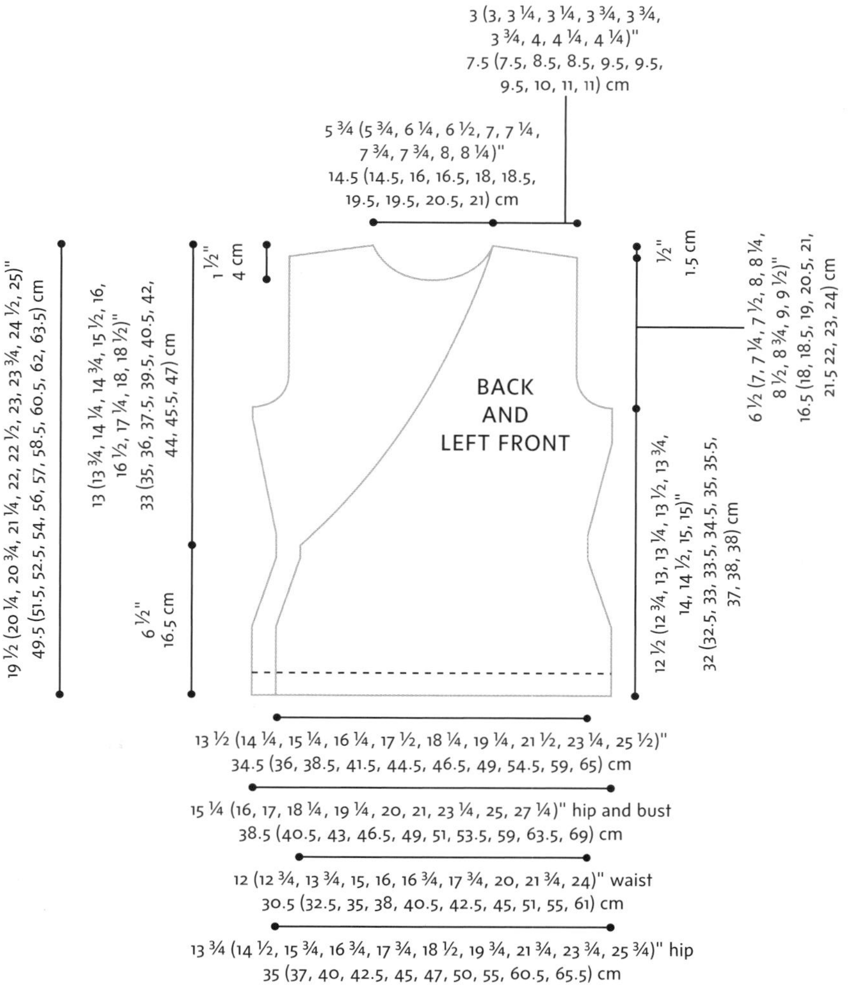
3 (3, 3 ¼, 3 ¼, 3 ¾, 3 ¾, 3 ¾, 4, 4 ¼, 4 ¼)"
7.5 (7.5, 8.5, 8.5, 9.5, 9.5, 9.5, 10, 11, 11) cm
5 ¾ (5 ¾, 6 ¼, 6 ½, 7, 7 ¼, 7 ¾, 7 ¾, 8, 8 ¼)"
14.5 (14.5, 16, 16.5, 18, 18.5, 19.5, 19.5, 20.5, 21) cm
19 ½ (20 ¼, 20 ¾, 21 ¼, 22, 22 ½, 23, 23 ¾, 24 ½, 25)"
49.5 (51.5, 52.5, 54, 56, 57, 58.5, 60.5, 62, 63.5) cm
13 (13 ¾, 14 ¼, 14 ¾, 15 ½, 16, 16 ½, 17 ¼, 18, 18 ½)"
33 (35, 36, 37.5, 39.5, 40.5, 42, 44, 45.5, 47) cm
6 ½"
16.5 cm
1 ½"
4 cm
½"
1.5 cm
6 ½ (7, 7 ¼, 7 ½, 8, 8 ¼, 8 ½, 8 ¾, 9, 9 ½)"
16.5 (18, 18.5, 19, 20.5, 21, 21.5 22, 23, 24) cm
12 ½ (12 ¾, 13, 13 ¼, 13 ½, 13 ¾, 14, 14 ½, 15, 15)"
32 (32.5, 33, 33.5, 34.5, 35, 35.5, 37, 38, 38) cm
BACK AND LEFT FRONT
13 ½ (14 ¼, 15 ¼, 16 ¼, 17 ½, 18 ¼, 19 ¼, 21 ½, 23 ¼, 25 ½)"
34.5 (36, 38.5, 41.5, 44.5, 46.5, 49, 54.5, 59, 65) cm
15 ¼ (16, 17, 18 ¼, 19 ¼, 20, 21, 23 ¼, 25, 27 ¼)" hip and bust
38.5 (40.5, 43, 46.5, 49, 51, 53.5, 59, 63.5, 69) cm
12 (12 ¾, 13 ¾, 15, 16, 16 ¾, 17 ¾, 20, 21 ¾, 24)" waist
30.5 (32.5, 35, 38, 40.5, 42.5, 45, 51, 55, 61) cm
13 ¾ (14 ½, 15 ¾, 16 ¾, 17 ¾, 18 ½, 19 ¾, 21 ¾, 23 ¾, 25 ¾)" hip
35 (37, 40, 42.5, 45, 47, 50, 55, 60.5, 65.5) cm

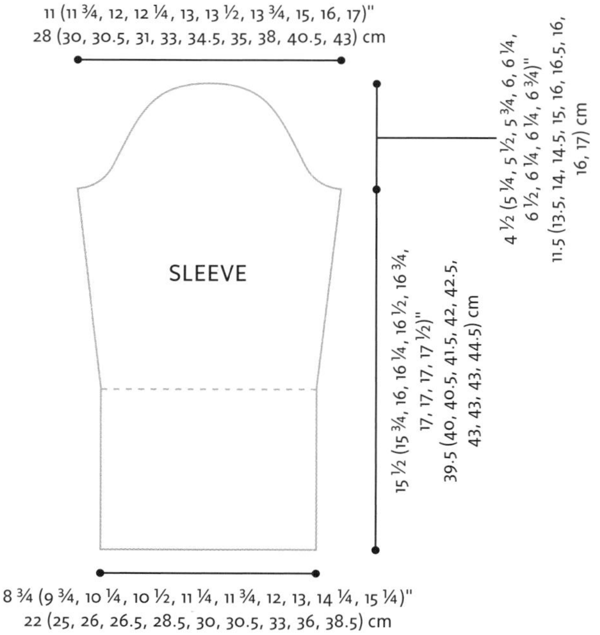
11 (11 ¾, 12, 12 ¼, 13, 13 ½, 13 ¾, 15, 16, 17)"
28 (30, 30.5, 31, 33, 34.5, 35, 38, 40.5, 43) cm
4 ½ (5 ¼, 5 ½, 5 ¾, 6, 6 ¼, 6 ½, 6 ¼, 6 ¼, 6 ¾)"
11.5 (13.5, 14, 14.5, 15, 16, 16.5, 16, 16, 17) cm
SLEEVE
15 ½ (15 ¾, 16, 16 ¼, 16 ½, 16 ¾, 17, 17, 17, 17 ½)"
39.5 (40, 40.5, 41.5, 42, 42.5, 43, 43, 43, 44.5) cm
8 ¾ (9 ¾, 10 ¼, 10 ½, 11 ¼, 11 ¾, 12, 13, 14 ¼, 15 ¼)"
22 (25, 26, 26.5, 28.5, 30, 30.5, 33, 36, 38.5) cm

Wide, shallow boatneck adds width to the shoulders.

Flutter sleeves broaden the torso, narrow the waist, and draw the eye upward.

Neat, plain-faced hem keeps the hip-line simple.

Jess is wearing size 34–35" (86.5–89 cm) with approximately ½" (1.5 cm) of positive ease in the upper torso.

# FLUTTER PULLOVER

The body of this delicately cabled sweater is kept interesting by repeating the sleeve cables on the sides, which also provides a nice outline for the figure. To accommodate the cable placement, this sweater is constructed in one piece to the armholes and then split into front and back.

## SIZES

To fit upper torso sizes 28–29 (30–31, 32–33, 34–35, 36–37, 38–39, 40–41, 44–45, 48–49, 52–53)" [71–73.5 (76–78.5, 81.5–84, 86.5–89, 91.5–94, 96.5–99, 101.5–104, 112–114.5, 122–124.5, 132–134.5) cm]

## FINISHED MEASUREMENTS

30 (32, 34, 36, 38, 40, 42, 46, 50, 54)"/ [76 (81.5, 86.5, 91.5, 96.5, 101.5, 106.5, 117, 127, 137) cm] chest

*Note: Sweater is intended to be worn with 1-2" (2.5-5 cm) positive ease in the upper torso.*

## YARN

SweetGeorgia Yarns, Inc. Merino Silk Fine [50% fine merino wool / 50% cultivated silk; 380 yards (347 meters) / 100 grams]: 3 (3, 3, 4, 4, 4, 5, 5, 5) skeins Coastal

## NEEDLES

One 24" (60 cm) long circular (circ) needle size US 4 (3.5 mm)

One 24" (60 cm) long circular needle size US 3 (3.25 mm)

Change needle size if necessary to obtain correct gauge.

## NOTIONS

Stitch markers; cable needle (cn); stitch holder

## GAUGE

24 sts and 32 rows = 4" (10 cm) in Stockinette stitch (St st), using larger needle

## ABBREVIATIONS

**MB (Make Bobble):** [K1, p1, k1, p1, k1, p1, k1] in same st to increase to 7 sts, pass second, third, fourth, fifth, sixth, then seventh sts one at a time over first st and off needle.

**T3F-p:** Slip 2 sts to cn, hold to front, p1, k2 from cn.

**T3B-p:** Slip next st to cn, hold to back, k2, p1 from cn.

**C4F-p:** Slip 2 sts to cn, hold to front, p2, k2 from cn.

**C4B-p:** Slip 2 sts to cn, hold to back, k2, p2 from cn.

**C4F:** Slip 2 sts to cn, hold to front, k2, k2 from cn.

**C4B:** Slip 2 sts to cn, hold to back, k2, k2 from cn.

## STITCH PATTERN

*Lorgnette Cable (see Chart)*

(panel of 12 sts; 40-rnd repeat)

**Rnds 1-3:** P2, k2, p4, k2, p2.

**Rnd 4:** P2, C4F-p, C4B-p, p2.

**Rnd 5 and all Odd-Numbered Rnds:** Knit the knit sts and purl the purl sts as they face you; purl Bobbles.

**Rnd 6:** P4, C4F-p, p4.

**Rnd 8:** P6, T3F-p, p3.

**Rnd 10:** P7, T3F-p, p2.

**Rnd 12:** P3, MB, p4, k2, p2.

**Rnd 14:** P7, T3B-p, p2.

**Rnd 16:** P6, T3B-p, p3.

**Rnd 18:** P4, C4F, p4.

**Rnd 20:** P2, C4B-p, C4F-p, p2.

**Rnd 22:** Repeat Rnd 2.

**Rnd 24:** Repeat Rnd 4.

**Rnd 26:** P4, C4B-p, p4.

**Rnd 28:** P3, T3B-p, p6.

**Rnd 30:** P2, T3B-p, p7.

**Rnd 32:** P2, k2, p3, MB, p4.

**Rnd 34:** P2, T3F-p, p7.

**Rnd 36:** P3, T3F-p, p6.

**Rnd 38:** P4, C4B, p4.

**Rnd 40:** Repeat Rnd 20.

Repeat Rnds 1-40 for Lorgnette Cable.

## Lorgnette Cable

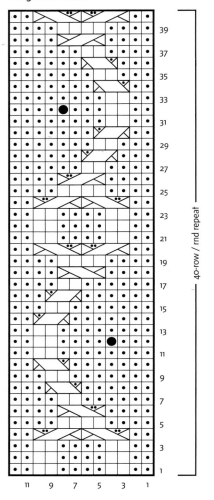

40-row / rnd repeat

Row numbers (right side, odd): 39, 37, 35, 33, 31, 29, 27, 25, 23, 21, 19, 17, 15, 13, 11, 9, 7, 5, 3, 1

Column numbers (bottom): 11, 9, 7, 5, 3, 1

### KEY

| | |
|---|---|
| ☐ | Knit on RS, purl on WS. |
| · | Purl on RS, knit on WS. |
| ● | MB |
| ◺◿ | T3F-p |
| ◹◸ | T3B-p |
| ◺◿ | C4F-p |
| ◹◸ | C4B-p |
| ◺◿ | C4F |
| ◹◸ | C4B |

## NOTES

Unless otherwise specified, decreases should be worked to match the slant of the edge being shaped, as follows: For left-slanting edges: On RS rows, k1, ssk, work to end; on WS rows, work to last 3 sts, ssp, p1. For right-slanting edges: On RS rows, work to last 3 sts, k2tog, k1; on WS rows, p1, p2tog, work to end. Increases should also be worked to match the slant of the edge being shaped, as follows: For right-slanting edges: On RS rows, work 1 st, M1-r, work to end; on WS rows, work to last st, M1-p, work 1 st. For left-slanting edges: On RS rows, work to last st, M1-l, work 1 st; on WS rows, work 1 st, M1-p-l, work to end.

## BODY

Using smaller needle, CO 180 (192, 204, 216, 228, 240, 252, 276, 300, 324) sts. Join for working in the rnd, being careful not to twist sts; pm for beginning of rnd. Begin St st; work even until piece measures 1½'' (4 cm) from the beginning.

**Next Rnd:** *[K2, M1] twice, k82 (88, 94, 100, 106, 112, 118, 130, 142, 154), [K2, M1] twice; repeat from * once—188 (200, 212, 224, 236, 248, 260, 284, 308, 332) sts.

**Turning Rnd:** Change to larger needle. K6, place marker for new beginning of rnd, p82 (88, 94, 100, 106, 112, 118, 130, 142, 154), pm, p12, pm, p82 (88, 94, 100, 106, 112, 118, 130, 142, 154), pm, purl to end.

**Next Rnd:** Work in St st to first marker, sm, work Lorgnette Cable (from text or Chart) to next marker, sm, work in St st to marker, sm, work Lorgnette Cable to end. Work even until piece measures 2'' (5 cm) from Turning Rnd.

**Next Rnd:** Work 25 (27, 29, 31, 33, 35, 37, 41, 45, 49) sts, place shaping marker, work 32 (34, 36, 38, 40, 42, 44, 48, 52, 56) sts, place shaping marker, work 31 (33, 35, 37, 39, 41, 43, 47, 51, 55) sts (to center of first cable panel), work 24 (25, 27, 28, 30, 31, 33, 36, 39, 42) sts, place shaping marker, work 46 (50, 52, 56,

58, 62, 64, 70, 76, 82) sts, place shaping marker, work 30 (31, 33, 34, 36, 37, 39, 42, 45, 48) sts. *Note: Back and Front shaping markers are not placed in the same position.*

## Shape Waist

**Decrease Rnd:** Decrease 4 sts this rnd, then every 8 rnds 4 times, as follows: [Work to 2 sts before shaping marker, ssk, sm, work to next shaping marker, sm, k2tog] twice, work to end—168 (180, 192, 204, 216, 228, 240, 264, 288, 312) sts remain. Work even until piece measures 7" (18 cm) from Turning Rnd.

## Shape Bust

**Increase Rnd:** Increase 4 sts this rnd, then every 10 rnds 4 times, as follows: [Work to shaping marker, M1-r, sm, work to next shaping marker, sm, M1-l] twice—188 (200, 212, 224, 236, 248, 260, 284, 308, 332) sts. Work even, removing shaping markers on first rnd, until piece measures 12 ¼ (12 ½, 12 ¾, 13, 13 ¼, 13 ½, 13 ¾, 14 ¼, 14 ¾, 14 ¾)" [31 (32, 32.5, 33, 33.5, 34.5, 35, 36, 37.5, 37.5) cm] from Turning Rnd, ending 6 sts before end of last rnd.

**Next Rnd:** Place marker for new beginning of rnd, continuing in patterns as established, work to second marker, removing original beginning-of-rnd marker and second marker as you come to them, work 6 sts, pm for side, work to end, removing third and fourth markers; you should now have a marker in the center of each cable panel.

**Next Rnd:** Change to St st. *[K2tog, k1] twice, knit to 6 sts before next marker, [ssk, k1] twice, sm; repeat from * to end—180 (192, 204, 216, 228, 240, 252, 276, 300, 324) sts remain; place last 90 (96, 102, 108, 114, 120, 126, 138, 150, 162) sts worked on st holder for Front.

The body of Flutter is largely worked in Stockinette, providing a wealth of modification opportunities. Proportional shapes might consider narrowing the neckline and/or narrowing the sleeves. Top-heavy shapes wanting to knit Flutter could both narrow the neckline and modify the sleeves to either a bell or straight shape, perhaps with the cable focused near the cuff rather than reaching all the way to the shoulder. Busty knitters could deepen the neckline into a scoop, square, or even V shape.

## BACK

### Shape Armholes

**Next Row (RS):** Working back and forth on Back sts only, BO 6 (6, 6, 6, 6, 8, 10, 12, 14) sts at beginning of next 2 rows, 2 (2, 2, 2, 2, 4, 4, 6, 8, 10) sts at beginning of next 2 rows, then decrease 1 st each side every other row 2 (4, 5, 7, 7, 6, 6, 7, 6) times—70 (72, 76, 78, 84, 88, 90, 94, 96, 102) sts remain. Work even until armhole measures 5 ½ (6, 6 ¼, 6 ½, 7, 7 ¼, 7 ½, 7 ¾, 8, 8 ½)" [14 (15, 16, 16.5, 18, 18.5, 19, 19.5, 20.5, 21.5) cm], ending with a WS row.

### Shape Neck

**Next Row (RS):** K13 (13, 14, 14, 15, 16, 16, 17, 17, 18), join a second ball of yarn, BO center 44 (46, 48, 50, 54, 56, 58, 60, 62, 66) sts, knit to end. Working both sides at the same time, decrease 1 st each neck edge every other row twice—11 (11, 12, 12, 13, 14, 14, 15, 15, 16) sts remain each side for shoulders. Work even until armhole measures 6 ½ (7, 7 ¼, 7 ½, 8, 8 ¼, 8 ½, 8 ¾, 9, 9 ½)" [16.5 (18, 18.5, 19, 20.5, 21, 21.5, 22, 23, 24) cm], ending with a WS row.

### Shape Shoulders

**Next Row (RS):** BO 6 (6, 6, 6, 7, 7, 7, 8, 8, 8) sts at each armhole edge once, then 5 (5, 6, 6, 6, 7, 7, 7, 7, 8) sts once.

## FRONT

Transfer sts from st holder to larger needle.

### Shape Armholes

With RS facing, rejoin yarn. Shape armholes as for Back—70 (72, 76, 78, 84, 88, 90, 94, 96, 102) sts remain. Work even until armhole measures 4 (4 ½, 4 ¾, 5, 5 ½, 5 ¾, 6, 6 ¼, 6 ½, 7)" [10 (11.5, 12, 12.5, 14, 14.5, 15, 16, 16.5, 18) cm], ending with a WS row.

### Shape Neck

Shape neck as for Back—11 (11, 12, 12, 13, 14, 14, 15, 15, 16) sts remain each side for shoulders. Work even until armhole measures same as for Back to shoulder shaping, ending with a WS row. Shape shoulders as for Back.

## SLEEVES

Using smaller needle, CO 106 (112, 114, 118, 120, 126, 126, 132, 138, 144) sts. Begin St st; work even until piece measures 1 ½'' (4 cm) from the beginning, ending with a RS row.

**Turning Row (WS):** Change to larger needle. K7 (10, 9, 11, 10, 11, 11, 12, 13, 14), [pm, k12, pm, k8 (8, 9, 9, 10, 11, 11, 12, 13, 14)] 4 times, pm, k12, pm, knit to end.

**Next Row (RS):** Work in St st to first marker, [sm, work Lorgnette Cable to next marker, sm, work in Rev St st to next marker] 4 times, sm, work Lorgnette Cable to next marker, sm, work in St st to end. Work even for 1 row.

### Shape Sleeve and Cap

*Note: Sleeve and Cap shaping are worked at the same time; please read entire section through before beginning.*

**\*Decrease Row 1 (RS):** Work to marker after first cable panel, sm, p2tog, work to 2 sts before marker before last cable panel, p2tog-tbl, sm, work to end—104 (110, 112, 116, 118, 124, 124, 130, 136, 142) sts remain. Work even for 3 rows.

**Decrease Row 2 (RS):** Work to marker after second cable panel, sm, p2tog, work to 2 sts before marker before fourth cable panel, p2tog-tbl, sm, work to end—102 (108, 110, 114, 116, 122, 122, 128, 134, 140) sts remain. Work even for 3 rows.

Repeat from * 9 (9, 9, 9, 9, 10, 9, 9, 9, 9) times, then repeat Decrease Row 1 zero (1, 1, 1, 1, 0, 1, 1, 1, 1) time(s). AT THE SAME TIME, when piece measures 6 (6 ¼, 6 ½, 6 ¾, 7, 7, 7, 7 ¼, 7 ¼, 7 ½)" [15 (16, 16.5, 17, 18, 18, 18, 18.5, 18.5, 19) cm] from Turning Row, ending with a WS row, shape cap as follows:

**Next Row (RS):** BO 6 (6, 6, 6, 6, 6, 8, 10, 12, 14) sts at beginning of next 2 rows, 2 (2, 2, 2, 2, 4, 4, 6, 8, 9) sts at beginning of next 2 rows, decrease 1 st each side every 6 rows 1 (1, 1, 0, 1, 1, 2, 5, 6, 8) time(s), every 4 rows rows 1 (0, 0, 1, 0, 1, 1, 1, 1, 0) time(s), then every other row 9 (12, 13, 15, 16, 15, 13, 4, 2, 1) time(s), then BO 3 (3, 3, 3, 3, 3, 3, 4, 4, 4) sts at beginning of next 4 rows. BO remaining 16 (16, 16, 16, 16, 16, 16, 22, 22, 22) sts.

## FINISHING

Block pieces as desired. Sew shoulder seams. Set in Sleeves; sew side and Sleeve seams. Fold hems to WS at Turning Round/Row and sew to WS, being careful not to let sts show on RS.

### Neckband

With RS facing, using smaller needle and beginning at right shoulder, pick up and knit 1 st for every BO st, and 2 sts for every 3 rows around neck shaping. Join for working in the rnd; pm for beginning of rnd. Begin St st; work even for 7 rnds. BO all sts loosely.

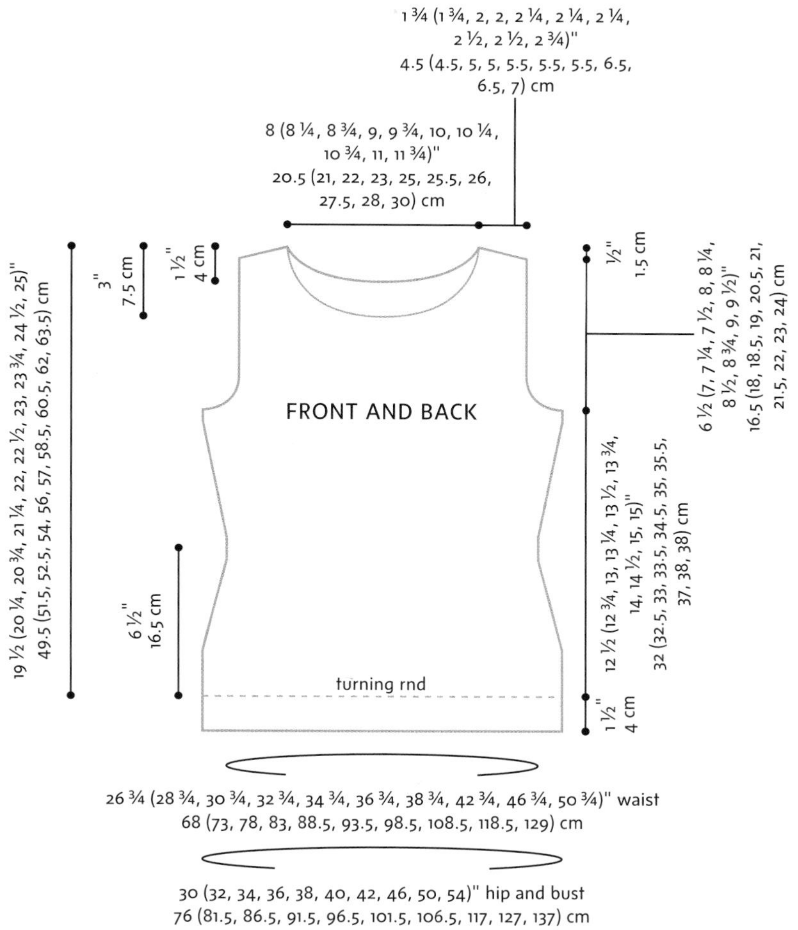
1 ¾ (1 ¾, 2, 2, 2 ¼, 2 ¼, 2 ¼, 2 ½, 2 ½, 2 ¾)"
4.5 (4.5, 5, 5, 5.5, 5.5, 5.5, 6.5, 6.5, 7) cm
8 (8 ¼, 8 ¾, 9, 9 ¾, 10, 10 ¼, 10 ¾, 11, 11 ¾)"
20.5 (21, 22, 23, 25, 25.5, 26, 27.5, 28, 30) cm
19 ½ (20 ¼, 20 ¾, 21 ¼, 22, 22 ½, 23, 23 ¾, 24 ½, 25)"
49.5 (51.5, 52.5, 54, 56, 57, 58.5, 60.5, 62, 63.5) cm
3"
7.5 cm
1 ½"
4 cm
½"
1.5 cm
6 ½ (7, 7 ¼, 7 ½, 8, 8 ¼, 8 ½, 8 ¾, 9, 9 ½)"
16.5 (18, 18.5, 19, 20.5, 21, 21.5, 22, 23, 24) cm
FRONT AND BACK
12 ½ (12 ¾, 13, 13 ¼, 13 ½, 13 ¾, 14, 14 ½, 15, 15)"
32 (32.5, 33, 33.5, 34.5, 35, 35.5, 37, 38, 38) cm
6 ½"
16.5 cm
turning rnd
1 ½"
4 cm
26 ¾ (28 ¾, 30 ¾, 32 ¾, 34 ¾, 36 ¾, 38 ¾, 42 ¾, 46 ¾, 50 ¾)" waist
68 (73, 78, 83, 88.5, 93.5, 98.5, 108.5, 118.5, 129) cm
30 (32, 34, 36, 38, 40, 42, 46, 50, 54)" hip and bust
76 (81.5, 86.5, 91.5, 96.5, 101.5, 106.5, 117, 127, 137) cm

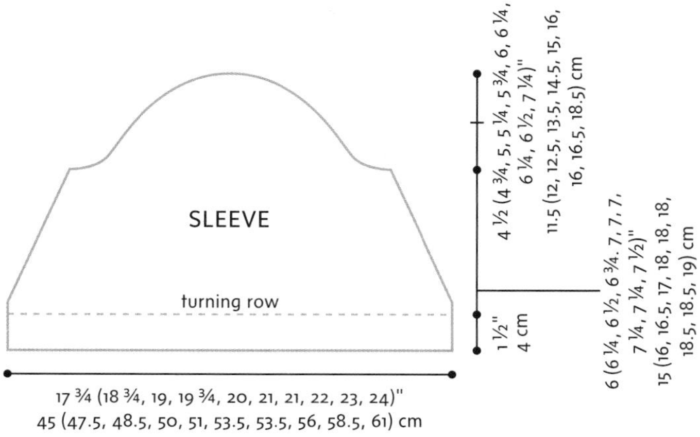
4 ½ (4 ¾, 5, 5 ¼, 5 ¾, 6, 6 ¼, 6 ¼, 6 ½, 7 ¼)"
11.5 (12, 12.5, 13.5, 14.5, 15, 16, 16, 16.5, 18.5) cm
SLEEVE
turning row
1 ½"
4 cm
6 (6 ¼, 6 ½, 6 ¾, 7, 7, 7, 7 ¼, 7 ¼, 7 ½)"
15 (16, 16.5, 17, 18, 18, 18, 18.5, 18.5, 19) cm
17 ¾ (18 ¾, 19, 19 ¾, 20, 21, 21, 22, 23, 24)"
45 (47.5, 48.5, 50, 51, 53.5, 53.5, 56, 58.5, 61) cm

The textured collar and short sleeves broaden the shoulders and bust.

The textured hem and shorter length draw the eye up higher than the widest part of a bottom-heavy figure.

Jess is wearing size 34" (86.5 cm) with approximately ½" (1.5 cm) of positive ease in the upper torso.

# ANDIE'S CARDIGAN

The front of this preppie cardigan is kept plain with applied I-Cord, and the hook-and-eye tape closure allows the cardigan to be flattering even when worn with negative ease. The cardigan can be worn in many ways—closed at the top, middle, bottom, or any combination—and waist shaping keeps the fit slim.

## SIZES

To fit upper torso sizes 28 (30, 32, 34, 36, 38, 40, 44, 48, 52)" [71 (76, 81.5, 86.5, 91.5, 96.5, 101.5, 112, 122, 132) cm]

## FINISHED MEASUREMENTS

30 (32, 35 ¼, 36 ¾, 38 ½, 40 ½, 42 ¾, 46, 51 ¼, 54 ½)" [76 (81.5, 89.5, 93.5, 98, 103, 108.5, 117, 130, 138.5) cm] chest

*Note: Cardigan is intended to be worn with approximately 2" (5 cm) positive ease in the upper torso.*

## YARN

Swans Island Worsted [100% organic merino wool; 250 yards (229 meters) / 100 grams]: 3 (3, 3, 4, 4, 4, 4, 5, 5, 6) skeins #216 Early Thyme

## NEEDLES

One pair straight needles size US 7 (4.5 mm)

One pair straight needles size US 8 (5 mm)

One 24" (60 cm) long circular (circ) needle size US 7 (4.5 mm)

One pair double-pointed needles (dpn) size US 7 (4.5 mm)

Change needle size if necessary to obtain correct gauge.

## NOTIONS

Stitch markers; ½" (1.5 cm) wide hook and eye tape approximately 20" (51 cm) long

## GAUGE

18 sts and 28 rows = 4" (10 cm) in Stockinette stitch (St st), using smaller needles

## STITCH PATTERN

### Linen Ridge Stitch

(even number of sts; 4-row repeat)

**Row 1 (RS):** Purl.

**Row 2:** K1, *slip 1 wyif, k1; repeat from * to last st, k1.

**Row 3:** Purl.

**Row 4:** K1, *k1, slip 1 wyif; repeat from * to last st, k1.

Repeat Rows 1-4 for Linen Ridge Stitch.

## NOTES

Unless otherwise specified, decreases should be worked to match the slant of the edge being shaped, as follows: For left-slanting edges: On RS rows, k1, ssk, work to end; on WS rows, work to last 3 sts, ssp, p1. For right-slanting edges: On RS rows, work to last 3 sts, k2tog, k1; on WS rows, p1, p2tog, work to end. Increases should also be worked to match the slant of the edge being shaped, as follows: For right-slanting edges: On RS rows, work 1 st, M1-r, work to end; on WS rows, work to last st, M1-p, work 1 st. For left-slanting edges: On RS rows, work to last st, M1-l, work 1 st; on WS rows, work 1 st, M1-p-l, work to end.

## BACK

Using larger needles, CO 68 (72, 78, 82, 86, 90, 96, 104, 114, 122) sts. Begin Linen Ridge Stitch; work even until piece measures 1 ½" (4 cm) from the beginning, ending with a WS row.

**Next Row (RS):** Change to smaller needles and St st; work even until piece measures 3" (7.5 cm) from the beginning, ending with a RS row.

**Next Row (WS):** P23 (24, 26, 27, 29, 30, 32, 35, 38, 41), pm, p22 (24, 26, 28, 28, 30, 32, 34, 38, 40), pm, purl to end.

### Shape Waist

**Decrease Row (RS):** Decrease 2 sts this row, then every 4 rows 3 times, as follows: Knit to 2 sts before marker, ssk, sm, knit to next marker, sm, k2tog, knit to

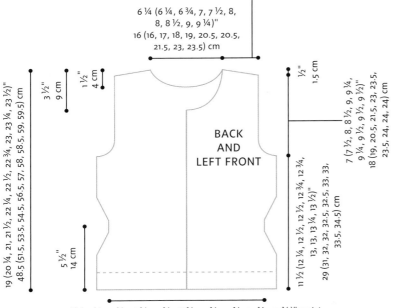

2 ¾ (3, 3, 3 ¼, 3 ¼, 3 ½, 3 ½, 3 ¾, 4)"
7 (7.5, 7.5, 7.5, 8.5, 8.5, 9, 9, 9.5, 10) cm

6 ¼ (6 ¼, 6 ¾, 7, 7 ½, 8,
8, 8 ½, 9, 9 ¼)"
16 (16, 17, 18, 19, 20.5, 20.5,
21.5, 23, 23.5) cm

3 ½"
9 cm

1 ½"
4 cm

½"
1.5 cm

BACK
AND
LEFT FRONT

7 (7 ½, 8, 8 ½, 9, 9 ¼,
9 ¼, 9 ½, 9 ½, 9 ½)"
18 (19, 20.5, 21.5, 23, 23.5,
23.5, 24, 24, 24) cm

19 (20 ¼, 21, 21 ½, 22 ¼, 22 ½, 22 ¾, 23, 23 ¼, 23 ½)"
48.5 (51.5, 53.5, 54.5, 56.5, 57, 58, 58.5, 59, 59.5) cm

11 ½ (12 ¼, 12 ½, 12 ½, 12 ¾, 12 ¾,
13, 13, 13 ¼, 13 ½)"
29 (31, 32, 32, 32.5, 32.5, 33, 33,
33.5, 34.5) cm

5 ½"
14 cm

13 ¼ (14 ¼, 15 ½, 16 ½, 17 ¼, 18 ¼, 19 ½, 21 ¼, 23 ½, 25 ¼)" waist
33.5 (36, 39.5, 42, 44, 46.5, 49.5, 54, 59.5, 64) cm

15 (16, 17 ¼, 18 ¼, 19, 20, 21 ¼, 23, 25 ¼, 27)" hip and bust
38 (40.5, 44, 46.5, 48.5, 51, 54, 58.5, 64, 68.5) cm

6 ¾ (7, 8, 8 ½, 9, 9 ¼, 9 ¾, 10 ¾, 12, 13)" waist
17 (18, 20.5, 21.5, 23, 23.5, 25, 27.5, 30.5, 33) cm

7 ½ (8, 9, 9 ¼, 9 ¾, 10 ¼, 10 ¾, 11 ½, 13, 13 ¾)" hip and bust
19 (20.5, 23, 23.5, 25, 26, 27.5, 29, 33, 35) cm

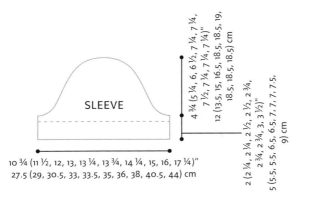

SLEEVE

4 ¾ (5 ¼, 6, 6 ½, 7 ¼, 7 ¼,
7 ½, 7 ¼, 7 ¼, 7 ¼)"
12 (13.5, 15, 16.5, 18.5, 18.5, 19,
18.5, 18.5, 18.5) cm

2 (2 ¼, 2 ¼, 2 ½, 2 ½, 2 ½, 2 ¾,
2 ¾, 2 ¾, 3, 3 ½)"
5 (5.5, 5.5, 6.5, 6.5, 7, 7, 7.5,
9) cm

10 ¾ (11 ½, 12, 13, 13 ¼, 13 ¾, 14 ¼, 15, 16, 17 ¼)"
27.5 (29, 30.5, 33, 33.5, 35, 36, 38, 40.5, 44) cm

end—60 (64, 70, 74, 78, 82, 88, 96, 106, 114) sts remain. Work even until piece measures 6" (15 cm) from the beginning, ending with a WS row.

Shape Bust

**Increase Row (RS):** Increase 2 sts this row, then every 8 rows 3 times, as follows: Knit to first marker, M1-r, sm, knit to second marker, sm, M1-l, knit to end—68 (72, 78, 82, 86, 90, 96, 104, 114, 122) sts. Work even, removing markers on first row, until piece measures 11 ½ (12 ¼, 12 ½, 12 ½, 12 ¾, 12 ¾, 13, 13, 13 ¼, 13 ½)" [29 (31, 32, 32, 32.5, 32.5, 33, 33, 33.5, 34.5) cm] from the beginning, ending with a WS row.

## Shape Armholes

**Next Row (RS):** BO 6 (6, 6, 6, 6, 6, 8, 8, 10) sts at beginning of next 2 rows, 0 (0, 2, 2, 2, 2, 2, 4, 6, 6) sts at beginning of next 2 rows, then decrease 1 st each side every other row 2 (3, 2, 3, 3, 4, 6, 5, 6, 6) times—52 (54, 58, 60, 64, 66, 68, 70, 74, 78) sts remain. Work even until armhole measures 6 (6 ½, 7, 7 ½, 8, 8 ¼, 8 ¼, 8 ½, 8 ½, 8 ½)" [15 (16.5, 18, 19, 20.5, 21, 21, 21.5, 21.5, 21.5) cm], ending with a WS row.

## Shape Neck

**Next Row (RS):** K14 (15, 16, 16, 17, 17, 18, 18, 19, 20), join a second ball of yarn, BO center 24 (24, 26, 28, 30, 32, 32, 34, 36, 38) sts, knit to end. Working both sides at the same time, work even for 1 row. Decrease 1 st at each neck edge every other row twice—12 (13, 14, 14, 15, 15, 16, 16, 17, 18) sts remain. Work even until armhole measures 7 (7 ½, 8, 8 ½, 9, 9 ¼, 9 ¼, 9 ½, 9 ½, 9 ½)" [18 (19, 20.5, 21.5, 23, 23.5, 23.5, 24, 24, 24) cm], ending with a WS row.

### Shape Shoulders

**Next Row (RS):** BO 6 (7, 7, 7, 8, 8, 8, 9, 9) sts at each armhole edge once, then 6 (6, 7, 7, 7, 7, 8, 8, 8, 9) sts once.

### LEFT FRONT

Using larger needles, CO 34 (36, 40, 42, 44, 46, 48, 52, 58, 62) sts. Begin Linen Ridge Stitch; work even until piece measures 1 ½" (4 cm) from the beginning, ending with a WS row.

**Next Row (RS):** Change to smaller needles and St st; work even until piece measures 3" (7.5 cm) from the beginning, ending with a RS row.

**Next Row (WS):** P17 (18, 20, 21, 22, 23, 24, 26, 29, 31), pm, purl to end.

### Shape Waist

**Decrease Row (RS):** Decrease 1 st this row, then every 4 rows 3 times, as follows: Knit to 2 sts before marker, ssk, sm, knit to end—30 (32, 36, 38, 40, 42, 44, 48, 54, 58) sts remain. Work even until piece measures 6" (15 cm) from the beginning, ending with a WS row.

### Shape Bust

**Increase Row (RS):** Increase 1 st this row, then every 8 rows 3 times, as follows: Knit to marker, M1-r, sm, knit to end—34 (36, 40, 42, 44, 46, 48, 52, 58, 62) sts. Work even, removing markers on first row, until piece measures 11 ½ (12 ¼, 12 ½, 12 ½, 12 ¾, 12 ¾, 13, 13, 13 ¼, 13 ½)" [29 (31, 32, 32, 32.5, 32.5, 33, 33, 33.5, 34.5) cm] from the beginning, ending with a WS row.

### Shape Armholes

**Next Row (RS):** BO 6 (6, 6, 6, 6, 6, 6, 8, 8, 10) sts at armhole edge once, 0 (0, 2, 2, 2, 2, 2, 4, 6, 6) sts once, then decrease 1 st at armhole edge every other row 2 (3, 2, 3, 3, 4, 6, 5, 6, 6) times—26 (27, 30, 31, 33, 34, 34, 35, 38, 40) sts remain. Work even until armhole measures 4 (4 ½, 5, 5 ½, 6, 6 ¼, 6 ¼, 6 ½,

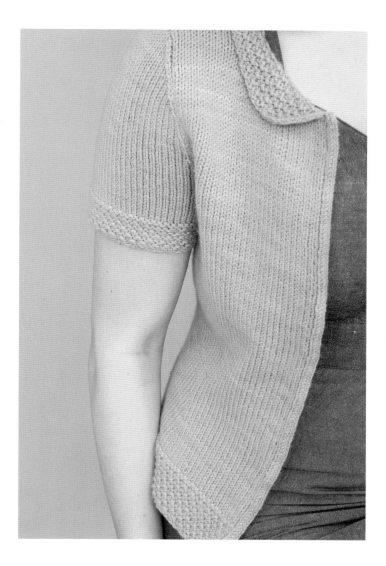

6 ½, 6 ½)" [10 (11.5, 12.5, 14, 15, 16, 16, 16.5, 16.5, 16.5) cm], ending with a RS row.

### Shape Neck

**Next Row (WS):** BO 7 (7, 8, 8, 9, 9, 9, 9, 10, 11) sts at neck edge once, 3 (3, 4, 5, 5, 5, 5, 5, 5, 6) sts once, decrease 1 st at neck edge every row 2 (2, 2, 2, 2, 3, 2, 3, 3, 3) times, then every other row 2 (2, 2, 2, 2, 2, 2, 2, 3, 2) times—12 (13, 14, 14, 15, 15, 16, 16, 17, 18) sts remain. Work even until armhole measures 7 (7 ½, 8, 8 ½, 9, 9 ¼, 9 ¼, 9 ½, 9 ½, 9 ½)" [18 (19, 20.5, 21.5, 23, 23.5, 23.5, 24, 24, 24) cm], ending with a WS row.

### Shape Shoulder

**Next Row (RS):** BO 6 (7, 7, 7, 8, 8, 8, 8, 9, 9) sts at armhole edge once, then 6 (6, 7, 7, 7, 7, 8, 8, 8, 9) sts once.

### RIGHT FRONT

Work as for Left Front until piece measures 3" (7.5 cm) from the beginning, ending with a RS row. Complete as for Left Front, reversing all shaping.

### SLEEVES

Using larger needles, CO 48 (52, 54, 58, 60, 62, 64, 68, 72, 78) sts. Begin Linen Ridge Stitch; work even until piece measures 1 ½" (4 cm) from the beginning, ending with a WS row.

**Next Row (RS):** Change to smaller needles and St st; work even until piece measures 2 (2 ¼, 2 ¼, 2 ½, 2 ½, 2 ¾, 2 ¾, 3, 3 ½)" [5 (5.5, 5.5, 6.5, 6.5, 7, 7, 7, 7.5, 9) cm] from the beginning, ending with a WS row.

### Shape Cap

**Next Row (RS):** BO 6 (6, 6, 6, 6, 6, 6, 8, 8, 10) sts at beginning of next 2 rows, 0 (0, 2, 2, 2, 2, 2, 4, 6, 6) sts at beginning of next 2 rows, decrease 1 st each side every 6 rows 3 (2, 4, 4, 4, 4, 4, 6, 6, 6) times, every 4 rows 0 (1, 0, 0, 1, 0, 0, 1, 1, 0) time(s), then every other row 5 (7, 5, 7, 7, 9, 10, 1, 1, 3) time(s), then BO 2 (2, 2, 2, 2, 2, 2, 3, 3, 3) sts at beginning of next 4 rows. BO remaining 12 (12, 12, 12, 12, 12, 12, 16, 16, 16) sts.

### FINISHING

Block pieces as desired. Sew shoulder seams. Set in Sleeves; sew side and Sleeve seams.

### Collar

With RS facing, using larger needles, and beginning at Right Front neck edge, pick up and knit 27 (27, 29, 30, 32, 32, 32, 32, 32, 34) sts to shoulder, 34 (34, 36, 38, 40, 42, 42, 44, 46, 48) sts along Back neck edge, then 27 (27, 29, 30, 32, 32, 32, 32, 32, 34) sts to Left Front neck edge—88 (88, 94, 98, 104, 106, 106, 108, 110, 116) sts. Begin Linen Ridge Stitch; work even for 2" (5 cm), ending with a WS row. Work 4 more rows, decreasing 1 st each side every row—80 (80, 86, 90, 96, 98, 98, 100, 102, 108) sts remain. BO all sts.

### Right Front I-Cord Edging

Using circular needle, pick up and knit 1 st per row up Right Front edge. Using dpn, CO 3 sts. *Do not turn; slide sts to opposite end of dpn. Using a second dpn and bringing yarn around behind dpn to right-hand side, k2, skp (1 st from I-Cord together with 1 st from circ needle). Repeat from * until all sts on circ needle have been worked. Thread tail through remaining sts, pull tight, and fasten off.

Repeat for Left Front edge. Sew hook-and-eye tape to WS of Fronts.

## MODIFICATION IDEAS

Andie is a snap to modify. Proportional knitters could either lengthen the sweater body, ensuring it ends at their widest hip point, or lengthen the sleeves to reduce the broadening effect on the shoulders. Top-heavy knitters could lengthen both the body and the sleeves, and perhaps block the collar a bit, folded to create a narrower line. Curvy knitters always look gorgeous in elbow-length sleeves, and busty knitters could add bust darts along the existing waist shaping lines. (For details, please see page 144.)

The cowl neckline broadens the shoulders and emphasizes the bust.

Shorter sleeves keep the focus above the hips.

Simple, ribbed hem draws the eye up.

Tessa is wearing size 40" (101.5 cm) with an additional 3" (7.5 cm) of bust darts and 2" (5 cm) of ease in the upper torso.

# STOKER COWL
## BY CARO SHERIDAN

This oversize cowl is a hugely comfortable "just throw it on" type of sweater, but the vertical waist shaping keeps it from looking boxy. The simple Stockinette stitch base provides an easy platform for modification.

. . . . . . . . . . . . . . . . . . . . . . . . . . . . .

### SIZES

To fit upper torso sizes 30 (32, 34, 36, 38, 40, 43, 46, 50, 54)" [76 (81.5, 86.5, 91.5, 96.5, 101.5, 109, 117, 127, 137) cm]

### FINISHED MEASUREMENTS

31 (33, 34 ½, 36 ½, 38, 40, 43 ½, 47, 50 ½, 54)" [78.5 (84, 87.5, 92.5, 96.5, 101.5, 110.5, 119.5, 128.5, 137) cm] chest

*Note: Cowl is intended to be worn with 0–1" (0–2.5 cm) positive ease in the upper torso.*

### YARN

Valley Yarns Stockbridge [50% superfine alpaca / 50% wool; 109 yards (100 meters) / 50 grams]: 8 (9, 9, 10, 10, 11, 12, 13, 14, 15) hanks Chocolate

### NEEDLES

One pair straight needles size US 7 (4.5 mm)

One 24" (60 cm) long circular (circ) needle size US 8 (5 mm)

One 24" (60 cm) long circular needle size US 10 (6 mm)

Change needle size if necessary to obtain correct gauge.

### NOTIONS

Stitch markers; stitch holder

### GAUGE

18 sts and 24 rows = 4" (10 cm) in Stockinette stitch (St st), using size US 7 (4.5 mm) needles

### STITCH PATTERN

#### 2x2 Rib

(multiple of 4 sts; 1-row/rnd repeat)

**Row/Rnd 1 (RS):** K2, *p2, k2; repeat from * to end.

**Row/Rnd 2:** Knit the knit sts and purl the purl sts as they face you.

Repeat Row/Rnd 2 for 2x2 Rib.

### NOTES

Unless otherwise specified, decreases should be worked to match the slant of the edge being shaped, as follows: For left-slanting edges: On RS rows, k1, ssk, work to end; on WS rows, work to last 3 sts, ssp, p1. For right-slanting edges: On RS rows, work to last 3 sts, k2tog, k1; on WS rows, p1, p2tog, work to end. Increases should also be worked to match the slant of the edge being shaped, as follows: For right-slanting edges: On RS rows, work 1 st, M1-r, work to end; on WS rows, work to last st, M1-p, work 1 st. For left-slanting edges: On RS rows, work to last st, M1-l, work 1 st; on WS rows, work 1 st, M1-p-l, work to end.

### BACK

Using US 7 (4.5 mm) needles, CO 70 (74, 78, 82, 86, 90, 98, 106, 114, 122) sts. Begin 2x2 Rib; work even until piece measures 2 ¾" (7 cm) from the beginning, ending with a WS row.

**Next Row (RS):** Change to St st; work even for 3 rows.

**Next Row (WS):** P23 (25, 26, 27, 29, 30, 33, 35, 38, 41), pm, p24 (24, 26, 28, 28, 30, 32, 36, 38, 40), pm, purl to end.

#### Shape Waist

**Decrease Row (RS):** Decrease 2 sts this row, then every 4 rows 3 times, as follows: Knit to 2 sts before first marker, ssk, sm, knit to next marker, sm, k2tog, knit to end—62 (66, 70, 74, 78, 82, 90, 98, 106, 114) sts remain. Work even until piece measures 7" (18 cm) from the beginning, ending with a WS row.

#### Shape Bust

**Increase Row (RS):** Increase 2 sts this row, then every 4 rows 3 times, as follows: Knit to first marker, M1-r, sm, knit to next marker, sm, M1-l, knit to end—70 (74, 78, 82, 86, 90, 98, 106, 114, 122) sts. Work even, removing markers on first row,

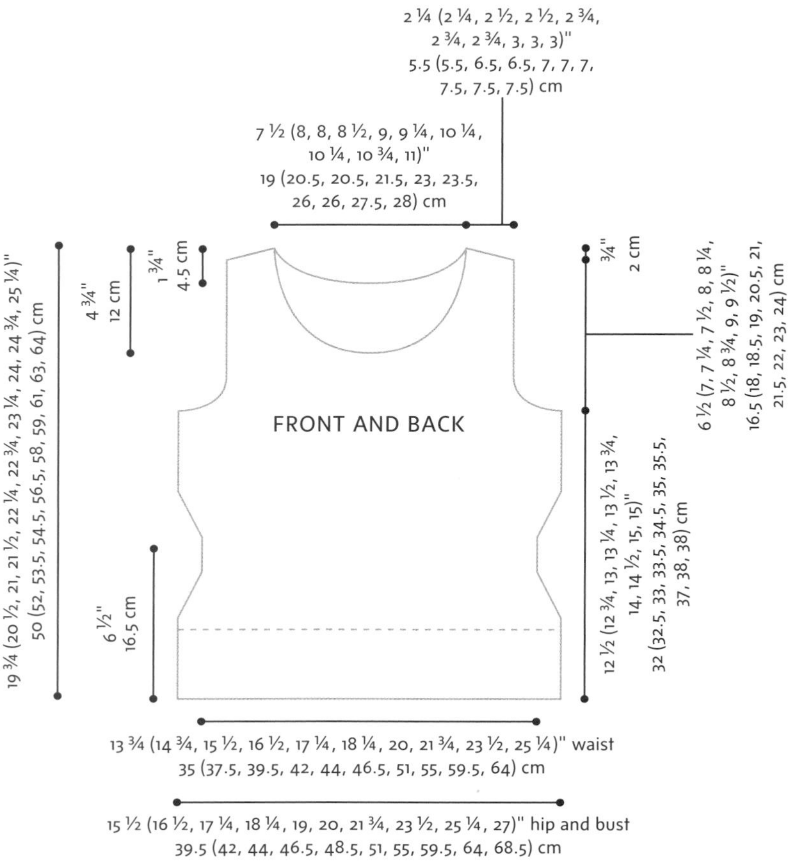
2 ¼ (2 ¼, 2 ½, 2 ½, 2 ¾, 2 ¾, 2 ¾, 3, 3, 3)"
5.5 (5.5, 6.5, 6.5, 7, 7, 7, 7.5, 7.5, 7.5) cm
7 ½ (8, 8, 8 ½, 9, 9 ¼, 10 ¼, 10 ¼, 10 ¾, 11)"
19 (20.5, 20.5, 21.5, 23, 23.5, 26, 26, 27.5, 28) cm
19 ¾ (20 ½, 21, 21 ½, 22 ¼, 22 ¾, 23 ¼, 24, 24 ¾, 25 ¼)"
50 (52, 53.5, 54.5, 56.5, 58, 59, 61, 63, 64) cm
4 ¾"
12 cm
1 ¾"
4.5 cm
¾"
2 cm
6 ½ (7, 7 ¼, 7 ½, 8, 8 ¼, 8 ½, 8 ¾, 9, 9 ½)"
16.5 (18, 18.5, 19, 20.5, 21, 21.5, 22, 23, 24) cm
FRONT AND BACK
12 ½ (12 ¾, 13, 13 ¼, 13 ½, 13 ¾, 14, 14 ½, 15, 15)"
32 (32.5, 33, 33.5, 34.5, 35, 35.5, 37, 38, 38) cm
6 ½"
16.5 cm
13 ¾ (14 ¾, 15 ½, 16 ½, 17 ¼, 18 ¼, 20, 21 ¾, 23 ½, 25 ¼)" waist
35 (37.5, 39.5, 42, 44, 46.5, 51, 55, 59.5, 64) cm
15 ½ (16 ½, 17 ¼, 18 ¼, 19, 20, 21 ¾, 23 ½, 25 ¼, 27)" hip and bust
39.5 (42, 44, 46.5, 48.5, 51, 55, 59.5, 64, 68.5) cm

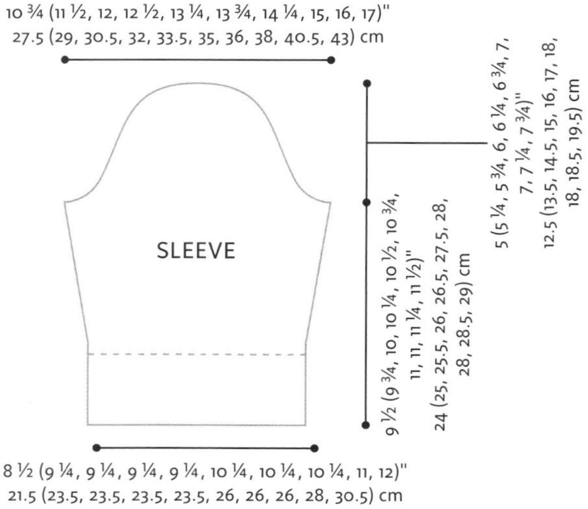
10 ¾ (11 ½, 12, 12 ½, 13 ¼, 13 ¾, 14 ¼, 15, 16, 17)"
27.5 (29, 30.5, 32, 33.5, 35, 36, 38, 40.5, 43) cm
5 (5 ¼, 5 ¾, 6, 6 ¼, 6 ¾, 7, 7, 7 ¼, 7 ¾)"
12.5 (13.5, 14.5, 15, 16, 17, 18, 18, 18.5, 19.5) cm
SLEEVE
9 ½ (9 ¾, 10, 10 ¼, 10 ½, 10 ¾, 11, 11, 11 ¼, 11 ½)"
24 (25, 25.5, 26, 26.5, 27.5, 28, 28, 28.5, 29) cm
8 ½ (9 ¼, 9 ¼, 9 ¼, 9 ¼, 10 ¼, 10 ¼, 10 ¼, 11, 12)"
21.5 (23.5, 23.5, 23.5, 23.5, 26, 26, 26, 28, 30.5) cm

until piece measures 12 ½ (12 ¾, 13, 13 ¼, 13 ½, 13 ¾, 14, 14 ½, 15, 15)" [32 (32.5, 33, 33.5, 34.5, 35, 35.5, 37, 38, 38) cm] from the beginning, ending with a WS row.

### Shape Armholes

**Next Row (RS):** BO 6 (6, 6, 6, 6, 6, 6, 8, 8, 10) sts at beginning of next 2 rows, 0 (0, 2, 2, 2, 2, 2, 4, 6, 6) sts at beginning of next 2 rows, then decrease 1 st each side every other row 2 (3, 2, 3, 3, 4, 6, 5, 6, 6) times—54 (56, 58, 60, 64, 66, 70, 72, 74, 78) sts remain. Work even until armhole measures 5 ½ (6, 6 ¼, 6 ½, 7, 7 ¼, 7 ½, 7 ¾, 8, 8 ½)" [14 (15, 16, 16.5, 18, 18.5, 19, 19.5, 20.5, 21.5) cm], ending with a WS row.

### Shape Neck

**Next Row (RS):** K12 (12, 13, 13, 14, 14, 14, 15, 15, 16), join a second ball of yarn, BO center 30 (32, 32, 34, 36, 38, 42, 42, 44, 46) sts, knit to end. Working both sides at the same time, work even for 1 row. Decrease 1 st at each neck edge every other row twice—10 (10, 11, 11, 12, 12, 12, 13, 13, 14) sts remain each side for shoulders. Work even for 1 row.

### Shape Shoulders

**Next Row (RS):** BO 5 (5, 6, 6, 6, 6, 6, 7, 7, 7) sts at each armhole edge once, then 5 (5, 5, 5, 6, 6, 6, 6, 6, 7) sts once.

## FRONT

Work as for Back until armhole measures 2 ½ (3, 3 ¼, 3 ½, 4, 4 ¼, 4 ½, 4 ¾, 5, 5 ½)" [6.5 (7.5, 8.5, 9, 10, 11, 11.5, 12, 12.5, 14) cm], ending with a WS row.

### Shape Neck

**Next Row (RS):** K15 (16, 17, 17, 19, 19, 20, 21, 21, 22), join a second ball of yarn, BO

center 24 (24, 24, 26, 26, 28, 30, 30, 32, 34) sts, knit
to end. Working both sides at the same time, work
even for 1 row. Decrease 1 st at each neck edge
every other row 5 (6, 6, 6, 7, 7, 8, 8, 8, 8) times—10
(10, 11, 11, 12, 12, 12, 13, 13, 14) sts remain each side for
shoulders. Work even until armhole measures same
as for Back to beginning of shoulder shaping; shape
shoulders as for Back.

## SLEEVES

Using size US 7 (4.5 mm) needles, CO 38 (42, 42, 42,
42, 46, 46, 46, 50, 54) sts. Begin 2x2 Rib; work even
until piece measures 2 ¾" (7 cm) from the beginning, ending with a WS row.

**Next Row (RS):** Change to St st; work even for 4
rows.

### Shape Sleeve

**Increase Row (RS):** Increase 1 st each side this row,
then every 6 (6, 6, 6, 4, 4, 4, 4, 4, 4) rows 4 (4, 5, 6,
8, 7, 8, 10, 10, 10) times—48 (52, 54, 56, 60, 62, 64,
68, 72, 76) sts. Work even until piece measures 9 ½
(9 ¾, 10, 10 ¼, 10 ½, 10 ¾, 11, 11, 11 ¼, 11 ½)" [24 (25,
25.5, 26, 26.5, 27.5, 28, 28, 28.5, 29) cm] from the
beginning, ending with a WS row.

### Shape Cap

**Next Row (RS):** BO 6 (6, 6, 6, 6, 6, 8, 8, 10) sts at
beginning of next 2 rows, 0 (0, 2, 2, 2, 2, 2, 4, 6, 6)
sts at beginning of next 2 rows, decrease 1 st each

side every 6 rows 1 (1, 2, 2, 1, 1, 1, 4, 5, 5) time(s),
every 4 rows 1 (0, 0, 0, 1, 1, 1, 1, 0, 1) time(s), then
every other row 6 (9, 7, 8, 10, 11, 12, 3, 3, 2) times,
then BO 2 (2, 2, 2, 2, 2, 2, 3, 3, 3) sts at beginning of
next 4 rows. BO remaining 12 (12, 12, 12, 12, 12, 16,
16, 16) sts.

## FINISHING

Sew shoulder seams. Set in Sleeves. Sew side and
Sleeve seams. Block as desired.

### Cowl Collar

With RS facing, using size US 8 (5 mm) needle,
beginning at right Back shoulder, pick up and knit 1
st for each BO st, and 2 sts for every 3 rows around
neck shaping, making sure to end with a number
divisible by 4. Join for working in the rnd; pm for
beginning of rnd. Begin 2x2 Rib; work even until
piece measures 6" (15 cm) from the pick-up row. Change
to size US 10 (6 mm) needle; work even until piece
measures 12" (30.5 cm) from pick-up row. BO all sts
in pattern.

# 4

# PROPORTIONAL
# SHAPES

Are you the classic hourglass shape? Do you possess a bust *and* a booty? Or maybe you're straight-up statuesque? Welcome to the Proportional club! Like Ms. Average, your top and bottom appear proportional to each other, but your similarity to her figure may end there—the proportional group encompasses a diverse set of shapes, all of them with their own particular quirks. It's time to embrace those quirks, and read on!

Jenn (right) has narrow shoulders, slim hips, and a straighter shape; Elora (middle) has broad shoulders, larger hips, and a curvy waist; and DeeDee (left) has a large bust and hips with a thicker middle.

## Welcome to the Proportional Club

If the photo you took of yourself from the front (see page 11) revealed that your shoulder or bust region is exactly the same width or just a smidge smaller than your hip line, then you possess a proportional shape. This balance comes in a wide range of packages but generally speaking, a proportional shape usually has an upper torso and/or bust measurement of nearly equal circumference to the hip. Don't get too hung up on the measurements, though! It's really your outline that matters.

The balance between the top and bottom of your body is the hallmark of a proportional figure, but there can be several variations on this theme:

- A very curvy figure, with large bust and hips
- An allover slender, boyish figure
- A thicker-middled shape (known as an "apple" in plant parlance)

## Perfect Proportional Sweaters

When selecting a sweater pattern, you will want to find a design that preserves the appearance of your already balanced figure, then modify that pattern as needed for fit. That said, proportional figures are flattered by clothing that is itself balanced—for instance, a shoulder-broadening element paired with a hip-broadening element, or a narrow, plain neckline combined with a very plain hem.

Since horizontal visual elements broaden a region of the wearer's body and vertical visual elements narrow it, proportional shapes are flattered by sweaters that, when laid flat on a table, appear the same width at their hem and at their neckline.

The proportional group, then, has the most flexibility in terms of design elements, since balance can be achieved in many ways: wide bands of ribbing at the hem combined with a large collar; a narrow, deep V-neck paired with a plain hem; a wider cowl neckline combined with slightly flared sleeves. Any sweater design element imaginable can be balanced in order to flatter a proportional shape.

## Less Ideal Choices

As for all shapes, there are sweater elements that will throw a proportional shape out of proportion. The following styles tend to be less flattering for proportional figures:

- Broad, shallow necklines (like boatnecks) widen the shoulders and lengthen the appearance of the bust, so they should not be combined with a shorter length.
- Deep, narrow necklines combined with longer sweater lengths tend to exaggerate the width of a proportional figure's bottom, which can be unflattering.
- Proportional shapes, due to their inherently balanced figure, are especially prone to looking boxy in sweaters that do not include waist shaping.

Elora's hips are just a bit wider than her bust, so she falls into the proportional category.

## Common Modifications

Have a pattern in hand? All set to knit your favorite sweater? Before you get started, consider the following common modifications for proportional shapes and check out Chapter 6 for instructions if any apply to you.

- Proportional shapes always require waist shaping and may need more than the pattern specifies (see page 147).

- Bust darts are a frequent requirement for proportional shapes (see page 151).

- Proportional shapes, like others, may need to shorten or lengthen a sweater or its sleeves (see page 148).

## Flattering Features for Proportional Shapes

To flatter a proportional figure, look for sweater patterns with the following features. (Note that the design features in each row are intended to be used in combination for optimal balance.)

| | LENGTHS | NECKLINES | SLEEVES |
|---|---|---|---|
|  | Keep the length at high hip or mid-hip, and use a vertical trim to accentuate curves. | Deep, narrow necklines | Elbow-length or longer sleeves to preserve the sweater's balance |
|  | Include an eye-catching hem treatment to balance the neckline. | Wide necklines, including wide collars or cowls | Three-quarter-length sleeves, which draw attention to the waist |
|  | Keep the length shorter or average with relatively plain hem treatments. | Crew necklines or turtlenecks | Any sleeve length will complement a plain hem and neckline. |

The plain crew neckline and plain ribbed hem balance one another.

The cable panels provide a nice vertical line that slims the torso.

Cables on the sleeve draw the eye up to the face.

Jenn is wearing size 32–33" (81–83.5 cm) with approximately 1" (2.5 cm) of positive ease in the upper torso.

# CLASSIC PULLOVER

The clean lines of this sweater are my take on a classic cabled pullover. The cables provide figure-flattering features (and are fun to knit), and the waist shaping ensures a nice trim fit, keeping a smaller-busted proportional figure in balance.

. . . . . . . . . . . . . . . . . . . . . . . .

## SIZES

To fit upper torso sizes 28–29 (30–31, 32–33, 34–35, 36–37, 38–39, 40–41, 44–45, 48–49, 52–53)" [71–73.5 (76–78.5, 81.5–84, 86.5–89, 91.5–94, 96.5–99, 101.5–104, 112–114.5, 122–124.5, 132–134.5) cm]

## FINISHED MEASUREMENTS

30 ½ (32, 34 ½, 36, 38 ½, 40, 42 ½, 46 ½, 50 ½, 54 ½)" [77.5 (81.5, 87.5, 91.5, 98, 101.5, 108, 118, 128.5, 138.5) cm] chest

*Note: Sweater is intended to be worn with 1-2" (2.5-5 cm) positive ease in the upper torso.*

## YARN

Bijou Basin Ranch Bijou Spun Bijou Bliss [50% yak down / 50% cormo wool; 150 yards (137 meters) / 2 ounces (56 grams)]: 7 (7, 8, 9, 9, 10, 10, 11, 12, 13) hanks #13 Steel

## NEEDLES

One pair straight needles size US 7 (4.5 mm)

One 24" (60 cm) long circular (circ) needle size US 7 (4.5 mm)

Change needle size if necessary to obtain correct gauge.

## NOTIONS

Stitch markers; cable needle (cn)

## GAUGE

20 sts and 28 rows = 4" (10 cm) in Stockinette stitch (St st)

## NOTES

Unless otherwise specified, decreases should be worked to match the slant of the edge being shaped, as follows: For left-slanting edges: On RS rows, k1, ssk, work to end; on WS rows, work to last 3 sts, ssp, p1. For right-slanting edges: On RS rows, work to last 3 sts, k2tog, k1; on WS rows, p1, p2tog, work to end. Increases should also be worked to match the slant of the edge being shaped, as follows: For right-slanting edges: On RS rows, work 1 st, M1-r, work to end; on WS rows, work to last st, M1-p, work 1 st. For left-slanting edges: On RS rows, work to last st, M1-l, work 1 st; on WS rows, work 1 st, M1-p-l, work to end.

## STITCH PATTERNS

### 3x3 Rib Flat

(multiple of 6 sts + 3; 1-row repeat)

**Row 1 (WS):** P3, *k3, p3; repeat from * to end.

**Row 2:** Knit the knit sts and purl the purl sts as they face you.

Repeat Row 2 for 3x3 Rib Flat.

### 3x3 Rib in the Rnd

(multiple of 6 sts; 1-rnd repeat)

**All Rnds:** *K3, p3; repeat from * to end.

## BACK

CO 75 (81, 87, 93, 99, 99, 105, 117, 123, 135) sts. Begin 3x3 Rib Flat; work even until piece measures 2 ½" (6.5 cm) from the beginning, ending with a WS row.

**Next Row (RS):** Change to St st, decreasing 0 (1, 1, 3, 3, 0, 0, 1, 0, 0) or increasing 1 (0, 0, 0, 0, 1, 1, 0, 3, 1) st(s) evenly on first row—76 (80, 86, 90, 96, 100, 106, 116, 126, 136) sts. Work even until piece measures 3 ½" (9 cm) from the beginning, ending with a RS row.

**Next Row (WS):** P25 (27, 29, 30, 32, 33, 35, 39, 42, 45), pm, p26 (26, 28, 30, 32, 34, 36, 38, 42, 46), pm, purl to end.

### Shape Waist

**Decrease Row (RS):** Decrease 2 sts this row, then every 6 rows 3 times, as follows: Knit to 2 sts before first marker, ssk, sm, knit to next marker, sm, k2tog, knit to end—68 (72, 78, 82, 88, 92, 98, 108, 118, 128) sts remain. Work even until piece measures 7" (18 cm) from the beginning, ending with a WS row.

### Shape Bust

**Increase Row (RS):** Increase 2 sts this row, then every 8 rows 3 times, as follows: Knit to first marker, M1-r, sm, knit to next marker, sm, M1-l, knit to end—76 (80, 86, 90, 96, 100, 106, 116, 126, 136) sts. Work even, removing markers on first row, until piece measures 12 ½ (12 ¾, 13, 13 ¼, 13 ½, 13 ¾, 14, 14 ½, 15, 15)" [32 (32.5, 33, 33.5, 34.5, 35, 35.5, 37, 38, 38) cm] from the beginning, ending with a WS row.

### Shape Armholes

**Next Row (RS):** BO 6 (6, 6, 6, 6, 6, 6, 8, 10, 12) sts at beginning of next 2 rows, 0 (2, 2, 2, 2, 2, 4, 6, 8, 8) sts at beginning of next 2 rows, then decrease 1 st each side every other row 3 (2, 3, 4, 4, 5, 5, 5, 5, 5) times—58 (60, 64, 66, 72, 74, 76, 78, 80, 86) sts remain. Work even until armhole measures 5 ½ (6, 6 ¼, 6 ½, 7, 7 ¼, 7 ½, 7 ¾, 8, 8 ½)" [14 (15, 16, 16.5, 18, 18.5, 19, 19.5, 20.5, 21.5) cm], ending with a WS row.

### Shape Neck

**Next Row (RS):** K18 (19, 20, 21, 22, 23, 23, 24, 24, 26), join a second ball of yarn, BO center 22 (22, 24, 24, 28, 28, 30, 30, 32, 34) sts, knit to end. Working both sides at the same time, work even for 1 row. Decrease 1 st at each neck edge every other row twice—16 (17, 18, 19, 20, 21, 21, 22, 22, 24) sts remain each side for shoulders. Work even until armhole measures 6 ½ (7, 7 ¼, 7 ½, 8, 8 ¼, 8 ½, 8 ¾, 9, 9 ½)" [16.5 (18, 18.5, 19, 20.5, 21, 21.5, 22, 23, 24) cm], ending with a WS row.

### Shape Shoulders

**Next Row (RS):** BO 8 (9, 9, 10, 10, 11, 11, 11, 11, 12) sts at each armhole edge once, then 8 (8, 9, 9, 10, 10, 10, 11, 11, 12) sts once.

## FRONT

CO 104 (104, 116, 116, 116, 128, 128, 140, 152, 164) sts.

**Next Row (RS):** P2, work 3x3 Rib Flat, beginning with k3, over next 18 (18, 24, 24, 24, 30, 30, 36, 42, 48) sts, pm, work Left Windblown Cable from Chart over next 18 sts, pm, work Ensign's Braid from Chart over next 28 sts, pm, work Right Windblown Cable from Chart over next 18 sts, pm, work 3x3 Rib Flat to last 2 sts, purl to end. Work even, working sts between markers in cable patterns, and remaining sts in rib as established, until piece measures 2 ½" (6.5 cm), ending with a WS row.

**Next Row (RS):** Work in St st to first marker, decreasing 2 (0, 3, 1, 0, 2, 0, 0, 1, 2) or increasing 0 (0, 0, 0, 2, 0, 1, 0, 0, 0) st(s) evenly to marker, sm, work as established to last marker, work in St st to end, decreasing 2 (0, 3, 1, 0, 2, 0, 0, 1, 2) or increasing 0 (0, 0, 0, 2, 0, 1, 0, 0, 0) st(s) evenly to end—100 (104, 110, 114, 120, 124, 130, 140, 150, 160) sts. Work even until piece measures 3 ½" (9 cm) from the beginning, ending with a WS row.

### Shape Waist

**Decrease Row (RS):** Decrease 2 sts this row, then every 6 rows 3 times, as follows: Knit to 3 sts before first marker, ssk, k1, sm, knit to next marker, sm, k1, k2tog, knit to end—92 (96, 102, 106, 112, 116, 122, 132, 142, 152) sts remain. Work even until piece measures 7" (18 cm) from the beginning, ending with a WS row.

### Shape Bust

**Increase Row (RS):** Increase 2 sts this row, then every 8 rows 3 times, as follows: Knit to 1 st before first marker, M1-r, sm, knit to next marker, sm, k1, M1-l, knit to end—100 (104, 110, 114, 120, 124, 130, 140, 150, 160) sts. Work even, removing markers on first row, until piece measures 12 ½ (12 ¾, 13, 13 ¼, 13 ½, 13 ¾, 14, 14 ½, 15, 15)" [32 (32.5, 33, 33.5, 34.5, 35, 35.5, 37, 38, 38) cm] from the beginning, ending with a WS row.

## Left Windblown Cable

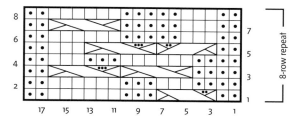

8-row repeat

## Right Windblown Cable

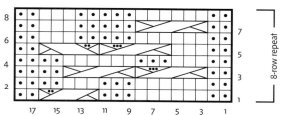

8-row repeat

## KEY

| | |
|---|---|
| ☐ | Knit on RS, purl on WS. |
| ⊡ | Purl on RS, knit on WS. |

Slip 3 sts to cn, hold to front, p1, k3 from cn.

Slip 1 st to cn, hold to back, k3, p1 from cn.

Slip 3 sts to cn, hold to front, p2, k3 from cn.

Slip 2 sts to cn, hold to back, k3, p2 from cn.

Slip 3 sts to cn, hold to front, k3, k3 from cn.

Slip 3 sts to cn, hold to back, k3, k3 from cn.

Slip 3 sts to cn, hold to front, p3, k3 from cn.

Slip 3 sts to cn, hold to back, k3, p3 from cn.

## Ensign's Braid

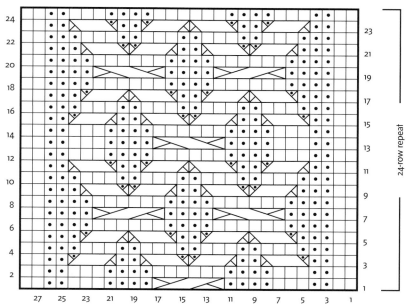

24-row repeat

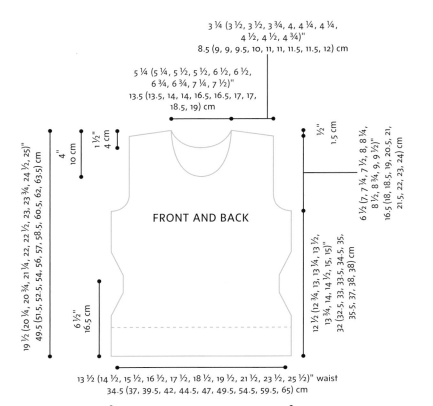

3 ¼ (3 ½, 3 ½, 3 ¾, 4, 4 ¼, 4 ¼, 4 ½, 4 ½, 4 ¾)"
8.5 (9, 9, 9.5, 10, 11, 11, 11.5, 11.5, 12) cm

5 ¼ (5 ¼, 5 ½, 5 ½, 6 ½, 6 ½, 6 ¾, 6 ¾, 7 ¼, 7 ½)"
13.5 (13.5, 14, 14, 16.5, 16.5, 17, 17, 18.5, 19) cm

1 ½"
4 cm

4"
10 cm

½"
1.5 cm

6 ½ (7, 7 ¼, 7 ½, 8, 8 ¼, 8 ½, 8 ¾, 9, 9 ½)"
16.5 (18, 18.5, 19, 20.5, 21, 21.5, 22, 23, 24) cm

FRONT AND BACK

19 ½ (20 ¼, 20 ¾, 21 ¼, 22, 22 ½, 23, 23 ¾, 24 ½, 25)"
49.5 (51.5, 52.5, 54, 56, 57, 58.5, 60.5, 62, 63.5) cm

12 ½ (12 ¾, 13, 13 ¼, 13 ½, 13 ¾, 14, 14 ½, 15, 15)"
32 (32.5, 33, 33.5, 34.5, 35, 35.5, 37, 38, 38) cm

6 ½"
16.5 cm

13 ½ (14 ½, 15 ½, 16 ½, 17 ½, 18 ½, 19 ½, 21 ½, 23 ½, 25 ½)" waist
34.5 (37, 39.5, 42, 44.5, 47, 49.5, 54.5, 59.5, 65) cm

15 ¼ (16, 17 ¼, 18, 19 ¼, 20, 21 ¼, 23 ¼, 25 ¼, 27 ¼)" hip and bust
38.5 (40.5, 44, 45.5, 49, 51, 54, 59, 64, 69) cm

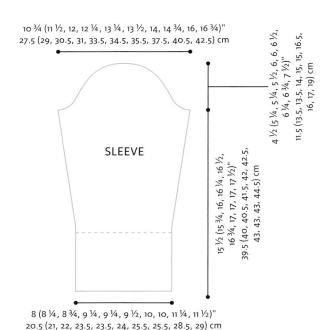

10 ¾ (11 ½, 12, 12 ¼, 13 ¼, 13 ½, 14, 14 ¾, 16, 16 ¾)"
27.5 (29, 30.5, 31, 33.5, 34.5, 35.5, 37.5, 40.5, 42.5) cm

4 ½ (5 ¼, 5 ¼, 5 ½, 6, 6 ½, 6 ¼, 6 ¾, 7 ½)"
11.5 (13.5, 13.5, 14, 15, 16.5, 16, 17, 19) cm

SLEEVE

15 ½ (15 ¾, 16, 16 ¼, 16 ½, 16 ¾, 17, 17, 17 ½)"
39.5 (40, 40.5, 41.5, 42, 42.5, 43, 43, 44.5) cm

8 (8 ¼, 8 ¾, 9 ¼, 9 ¼, 9 ½, 10, 10, 11 ¼, 11 ½)"
20.5 (21, 22, 23.5, 23.5, 24, 25.5, 25.5, 28.5, 29) cm

## Shape Armholes

**Next Row (RS):** BO 6 (6, 6, 6, 6, 6, 8, 10, 12) sts at beginning of next 2 rows, 0 (2, 2, 2, 2, 2, 4, 6, 8) sts at beginning of next 2 rows, then decrease 1 st each side every other row 3 (2, 3, 4, 4, 5, 5, 5, 5) times—82 (84, 88, 90, 96, 98, 100, 102, 104, 110) sts remain. Work even until armhole measures 3 (3 ½, 3 ¾, 4, 4 ½, 4 ¾, 5, 5 ¼, 5 ½, 6)" [7.5 (9, 9.5, 10, 11.5, 12, 12.5, 13.5, 14, 15) cm], ending with a WS row.

## Shape Neck

**Next Row (RS):** Work 26 (27, 28, 29, 31, 32, 33, 34, 34, 36) sts, join a second ball of yarn, BO center 30 (30, 32, 32, 34, 34, 34, 34, 36, 38) sts, work to end. Working both sides at the same time, work even for 1 row. Decrease 1 st at each neck edge every row 7 (7, 7, 7, 8, 8, 9, 9, 9, 9) times, then every other row 3 times—16 (17, 18, 19, 20, 21, 21, 22, 22, 24) sts remain each side for shoulders. Work even until armhole measures same as for Back to shoulder shaping; shape shoulders as for Back.

## LEFT SLEEVE

CO 46 (46, 58, 58, 58, 58, 58, 58, 70, 70) sts.

**Next Row (WS):** P2, work in 3x3 Rib Flat over next 12 (12, 18, 18, 18, 18, 18, 18, 24, 24) sts, pm, work Left Windblown Cable, beginning with Row 2, over next 18 sts, pm, work 3x3 Rib Flat to last 2 sts, purl to end. Work even, working sts between markers in Cable pattern, and remaining sts in rib as established, until piece measures 5" (12.5 cm) from the beginning, ending with a WS row.

**Next Row (RS):** Work in St st to first marker, decreasing 0 (0, 3, 2, 2, 1, 0, 0, 3, 2) or increasing 1 (2, 0, 0, 0, 0, 0, 0, 0, 0) st(s) evenly to marker, sm, work to next marker, work

in St st to end, decreasing 0 (0, 3, 2, 2, 1, 0, 0, 3, 2) or increasing 1 (2, 0, 0, 0, 0, 0, 0, 0, 0) st(s) evenly to end—48 (50, 52, 54, 54, 56, 58, 58, 64, 66). Work even for 1 row.

### Shape Sleeve

**Next Row (RS):** Continuing to work sts between markers in Cable pattern, and remaining sts in St st, increase 1 st each side this row, then every 10 (10, 10, 10, 8, 8, 8, 6, 6, 6) rows 6 (7, 7, 7, 9, 9, 9, 11, 11, 12) times—62 (66, 68, 70, 74, 76, 78, 82, 88, 92) sts. Work even until piece measures 15 ½ (15 ¾, 16, 16 ¼, 16 ½, 16 ¾, 17, 17, 17, 17 ½)" [39.5 (40, 40.5, 41.5, 42, 42.5, 43, 43, 43, 44.5) cm] from the beginning, ending with a WS row.

### Shape Cap

**Next Row (RS):** BO 6 (6, 6, 6, 6, 6, 6, 8, 10, 12) sts at beginning of next 2 rows, 0 (2, 2, 2, 2, 2, 4, 6, 7, 7) sts at beginning of next 2 rows, decrease 1 st each side every 6 rows 1 (2, 1, 1, 1, 1, 2, 5, 6, 7) time(s), every 4 rows 0 (0, 1, 1, 1, 0, 1, 0, 0, 0) time(s), then

every other row 9 (8, 9, 10, 12, 14, 11, 3, 2, 1) time(s), then BO 3 (3, 3, 3, 3, 3, 3, 4, 4, 4) sts at beginning of next 4 rows. BO remaining 18 (18, 18, 18, 18, 18, 18, 22, 22, 22) sts.

### RIGHT SLEEVE

Work as for Left Sleeve, substituting Right Windblown Cable for Left Windblown Cable.

### FINISHING

Block pieces as desired. Sew shoulder seams. Set in Sleeves; sew side and Sleeve seams.

### Neckband

With RS facing, using circ needle, and beginning at right shoulder, pick up and knit 38 (38, 40, 40, 44, 44, 46, 46, 48, 50) sts along Back neck, then 70 (70, 74, 74, 76, 76, 74, 74, 78, 82) sts along Front neck—108 (108, 114, 114, 120, 120, 120, 120, 126, 132) sts. Join for working in the rnd; pm for beginning of rnd. Begin 3x3 Rib in the Rnd; work even for ½" (1.5 cm). BO all sts in pattern.

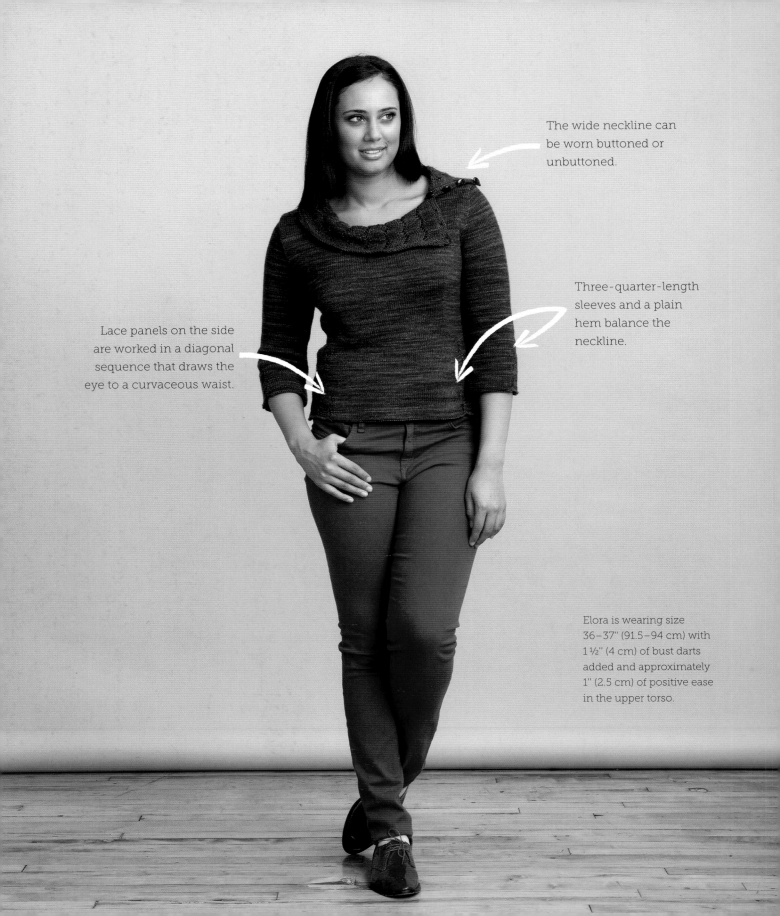

The wide neckline can be worn buttoned or unbuttoned.

Three-quarter-length sleeves and a plain hem balance the neckline.

Lace panels on the side are worked in a diagonal sequence that draws the eye to a curvaceous waist.

Elora is wearing size 36–37" (91.5–94 cm) with 1½" (4 cm) of bust darts added and approximately 1" (2.5 cm) of positive ease in the upper torso.

# HOLLOWAY PULLOVER

This eye-catching sweater flatters a classic hourglass figure without exposing a lot of skin. The body, largely in plain Stockinette stitch, allows for flexible waist and bust shaping.

. . . . . . . . . . . . . . . . . . . . . . . . . . . . . . . . . . . . . . . . . .

## SIZES

To fit upper torso sizes 28–29 (30–31, 32–33, 34–35, 36–37, 38–39, 40–41, 44–45, 48–49, 52–53)" [71–73.5 (76–78.5, 81.5–84, 86.5–89, 91.5–94, 96.5–99, 101.5–104, 112–114.5, 122–124.5, 132–134.5) cm]

## FINISHED MEASUREMENTS

30 (32, 34, 36, 38, 40, 42, 46, 50, 54)" [76 (81.5, 86.5, 91.5, 96.5, 101.5, 106.5, 117, 127, 137) cm] chest

*Note: Pullover is intended to be worn with 1-2" (2.5-5 cm) positive ease in the upper torso.*

## YARN

The Plucky Knitter Primo Sport [75% merino wool / 20% cashmere / 5% nylon; 275 yards (251 meters) / 100 grams]: 5 (5, 5, 6, 6, 6, 7, 7, 8, 9) hanks Poppycock

## NEEDLES

One pair straight needles size US 3 (3.25 mm)

One 24" (60 cm) long circular (circ) needle size US 3 (3.25 mm)

One 24" (60 cm) long circular needle size US 4 (3.5 mm)

One 24" (60 cm) long circular needle size US 5 (3.75 mm)

Change needle size if necessary to obtain correct gauge.

## NOTIONS

Stitch markers; four ½" (13 mm) buttons

## GAUGE

24 sts and 32 rows = 4" (10 cm) in Stockinette stitch (St st), using smaller needles

## NOTES

Front and Back begin with a 1" hem that is worked across the center of the piece, then stitches are cast on to either side for the lace panels. Unless otherwise specified, decreases should be worked to match the slant of the edge being shaped, as follows: For left-slanting edges: On RS rows, k1, ssk, work to end; on WS rows, work to last 3 sts, ssp, p1. For right-slanting edges: On RS rows, work to last 3 sts, k2tog, k1; on WS rows, p1, p2tog, work to end. Increases should also be worked to match the slant of the edge being shaped, as follows: For right-slanting edges: On RS rows, work 1 st, M1-r, work to end; on WS rows, work to last st, M1-p, work 1 st. For left-slanting edges: On RS rows, work to last st, M1-l, work 1 st; on WS rows, work 1 st, M1-p-l, work to end.

## STITCH PATTERN

### Herringbone Lace

(multiple of 8 sts; 12-row repeat)

**Rows 1, 3, and 5 (RS):** *Ssk, k2, yo, k4; repeat from * to end.

**Row 2 and all WS Rows:** Purl.

**Rows 7, 9, and 11:** *K3, yo, k2, k2tog, k1; repeat from * to end.

**Row 12:** Purl.

Repeat Rows 1-12 for Herringbone Lace.

## BACK

Using smaller needles, CO 38 (44, 50, 56, 62, 68, 74, 86, 98, 110) sts. Begin St st; work even until piece measures 1" (2.5 cm) from the beginning, ending with a RS row.

**Next Row (WS):** CO 26 sts, knit to end (Turning Row), CO 26 sts—90 (96, 102, 108, 114, 120, 126, 138, 150, 162) sts.

**Next Row:** K2 (edge sts, keep in St st), [work Herringbone Lace (from text or Chart), beginning with Row 1, over next 8 sts, pm] 3 times, knit to last 26 sts, [pm, work Herringbone Lace, beginning with Row 7, over next 8 sts] 3 times, k2 (edge sts, keep in St st). Work even, working Herringbone Lace on sides as established, and St st between center markers, until piece measures 2 ½" (6.5 cm) from Turning Row, ending with a WS row.

**Next Row (RS):** K2, work in Herringbone Lace as established to second marker, sm, work in St st to fifth marker, removing third and fourth markers, sm, work in Herringbone Lace as established to last 2 sts, k2 (4 markers remain).

**Next Row:** [Work 30 (32, 34, 36, 38, 40, 42, 46, 50, 54) sts, pm] twice, work to end.

### Shape Waist

**Decrease Row (RS):** Decrease 2 sts this row, then every 8 rows 4 times, as follows: Work to 2 sts before third marker, ssk, sm, knit to next marker, sm, k2tog, work to end—80 (86, 92, 98, 104, 110, 116, 128, 140, 152) sts remain. Work even until piece measures 7 ½" (19 cm) from Turning Row, ending with a RS row.

**Next Row (WS):** P2, work in Herringbone Lace as established to first marker, sm, work in St st to last marker, removing second and fifth markers, work in Herringbone Lace as established to last 2 sts, p2 (4 markers remain).

### Shape Bust

**Increase Row (RS):** Increase 2 sts this row, then every 8 rows 4 times, as follows: Work to second marker, M1-r, sm, work to next marker, sm, M1-l, work to end—90 (96, 102, 108, 114, 120, 126, 138, 150, 162) sts. Work even, removing center 2 markers on first row, until piece measures 13 (13 ¼, 13 ½, 13 ¾, 14, 14 ¼, 14 ½, 15, 15 ½, 15 ½)" [33 (33.5, 34.5, 35, 35.5, 36, 37, 38, 39.5, 39.5) cm] from Turning Row, ending with a WS row, and removing remaining 2 markers on last row.

### Shape Armholes

**Next Row (RS):** BO 6 (6, 6, 6, 6, 6, 8, 10, 12, 14) sts at beginning of next 2 rows, 2 (2, 2, 2, 2, 4, 4, 6, 8, 10) sts at beginning of next 2 rows, then decrease 1 st each side every other row 2 (4, 5, 7, 7, 6, 6, 6, 7, 6) times—70 (72, 76, 78, 84, 88, 90, 94, 96, 102) sts remain. Work even until armhole measures 5 ½ (6, 6 ¼, 6 ½, 7, 7 ¼, 7 ½, 7 ¾, 8, 8 ½)" [14 (15, 16, 16.5, 18, 18.5, 19, 19.5, 20.5, 21.5) cm], ending with a WS row.

### Shape Neck

**Next Row (RS):** K20 (20, 22, 22, 23, 25, 25, 26, 26, 28), join a second ball of yarn, BO center 30 (32, 32, 34, 38, 38, 40, 42, 44, 46) sts, knit to end. Working both sides at the same time, work even for 1 row. Decrease 1 st at each neck edge every other row twice—18 (18, 20, 20, 21, 23, 23, 24, 24, 26) sts remain each side for shoulders. Work even until armhole measures 6 ½ (7, 7 ¼, 7 ½, 8, 8 ¼, 8 ½, 8 ¾, 9, 9 ½)" [16.5 (18, 18.5, 19, 20.5, 21, 21.5, 22, 23, 24) cm], ending with a WS row.

**Next Row (RS):** BO 9 (9, 10, 10, 11, 12, 12, 12, 12, 13) sts at each armhole edge once, then 9 (9, 10, 10, 10, 11, 11, 12, 12, 13) sts once.

**KEY**

| | |
|---|---|
| ☐ | Knit on RS, purl on WS. |
| ⊡ | Yo |
| ⊠ | K2tog |
| ⊠ | Ssk |

**Herringbone Lace**

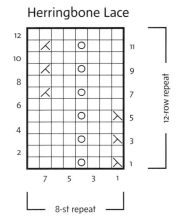

12-row repeat

8-st repeat

## FRONT

Work as for Back until piece measures 2 ½" (6.5 cm) from Turning Row, ending with a WS row.

**Next Row (RS):** K2, work in Herringbone Lace as established to second marker, sm, work in St st to fifth marker, removing third and fourth markers, sm, work in Herringbone Lace as established to last 2 sts, k2.

**Next Row:** Work 23 (24, 26, 27, 29, 30, 32, 35, 38, 41) sts, pm, work 44 (48, 50, 54, 56, 60, 62, 68, 74, 80) sts, pm, work to end. Work as for Back to beginning of armhole shaping, ending with a WS row, removing remaining markers on last row.

### Shape Armholes

**Next Row (RS):** Shape armholes as for Back—70 (72, 76, 78, 84, 88, 90, 94, 96, 102) sts remain. Work even until armhole measures 2 (2 ½, 2 ¾, 3, 3 ½, 3 ¾, 4, 4 ¼, 4 ½, 5)" [5 (6.5, 7, 7.5, 9, 9.5, 10, 11, 11.5, 12.5) cm], ending with a WS row.

### Shape Neck

**Next Row (RS):** Work 26 (27, 29, 29, 31, 33, 34, 35, 36, 38) sts, join a second ball of yarn, BO center 18 (18, 18, 20, 22, 22, 22, 24, 24, 26) sts, work to end. Working both sides at the same time, decrease 1 st at each neck edge every row 4 (5, 5, 5, 5, 5, 6, 6, 6, 6) times, every other row 2 (2, 2, 2, 3, 3, 3, 3, 3, 3) times, then every 4 rows 2 (2, 2, 2, 2, 2, 2, 3, 3) times—18 (18, 20, 20, 21, 23, 23, 24, 24, 26) sts remain each side for shoulders. Work even until armhole measures same as for Back to shoulder shaping; shape shoulders as for Back.

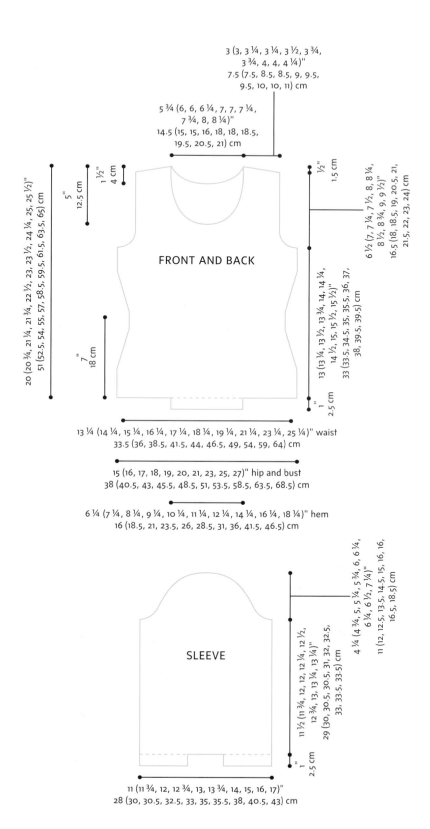

3 (3, 3 ¼, 3 ¼, 3 ½, 3 ¾, 3 ¾, 4, 4, 4 ¼)"
7.5 (7.5, 8.5, 8.5, 9, 9.5, 9.5, 10, 10, 11) cm

5 ¾ (6, 6, 6 ¼, 7, 7, 7 ¼, 7 ¾, 8, 8 ¼)"
14.5 (15, 15, 16, 18, 18, 18.5, 19.5, 20.5, 21) cm

5"
12.5 cm

1 ½"
4 cm

½"
1.5 cm

6 ½ (7, 7 ¼, 7 ½, 8, 8 ¼, 8 ½, 8 ¾, 9, 9 ½)"
16.5 (18, 18.5, 19, 20.5, 21, 21.5, 22, 23, 24) cm

**FRONT AND BACK**

20 (20 ¾, 21 ¼, 21 ¾, 22 ½, 23, 23 ½, 24 ¼, 25, 25 ½)"
51 (52.5, 54, 55, 57, 58.5, 59.5, 61.5, 63.5, 65) cm

7"
18 cm

13 (13 ¼, 13 ½, 13 ¾, 14, 14 ¼, 14 ½, 15, 15 ½, 15 ½)"
33 (33.5, 34.5, 35, 35.5, 36, 37, 38, 39.5, 39.5) cm

1"
2.5 cm

13 ¼ (14 ¼, 15 ¼, 16 ¼, 17 ¼, 18 ¼, 19 ¼, 21 ¼, 23 ¼, 25 ¼)" waist
33.5 (36, 38.5, 41.5, 44, 46.5, 49, 54, 59, 64) cm

15 (16, 17, 18, 19, 20, 21, 23, 25, 27)" hip and bust
38 (40.5, 43, 45.5, 48.5, 51, 53.5, 58.5, 63.5, 68.5) cm

6 ¼ (7 ¼, 8 ¼, 9 ¼, 10 ¼, 11 ¼, 12 ¼, 14 ¼, 16 ¼, 18 ¼)" hem
16 (18.5, 21, 23.5, 26, 28.5, 31, 36, 41.5, 46.5) cm

4 ¼ (4 ¾, 5, 5 ¼, 5 ¾, 6, 6 ¼, 6 ¼, 6 ½, 7 ¼)"
11 (12, 12.5, 13.5, 14.5, 15, 16, 16, 16.5, 18.5) cm

**SLEEVE**

11 ½ (11 ¾, 12, 12, 12 ¼, 12 ½, 12 ¾, 13, 13 ¼, 13 ¼)"
29 (30, 30.5, 30.5, 31, 32, 32.5, 33, 33.5, 33.5) cm

1"
2.5 cm

11 (11 ¾, 12, 12 ¾, 13, 13 ¾, 14, 15, 16, 17)"
28 (30, 30.5, 32.5, 33, 35, 35.5, 38, 40.5, 43) cm

## SLEEVES

Using smaller needles, CO 21 (23, 24, 26, 27, 29, 30, 33, 36, 39) sts. Begin St st; work even until piece measures 1" (2.5 cm) from the beginning, ending with a RS row. Break yarn and set aside for first side of hem. Repeat for second side of hem, leaving sts on the needle.

**Turning Row (WS):** Knit across second side of hem, pm, CO 24 sts for center of Sleeve, pm, knit across first side of hem—66 (70, 72, 76, 78, 82, 84, 90, 96, 102) sts.

**Next Row (RS):** Work in St st to first marker, sm, [work Herringbone Lace (from text or Chart), beginning with Row 1, over next 8 sts, pm] 3 times, omitting final pm, work in St st to end. Work even, working Herringbone Lace between markers, and remaining sts in St, until piece measures 2 ½" (6.5 cm) from Turning Row, ending with a WS row.

**Next Row (RS):** Work in St st to second marker, removing first marker, sm, work in Herringbone

Lace as established to next marker, sm, work in St st to end, removing last marker. Work even until piece measures 5 ½" (14 cm) from Turning Row, ending with a WS row.

**Next Row (RS):** Work in St st across all sts, removing remaining markers; work even until piece measures 11 ½ (11 ¾, 12, 12, 12 ¼, 12 ½, 12 ¾, 13, 13 ¼, 13 ¼)" [29 (30, 30.5, 30.5, 31, 32, 32.5, 33, 33.5, 33.5) cm] from Turning Row, ending with a WS row.

## Shape Cap

**Next Row (RS):** BO 6 (6, 6, 6, 6, 6, 8, 10, 12, 14) sts at beginning of next 2 rows, 2 (2, 2, 2, 2, 4, 4, 6, 8, 9) sts at beginning of next 2 rows, decrease 1 st each side every 6 rows 1 (1, 1, 0, 1, 1, 2, 5, 6, 8) time(s), every 4 rows 0 (0, 0, 1, 0, 1, 1, 1, 1, 0) time(s), then every other row 10 (12, 13, 15, 16, 15, 13, 4, 2, 1) time(s), then BO 3 (3, 3, 3, 3, 3, 3, 4, 4, 4) sts at beginning of next 4 rows. BO remaining 16 (16, 16, 16, 16, 16, 16, 22, 22, 22) sts.

## FINISHING

Block pieces as desired. Sew shoulders seams. Set in Sleeves; sew side and Sleeve seams. Fold hems to WS at Turning Row and sew to WS, being careful not to let sts shown on RS.

## Collar

With RS facing, using smallest circ needle, and beginning halfway between left shoulder seam and right-hand edge of center Front neck BO sts, pick up and knit 14 (14, 14, 14, 14, 14, 15, 15, 15, 15) sts along Left Front neck, 18 (18, 18, 20, 22, 22, 22, 24, 24, 26) sts in center Front neck BO sts, 28 (28, 28, 28, 28, 28, 30, 30, 30, 30) sts to right shoulder, 50 (52, 52, 54, 58, 58, 60, 62, 64, 66) sts along Back neck edge, then 14 (14, 14, 14, 14, 14, 15, 15, 15, 15) sts along remaining portion of Left Front neck edge—124 (126, 126, 130, 136, 136, 142, 146, 148, 152) sts.

**Next Row (RS):** K2 (3, 3, 1, 0, 0, 3, 1, 2, 0), work Herringbone Lace (from text or Chart), beginning

with Row 1, to last 2 (3, 3, 1, 0, 0, 3, 1, 2, 0) sts, knit to end. Note: Collar will be folded over to the RS when completed, so that what was WS of Collar will become RS. Work even until piece measures 1" (2.5 cm) from pick-up row. Change to size US 4 (3.5 mm) circ needle; work even until piece measures 3" (7.5 cm) from pick-up row. Change to size US 5 (3.75 mm) circ needle; work even until piece measures 5" (12.5 cm) from pick-up row, ending with a RS row. Change to Garter st (knit every row); work even for 8 rows. BO all sts.

## Button Band

With RS facing, using smallest needles, and beginning at edge of Collar closest to shoulder, pick up and knit 30 sts along side edge of Collar. Begin Garter st; work even for 8 rows. BO all sts.

## Buttonhole Band

With RS facing, using smallest needles, pick up and knit 30 sts along remaining side edge of Collar. Begin Garter st; work even for 3 rows.

**Buttonhole Row (RS):** [K5, yo, k2tog] 4 times, knit to end. Work even for 4 rows. BO all sts.

Sew buttons opposite buttonholes.

The deep, square neck-
line is balanced by a
wide, curved band of
textured stitches at the
hem and the sleeves.

Curved textured
panel draws eye
to waist.

Elora is wearing size
37–38" (94–96.5 cm) with
1½" (4 cm) of bust darts
added and a bit over 1"
(2.5 cm) of positive ease in
the upper torso.

# SQUARED CARDIGAN

This three-quarter-length sleeve cardigan is a perfect choice for curvaceous proportional figures with large busts. The waist is plain Stockinette, allowing for a wide variety of waist- and bust-shaping requirements.

- - - - - - - - - - - - - - - - - - - - - - - - - - - - - - - - - -

## SIZES

To fit upper torso sizes 29–30 (31–32, 33–34, 35–36, 37–38, 39–40, 41–42, 45–46, 49–50, 53–54)" [73.5-76 (78.5–81.5, 84–86.5, 89–91.5, 94–96.5, 99–101.5, 104–106.5, 114.5–117, 124.5–127, 134.5–137) cm]

## FINISHED MEASUREMENTS

32 ¼ (34 ½, 35 ¼, 38 ¼, 40 ½, 41 ¼, 44, 47 ¾, 51 ¾, 55 ½)" [82 (87.5, 89.5, 97, 103, 105, 112, 121.5, 131.5, 141) cm] chest

*Note: Cardigan is intended to be worn with ½-1" (1.5-2.5 cm) positive ease in the upper torso.*

## YARN

Blue Moon Fiber Arts Socks that Rock Heavyweight [100% superwash merino wool; 350 yards (320 meters) / 7 ounces (198 grams)]: 3 (3, 3, 4, 4, 4, 4, 5, 5) hanks Chestnutty

## NEEDLES

One pair straight needles size US 4 (3.5 mm)

One 24" (60 cm) long circular (circ) needle size US 4 (3.5 mm)

Change needle size if necessary to obtain correct gauge.

## NOTIONS

Stitch markers in 2 colors (A and B); 7 (7, 7, 7, 7, 8, 8, 8, 8, 8) ¾" (19 mm) buttons

## GAUGE

22 sts and 30 rows = 4" (10 cm) in Stockinette stitch (St st)

22 sts and 30 rows = 4" (10 cm) in Cabled Check Stitch

## NOTES

Unless otherwise specified, decreases should be worked to match the slant of the edge being shaped, as follows: For left-slanting edges: On RS rows, k1, ssk, work to end; on WS rows, work to last 3 sts, ssp, p1. For right-slanting edges: On RS rows, work to last 3 sts, k2tog, k1; on WS rows, p1, p2tog, work to end. Increases should also be worked to match the slant of the edge being shaped, as follows: For right-slanting edges: On RS rows, work 1 st, M1-r, work to end; on WS rows, work to last st, M1-p, work 1 st. For left-slanting edges: On RS rows, work to last st, M1-l, work 1 st; on WS rows, work 1 st, M1-p-L, work to end.

## ABBREVIATIONS

**LT:** Knit into back of second st, then knit first and second sts together through back loop, slip both sts from left-hand needle together.

**RT:** K2tog, but do not drop sts from left-hand needle, insert right-hand needle between 2 sts just worked and knit first st again, slip both sts from left-hand needle together.

## STITCH PATTERN

### Cabled Check Stitch

(multiple of 4 sts; 8-row repeat)

**Row 1 (RS):** *LT, p2; repeat from * to end.

**Rows 2 and 3:** *K2, p2; repeat from * to end.

**Rows 4, 6, and 7:** *P2, k2; repeat from * to end.

**Row 5:** *P2, RT; repeat from * to end.

**Row 8:** Repeat Row 2.

Repeat Rows 1-8 for Cabled Check.

## BACK

CO 84 (88, 92, 100, 104, 108, 116, 128, 136, 148) sts. Begin Cabled Check; work even until piece measures 2 ½" (6.5 cm) from the beginning, ending with a RS row.

**Next Row (WS):** Work 20 (20, 24, 24, 28, 28, 32, 32, 32, 36) sts, pm (color A) for Cabled Check shaping, work 44 (48, 44,

52, 48, 52, 52, 64, 72, 76) sts, pm (color A) for Cabled Check shaping, work to end.

### Shape Cabled Check and Waist

*Note: Cabled Check and waist shaping are worked at the same time; please read entire section through before beginning.*

**Rows 1, 3, 5, and 7 (RS):** Work in Cabled Check to first marker, sm, work in St st to next marker, sm, work in Cabled Check to end.

**Row 2:** Work even, moving markers 6 (6, 8, 8, 10, 10, 10, 10, 10, 12) sts closer to each side edge.

**Row 4:** Work 28 (29, 31, 33, 35, 36, 39, 43, 45, 49) sts, moving A marker 6 (6, 8, 8, 10, 10, 10, 10, 10, 12) sts closer to beginning of row, pm (color B) for waist shaping, work to last 28 (29, 31, 33, 35, 36, 39, 43, 45, 49) sts, pm (color B) for waist shaping, work to end, moving A marker 6 (6, 8, 8, 10, 10, 10, 10, 10, 12) sts closer to end of row.

**Rows 6 and 8:** Work even, moving A markers 2 (2, 2, 2, 2, 2, 4, 4, 4, 4) sts closer to each side edge—4 sts remain in Cabled Check at each end of row after Row 8.

**Row 9:** Work in Cabled Check to first A marker, sm, work in St st to second A marker, sm, work in Cabled Check to end.

**Row 10:** Work even, removing A markers.

**Row 11:** Change to St st across all sts.

AT THE SAME TIME, beginning on Row 5 of Cabled Check shaping, work waist shaping as follows:

**Decrease Row (RS):** Continuing to shape Cabled Check, decrease 2 sts this row, then every 6 rows 4 times, as follows: Work to 2 sts before first B marker, ssk, sm, knit to next B marker, sm, k2tog, work to end—74 (78, 82, 90, 94, 98, 106, 118, 126, 138) sts remain. Work even until piece measures 7" (18 cm) from the beginning, ending with a WS row.

### Shape Bust

**Increase Row (RS):** Increase 2 sts this row, then every 8 rows 4 times, as follows: Knit to first marker, M1-r, sm, work to second marker, sm, M1-l, knit to end—84 (88, 92, 100, 104, 108, 116, 128, 136, 148) sts. Work even, removing markers on first row, until piece measures 12 ½ (12 ¾, 13, 13 ¼, 13 ½, 13 ¾, 14, 14 ½, 15, 15)" [32 (32.5, 33, 33.5, 34.5, 35, 35.5, 37, 38, 38) cm] from the beginning, ending with a WS row.

### Shape Armholes

**Next Row (RS):** BO 6 (6, 6, 6, 6, 6, 8, 10, 12) sts at beginning of next 2 rows, 2 (2, 2, 2, 2, 2, 4, 6, 8, 8) sts at beginning of next 2 rows, then decrease 1 st each side every other row 2 (3, 3, 6, 5, 6, 6, 7, 6, 7) times—64 (66, 70, 72, 78, 80, 84, 86, 88, 94) sts remain. Work even until armhole measures 5 ½ (6, 6 ¼, 6 ½, 7, 7 ¼, 7 ½, 7 ¾, 8, 8 ½)" [14 (15, 16, 16.5, 18, 18.5, 19, 19.5, 20.5, 21.5) cm], ending with a WS row.

### Shape Neck

**Next Row (RS):** K20 (21, 22, 22, 24, 24, 26, 26, 27, 28) sts, join a second ball of yarn, BO center 24 (24, 26, 28, 30, 32, 32, 34, 34, 38) sts, knit to end. Working both sides at the same time, work even for 1 row. Decrease 1 st at each neck edge every other row twice—18 (19, 20, 20, 22, 22, 24, 24, 25, 26) sts remain each side for shoulders. Work even until armhole measures 6 ½ (7, 7 ¼, 7 ½, 8, 8 ¼, 8 ½, 8 ¾, 9, 9 ½)" [16.5 (18, 18.5, 19, 20.5, 21, 21.5, 22, 23, 24) cm], ending with a WS row.

### Shape Shoulders

**Next Row (RS):** BO 9 (10, 10, 10, 11, 11, 12, 12, 13, 13) sts at each armhole edge once, then 9 (9, 10, 10, 11, 11, 12, 12, 12, 13) sts once.

### LEFT FRONT

CO 44 (48, 48, 52, 56, 56, 60, 64, 72, 76) sts. Begin Cabled Check; work even until piece measures 2 ½" (6.5 cm) from the beginning, ending with a RS row.

**Next Row (WS):** Work 24 (28, 24, 28, 28, 28, 28, 32, 40, 40) sts, pm (color A) for Cabled Check shaping, work to end.

## Shape Cabled Check and Waist

*Note: Cabled Check and waist shaping are worked at the same time; please read entire section through before beginning.*

**Rows 1, 3, 5, and 7 (RS):** Work in Cabled Check to marker, sm, work in St st to end.

**Row 2:** Work even, moving marker 6 (6, 8, 8, 10, 10, 10, 10, 12) sts closer to armhole edge.

**Row 4:** P22 (24, 24, 26, 28, 28, 30, 32, 36, 38), pm (color B) for waist shaping, work to end, moving A marker 6 (6, 8, 8, 10, 10, 10, 10, 12) sts closer to end of row.

**Rows 6 and 8:** Work even, moving A marker 2 (2, 2, 2, 2, 2, 4, 4, 4, 4) sts closer to armhole edge—4 sts remain in Cabled Check at end of row after Row 8.

**Row 9:** Work in Cabled Check to A marker, sm, work in St st to end.

**Row 10:** Work even, removing A marker.

**Row 11:** Change to St st across all sts.

AT THE SAME TIME, beginning on Row 5 of Cabled Check shaping, work waist shaping as follows:

**Decrease Row (RS):** Continuing to shape Cabled Check, decrease 1 st this row, then every 6 rows 4 times, as follows: Work to 2 sts before B marker, ssk, sm, work to end—39 (43, 43, 47, 51, 51, 55, 59, 67, 71) sts remain. Work even until piece measures 7" (18 cm) from the beginning, ending with a WS row.

## Shape Bust

**Increase Row (RS):** Increase 1 st this row, then every 6 rows 4 times, as follows: Work to marker, M1-r, sm, work to end—44 (48, 48, 52, 56, 56, 60, 64, 72, 76) sts. Work even, removing marker, until piece measures 12 ½

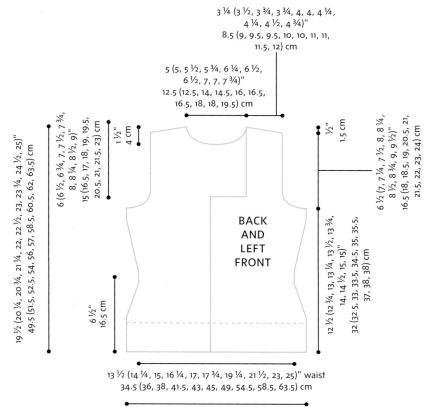

3 ¼ (3 ½, 3 ¾, 3 ¾, 4, 4, 4 ¼, 4 ¼, 4 ½, 4 ¾)"
8.5 (9, 9.5, 9.5, 10, 10, 11, 11, 11.5, 12) cm

5 (5, 5 ½, 5 ¾, 6 ¼, 6 ½, 6 ½, 7, 7, 7 ¾)"
12.5 (12.5, 14, 14.5, 16, 16.5, 16.5, 18, 18, 19.5) cm

1 ½"
4 cm

½"
1.5 cm

6 (6 ½, 6 ¾, 7, 7 ½, 7 ¾, 8, 8 ¼, 8 ½, 9)"
15 (16.5, 17, 18, 19, 19.5, 20.5, 21, 21.5, 23) cm

6 ½ (7, 7 ¼, 7 ½, 8, 8 ¼, 8 ½, 8 ¾, 9, 9 ½)"
16.5 (18, 18.5, 19, 20.5, 21, 21.5, 22, 23, 24) cm

**BACK AND LEFT FRONT**

12 ½ (12 ¾, 13, 13 ¼, 13 ½, 13 ¾, 14, 14 ½, 15, 15)"
32 (32.5, 33, 33.5, 34.5, 35, 35.5, 37, 38, 38) cm

19 ½ (20 ¼, 20 ¾, 21 ¼, 22, 22 ½, 23, 23 ¾, 24 ½, 25)"
49.5 (51.5, 52.5, 54, 56, 57, 58.5, 60.5, 62, 63.5) cm

6 ½"
16.5 cm

13 ½ (14 ¼, 15, 16 ¼, 17, 17 ¾, 19 ¼, 21 ½, 23, 25)" waist
34.5 (36, 38, 41.5, 43, 45, 49, 54.5, 58.5, 63.5) cm

15 ¼ (16, 16 ¾, 18 ¼, 19, 19 ¾, 21, 23 ¼, 24 ¾, 27)" hip and bust
38.5 (40.5, 42.5, 46.5, 48.5, 50, 53.5, 59, 63, 68.5) cm

7 (7 ¾, 7 ¾, 8 ½, 9 ¼, 9 ¼, 10, 10 ¾, 12 ¼, 13)" waist
18 (19.5, 19.5, 21.5, 23.5, 23.5, 25.5, 27.5, 31, 33) cm

8 (8 ¾, 8 ¾, 9 ½, 10 ¼, 10 ¼, 11, 11 ¾, 13, 13 ¾)" hip and bust
20.5 (22, 22, 24, 26, 26, 28, 30, 33, 35) cm

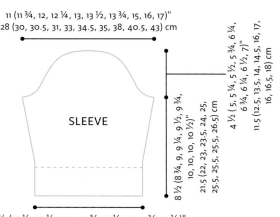

11 (11 ¾, 12, 12 ¼, 13, 13 ½, 13 ¾, 15, 16, 17)"
28 (30, 30.5, 31, 33, 34.5, 35, 38, 40.5, 43) cm

4 ½ (5, 5 ¼, 5 ½, 5 ¾, 6 ¼, 6 ¾, 6 ¼, 6 ½, 7)"
11.5 (12.5, 13.5, 14, 14.5, 16, 17, 16, 16.5, 18) cm

**SLEEVE**

8 ½ (8 ¾, 9, 9 ¼, 9 ½, 9 ¾, 10, 10, 10 ½)"
21.5 (22, 23, 23.5, 24, 25, 25.5, 25.5, 26.5) cm

9 ½ (10 ¼, 10 ¼, 11, 11, 11 ¾, 12 ¼, 13, 13 ¾, 15 ¼)"
24 (26, 26, 28, 28, 30, 31, 33, 35, 38.5) cm

## MODIFICATION IDEAS

(12 ¾, 13, 13 ¼, 13 ½, 13 ¾, 14, 14 ½, 15, 15)" [32 (32.5, 33, 33.5, 34.5, 35, 35.5, 37, 38, 38) cm] from the beginning, ending with a WS row.

### Shape Armhole and Neck

*Note: Armhole and neck shaping are worked at the same time; please read entire section through before beginning.*

**Next Row (RS):** BO 6 (6, 6, 6, 6, 6, 8, 10, 12) sts at armhole edge once, 2 (2, 2, 2, 2, 2, 4, 6, 8) sts once, then decrease 1 st at armhole edge every other row 2 (3, 3, 6, 5, 6, 6, 7, 6, 7) times and, AT THE SAME TIME, when armhole measures 1" (2.5 cm), shape neck as follows:

**Next Row (WS):** BO 16 (18, 17, 18, 21, 20, 20, 19, 23, 23) sts, work to end—18 (19, 20, 20, 22, 22, 24, 24, 25, 26) sts remain when all shaping is complete. Work even until armhole measures 6 ½ (7, 7 ¼, 7 ½, 8, 8 ¼, 8 ½, 8 ¾, 9, 9 ½)" [16.5 (18, 18.5, 19, 20.5, 21, 21.5, 22, 23, 24) cm], ending with a WS row.

### Shape Shoulder

**Next Row (RS):** BO 9 (10, 10, 10, 11, 11, 12, 12, 13, 13) sts at armhole edge once, then 9 (9, 10, 10, 11, 11, 12, 12, 12, 13) sts once.

### RIGHT FRONT

Work as for Left Front until piece measures 2 ½" (6.5 cm) from the beginning, ending with a RS row.

**Next Row (WS):** Work 20 (20, 24, 24, 28, 28, 32, 32, 32, 36) sts, pm (color A) for Cabled Check shaping, work to end.

Complete as for Left Front, reversing st patterns and all shaping.

### SLEEVES

CO 52 (56, 56, 60, 60, 64, 68, 72, 76, 84) sts. Begin Cabled Check; work even until piece measures 2 ½" (6.5 cm) from the beginning, ending with a RS row.

**Next Row (WS):** Work 20 (24, 24, 24, 24, 28, 28, 32, 32, 36) sts, pm, work 12 (8, 8, 12, 12, 8, 12, 8, 12, 12) sts, pm, work to end.

### Shape Cabled Check and Sleeve

*Note: Cabled Check and Sleeve shaping are worked at the same time; please read entire section through before beginning.*

**Row 1 (RS):** Work in St st over next 12 (12, 12, 12, 12, 16, 16, 16, 16, 20) sts, work in Cabled Check to last 12 (12, 12, 12, 12, 16, 16, 16, 16, 20) sts, work in St st to end.

**Rows 2-4:** Work even.

**Row 5:** Work in St st to 4 (4, 4, 4, 4, 4, 8, 8, 8) sts before first marker, sm, work in Cabled Check to 4 (4, 4, 4, 4, 4, 8, 8, 8) sts past next marker, work in St st to end.

**Rows 6-8:** Work even.

**Row 9:** Work in St st to first marker, sm, work in Cabled Check to next marker, work in St st to end.

**Rows 10-12:** Work even.

**Row 13:** Change to St st across all sts.

AT THE SAME TIME, beginning on Row 5 of Cabled Check shaping, work Sleeve shaping as follows:

**Increase Row (RS):** Continuing to shape Cabled Check, increase 1 st each side this row, then every 6 (6, 6, 6, 8, 8, 8, 8, 8) rows 3 (3, 4, 3, 5, 4, 3, 4, 5, 4) times—60 (64, 66, 68, 72, 74, 76, 82, 88, 94) sts. Work even until piece measures 8 ½ (8 ¾, 9, 9 ¼,

9 ½, 9 ¾, 10, 10, 10, 10 ½)" [21.5 (22, 23, 23.5, 24, 25, 25.5, 25.5, 25.5, 26.5) cm] from the beginning, ending with a WS row.

## Shape Cap

**Next Row (RS):** BO 6 (6, 6, 6, 6, 6, 8, 10, 12) sts at beginning of next 2 rows, 2 (2, 2, 2, 2, 2, 4, 6, 8, 8) sts at beginning of next 2 rows, decrease 1 st each side every 6 rows 1 (1, 1, 1, 0, 0, 2, 5, 6, 6) time(s), every 4 rows 0 (0, 0, 0, 1, 1, 0, 0, 0, 1) time(s), then every other row 10 (12, 13, 14, 16, 17, 15, 4, 2, 2) times, then BO 2 (2, 2, 2, 2, 2, 2, 4, 4, 4) sts at beginning of next 4 rows. BO remaining 14 (14, 14, 14, 14, 14, 14, 20, 20, 20) sts.

## FINISHING

Block pieces as desired. Sew shoulder seams. Set in Sleeves; sew side and Sleeve seams.

## Neckband

With RS facing, using circ needle, and beginning at Right Front neck edge, pick up and knit 16 (18, 17, 18, 21, 20, 20, 19, 23, 23) sts along BO portion of Right Front neck edge, pm, 31 (33, 35, 36, 39, 40, 42, 43, 44, 47) sts to shoulder, 40 (40, 42, 44, 46, 48, 48, 50, 50, 54) sts along Back neck, 31 (33, 35, 36, 39, 40, 42, 43, 44, 47) sts to Left Front BO sts, pm, then 16 (18, 17, 18, 21, 20, 20, 19, 23, 23) sts to Left Front neck edge—134 (142, 146, 152, 166, 168, 172, 174, 184, 194) sts. Begin St st; work even for 1 row.

**Decrease Row (RS):** Continuing in St st, decrease 4 sts this row, then every other row twice, as follows: [Knit to 1 st before marker, s2kp2, removing marker, reposition marker to before s2kp2] twice, knit to end—122 (130, 134, 140, 154, 156, 160, 162, 172, 182) sts remain. BO all sts, allowing edge to roll.

## Button Band

With RS facing, and beginning at Left Front neck edge, pick up and knit 76 (76, 76, 80, 80, 80, 84, 84, 88, 88) sts along Left Front edge, picking up first st from Neckband. Begin Cabled Check, beginning

with Row 2; work even until piece measures 1" (2.5 cm) from pick-up row, ending with a RS row. BO all sts in pattern.

## Buttonhole Band

With RS facing, and beginning at lower Right Front edge, pick up and knit 76 (76, 76, 80, 80, 80, 84, 84, 88, 88) sts along Right Front edge, picking up final st from Neckband. Begin Cabled Check, beginning with Row 2; work even until piece measures ½" (1.5 cm) from pick-up row, ending with a WS row. Place markers for 7 (7, 7, 7, 7, 8, 8, 8, 8, 8) buttons, the first ¾" (2 cm) below Neckband, the last ¾" (2 cm) from bottom edge, and the remaining buttons evenly spaced between.

**Buttonhole Row (RS):** *Work to marker, remove marker, [slip next st purlwise to right-hand needle, pass second st on right-hand needle over first st] 3 times, slip last st from right-hand needle to left-hand needle, turn. Using Cable CO (see Special Techniques, page 159), CO 4 sts onto left-hand needle, turn. Slip first st on left-hand needle to right-hand needle, pass second st (fourth CO st) on right-hand needle over first st to close buttonhole. Repeat from * for remaining markers, work to end. Complete as for Button Band.

Sew buttons opposite buttonholes.

## BUST DARTS

The sample shown has bust darts added to each Front. The pattern calls for you to increase 1 stitch at the bust every 6 rows 5 times (see Increase Row under Shape Bust for Left and Right Fronts). In order to add bust darts to the sample, Increase Rows were worked at the bust every 4 rows instead of every 6, until a total of 9 bust Increase Rows were worked, instead of 4; this resulted in an extra 4 stitches at the bust. In order to get rid of those 4 extra stitches and end the neck shaping with the number of stitches required for the shoulders, those 4 stitches were added to the initial neck bind-off (see Shape Armhole and Neck).

The coin closure and thin opening slim the torso.

The slightly wide V-neck is balanced by long sleeves.

A perpendicular line of trim at the hem broadens the shoulders and the hips, and shrinks the waist

DeeDee is wearing size 41" (104 cm) with zero ease in the upper torso.

# COIN CABLE CARDIGAN
## BY ELINOR BROWN

This cardigan is especially flattering to a thicker-middled proportional shape. Waist shaping placed only on the back of the cardigan provides a flattering fit without being tight.

. . . . . . . . . . . . . . . . . . . . . . . . . . . . .

### SIZES

To fit upper torso sizes 29 (31, 33, 35, 37, 39, 41, 45, 49, 53)" [73.5 (78.5, 84, 89, 94, 99, 104, 114.5, 124.5, 134.5) cm]

### FINISHED MEASUREMENTS

30 ¼ (32 ½, 34 ½, 36 ¾, 38 ¾, 41, 43, 47 ¼, 51 ½, 55 ¾)" [77 (82.5, 87.5, 93.5, 98.5, 104, 109, 120, 131, 141.5) cm] chest, buttoned

*Note: Cardigan is intended to be worn with 1" (2.5 cm) positive ease in the upper torso.*

### YARN

Quince and Company Osprey [100% wool; 170 yards (155 meters) / 100 grams]: 4 (5, 5, 5, 6, 6, 7, 7, 8, 8) hanks Pomegranate

### NEEDLES

One 32" (80 cm) long or longer circular (circ) needle size US 9 (5.5 mm)

One set of three double-pointed needles (dpn) size US 9 (5.5 mm)

Change needle size if necessary to obtain correct gauge.

### NOTIONS

Crochet hook size US I/9 (5.5 mm); waste yarn; stitch markers; stitch holders; one ¾" (19 mm) button

### GAUGE

15 sts and 22 rows = 4" (10 cm) in Stockinette stitch (St st)

### NOTES

Unless otherwise specified, decreases should be worked to match the slant of the edge being shaped, as follows: For left-slanting edges: On RS rows, k1, ssk, work to end; on WS rows, work to last 3 sts, ssp, p1. For right-slanting edges: On RS rows, work to last 3 sts, k2tog, k1; on WS rows, p1, p2tog, work to end. Increases should also be worked to match the slant of the edge being shaped, as follows: For right-slanting edges: On RS rows, work 1 st, M1-r, work to end; on WS rows, work to last st, M1-p, work 1 st. For left-slanting edges: On RS rows, work to last st, M1-l, work 1 st; on WS rows, work 1 st, M1-p-l, work to end.

### ABBREVIATIONS

**T4B-kp:** Slip 2 sts to cn, hold to back, k1, p1, [k1, p1] from cn.

**T4F-kp:** Slip 2 sts to cn, hold to front, k1, p1, k2 from cn.

### STITCH PATTERN

#### Coin Cable

(panel of 12 sts; 6-row repeat)

**Row 1 (RS):** K2, T4B-kp, T4F-kp, k2.

**Rows 2 and 4:** K2, [p1, k1] 3 times, p2, k2.

**Rows 3 and 5:** K3, [p1, k1] 3 times, k3.

**Row 6:** Repeat Row 2.

Repeat Rows 1-6 for Coin Cable.

### BODY CABLE BAND

Using crochet hook, waste yarn and Provisional CO (see Special Techniques, page 159), CO 12 sts. Change to dpns and working yarn. Purl 1 row. Change to Coin Cable; work even until piece measures 28 ¼ (30 ½, 32 ½, 34 ¾, 36 ¾, 39, 41, 45 ¼, 49 ½, 53 ¾)" [72 (77.5, 82.5, 88.5, 93.5, 99, 104, 115, 125.5, 136.5) cm] from the beginning, ending with a WS row. Cut yarn; leave sts on dpn.

### LEFT FRONT CABLE BAND

Using dpn, CO 12 sts.

**Row 1 (WS):** Purl to last st, ssp (last st together with 1 st of Body Cable Band from dpn, making sure to work with WS of Body Cable Band facing).

**Row 2:** Begin Coin Cable. Work even for 1 row.

**Row 3:** Work in Coin Cable to last st, ssp (last st together with 1 st of Body Cable Band from dpn).

Repeat Rows 2 and 3 until all sts from Body Cable Band have been worked. Cut yarn and set aside.

### RIGHT FRONT CABLE BAND

Carefully unpick Provisional CO from Body Cable Band and place sts on dpn. Using circ needle, CO 12 sts. Purl 1 row.

**Row 1 (RS):** Work Coin Cable to last st, ssk (last st together with 1 st of Body Cable Band from dpn, making sure to work with RS of Body Cable Band facing).

**Row 2:** Work even.

Repeat Rows 1 and 2 until 1 st remains from Body Cable Band, ending with a WS row.

### BODY

**Next row (RS):** Work to last st, ssk (last st together with last remaining st of Body Cable Band), pick up and knit 106 (114, 122, 130, 138, 146, 154, 170, 186, 202) sts along long edge of Body Cable Band, work across 12 sts of Left Front Band—130 (138, 146, 154, 162, 170, 178, 194, 210, 226) sts. Working first and last 12 sts in Coin Cable as established, and remaining sts in St st, work even until piece measures 4 ¼" (11 cm) from bottom of Body Cable Band, ending with a RS row.

**Next Row (WS):** Work 55 (58, 61, 65, 68, 72, 75, 82, 89, 95) sts, pm, work 20 (22, 24, 24, 26, 26, 28, 30, 32, 36) sts, pm, work to end.

### Shape Waist

**Decrease Row (RS):** Decrease 2 sts this row, then every 6 rows twice, as follows: Knit to 2 sts before first marker, ssk, sm, knit to next marker, sm, k2tog,

knit to end—124 (132, 140, 148, 156, 164, 172, 188, 204, 220) sts remain. Work even until piece measures 9 ½" (24 cm) from the beginning, ending with a WS row.

### Shape Bust

**Increase Row (RS):** Increase 2 sts this row, then every 8 rows twice, as follows: Work to first marker, M1-r, sm, work to next marker, sm, M1-l, work to end—130 (138, 146, 154, 162, 170, 178, 194, 210, 226) sts. Work even, removing markers on first row, until piece measures 14 ¾ (15, 15 ¼, 15 ½, 15 ¾, 16, 16 ½, 16 ¾, 17, 17)" [37.5 (38, 38.5, 39.5, 40, 40.5, 42, 42.5, 43, 43) cm] from bottom of Body Cable Band, ending with a WS row.

### Divide for Armholes

**Next Row (RS):** Work 11 sts, ssk, k18 (20, 22, 25, 27, 27, 29, 34, 36, 38), place last 30 (32, 34, 37, 39, 39, 41, 46, 48, 50) sts worked on st holder for Right Front, BO 8 (8, 8, 8, 8, 12, 12, 12, 16, 20) sts, k52 (56, 60, 62, 66, 66, 70, 76, 80, 84) and place on st holder for Back, BO 8 (8, 8, 8, 8, 12, 12, 12, 16, 20) sts, work to 1 st before next marker, k2tog, work to end—30 (32, 34, 37, 39, 39, 41, 46, 48, 50) sts remain each Front; 52 (56, 60, 62, 66, 66, 70, 76, 80, 84) sts for Back.

### LEFT FRONT

### Shape Armhole and Neck

*Note: Armhole and neck shaping are worked at the same time; please read entire section through before beginning.*

Working on Left Front sts only, work even for 1 row.

**Next Row (RS):** BO 0 (0, 2, 2, 2, 2, 2, 4, 6, 6) sts at armhole edge once, then decrease 1 st at armhole edge every other row 3 (3, 2, 3, 4, 2, 3, 4, 3, 3) times. AT THE SAME TIME, beginning with first armhole shaping row, work neck shaping as follows:

**Decrease Row (RS):** Decrease 1 st at neck edge this row, every other row 7 (6, 5, 10, 9, 9, 10, 13, 12, 11) times, then every 4 rows 4 (5, 6, 4, 5, 5, 5, 4, 5,

6) times, as follows: Work to last 13 sts, k2tog, work to end—16 (18, 19, 18, 19, 21, 21, 21, 22, 24) sts remain when all shaping is complete. Work even until armhole measures 7 (7 ¼, 7 ½, 8, 8 ¼, 8 ½, 8 ¾, 9, 9 ½, 9 ¾)" [18 (18.5, 19, 20.5, 21, 21.5, 22, 23, 24, 25) cm], ending with a WS row.

### Shape Shoulder

**Next Row (RS):** BO 4 (6, 7, 6, 7, 9, 9, 9, 10, 12) sts; place remaining 12 sts on st holder for Back Neckband.

### BACK

With WS facing, rejoin yarn to sts on hold for Back. Continuing in St st, BO 0 (0, 2, 2, 2, 2, 2, 4, 6, 6) sts at beginning of next 2 rows, then decrease 1 st each side every other row 3 (3, 2, 3, 4, 2, 3, 4, 3, 3) times—46 (50, 52, 52, 54, 58, 60, 60, 62, 66) sts remain. Work even until armhole measures 5 ½ (5 ¾, 6, 6 ½, 6 ¾, 7, 7 ¼, 7 ½, 8, 8 ¼)" [14 (14.5, 15, 16.5, 17, 18, 18.5, 19, 20.5, 21) cm], ending with a WS row.

### Shape Neck

**Next Row (RS):** K7 (9, 10, 9, 10, 12, 12, 12, 13, 15), join a second ball of yarn, BO center 32 (32, 32, 34, 34, 34, 36, 36, 36, 36) sts, knit to end. Working both sides at the same time, work even for 1 row. Decrease 1 st at each neck edge every other row 3 times— 4 (6, 7, 6, 7, 9, 9, 9, 10 12) sts remain. Work even for 1 row.

### Shape Shoulders

**Next Row (RS):** BO 4 (6, 7, 6, 7, 9, 9, 9, 10, 12) sts at beginning of next 2 rows.

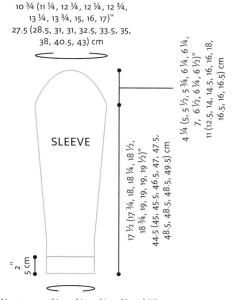

3 (3 ½, 3 ¾, 3 ½, 3 ¾, 4 ½, 4 ½, 4 ½, 4 ¾, 5 ¼)"
7.5 (9, 9.5, 9, 9.5, 11.5, 11.5, 11.5, 12, 13.5) cm

7 ¾ (7 ¾, 7 ¾, 8 ¼, 8 ¼, 8 ¼, 8 ¾, 8 ¾, 8 ¾, 8 ¾)"
19.5 (19.5, 19.5, 21, 21, 21, 22, 22, 22, 22) cm

7 (7 ¼, 7 ½, 7 ½, 8, 8 ¼, 8 ½, 8 ¾, 9, 9 ½, 9 ¾)"
18 (18.5, 19, 20.5, 21, 21.5, 22, 23, 24, 25) cm

1 ½"
4 cm

BACK AND FRONTS

21 ¾ (22 ¼, 22 ¾, 23 ½, 24, 24 ½, 25 ¼, 25 ¾, 26 ½, 26 ¾)"
55 (56.5, 58, 59.5, 61, 62, 64, 65.5, 67.5, 68) cm

14 ¾ (15, 15 ¼, 15 ½, 15 ¾, 16, 16 ½, 16 ¾, 17, 17)"
37.5 (38, 38.5, 39.5, 40, 40.5, 42, 42.5, 43, 43) cm

9"
23 cm

2"
5 cm

30 ¾ (32 ¾, 35, 37, 39 ¼, 41 ¼, 43, 43 ½, 47 ¾, 52, 56 ¼)" waist
78 (83, 89, 94, 99.5, 105, 110.5, 121.5, 132, 143) cm

32 ¼ (34 ½, 36 ½, 38 ¾, 40 ¾, 43, 45, 49 ¼, 53 ½, 57 ¾)" hip and bust
82 (87.5, 92.5, 98.5, 103.5, 109, 114.5, 125, 136, 146.5) cm

10 ¾ (11 ¼, 12 ¼, 12 ¼, 12 ¾, 13 ¼, 13 ¾, 15, 16, 17)"
27.5 (28.5, 31, 31, 32.5, 33.5, 35, 38, 40.5, 43) cm

4 ¼ (5, 5 ½, 5 ¾, 6 ¼, 6 ¼, 7, 6 ½, 6 ¼, 6 ½)"
11 (12.5, 14, 14.5, 16, 16, 18, 16.5, 16, 16.5) cm

SLEEVE

17 ½ (17 ¾, 18, 18 ¼, 18 ½, 18 ¾, 19, 19, 19, 19 ½)"
44.5 (45, 45.5, 46.5, 47, 47.5, 48.5, 48.5, 48.5, 49.5) cm

2"
5 cm

8 (8 ½, 9, 9, 9, 9 ½, 10 ¼, 10 ¼, 11 ¼, 11 ¾)"
20.5 (21.5, 23, 23, 23, 24, 26, 26, 28.5, 30) cm

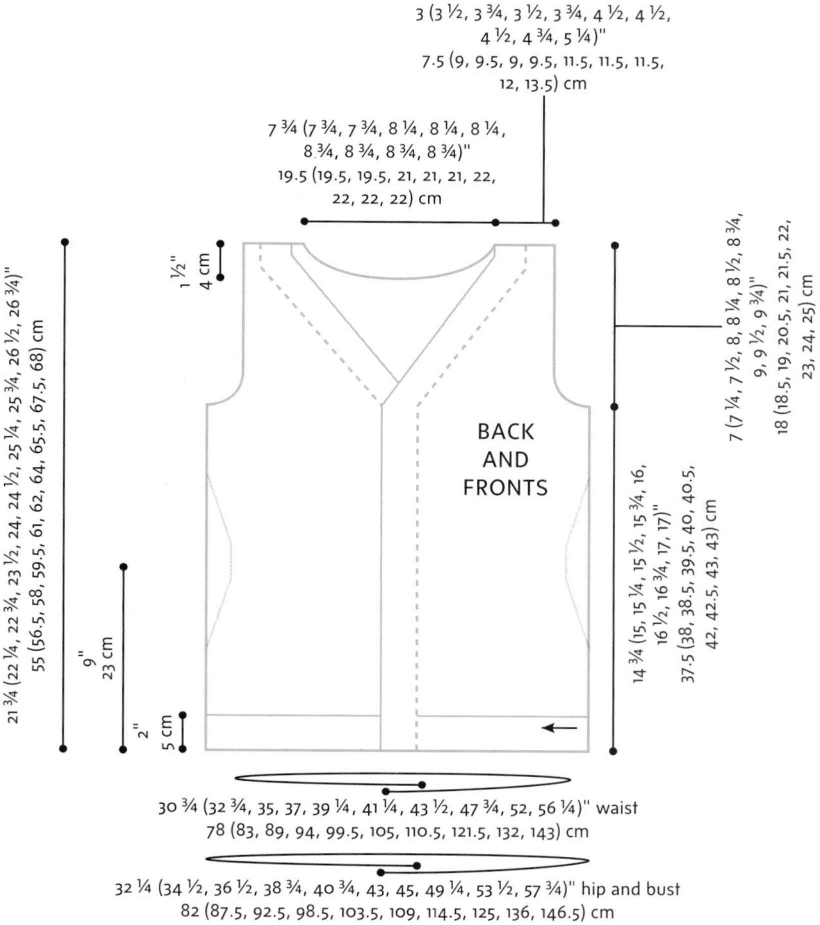

## RIGHT FRONT

With WS facing, rejoin yarn to sts on hold for Right Front. Complete as for Left Front, reversing st pattern and all shaping.

## SLEEVE CABLE BAND

Using crochet hook, waste yarn, and Provisional CO, CO 12 sts. Change to dpn and working yarn; purl 1 row.

**Next Row (RS):** Begin Coin Cable; work even until piece measures 8 (8 ½, 9, 9, 9, 9 ½, 10 ¼, 10 ¼, 11 ¼, 11 ¾)" [20.5 (21.5, 23, 23, 23, 24, 26, 26, 28.5, 30) cm] from the beginning, ending with a WS row. Cut yarn, leaving sts on dpn. Carefully unpick Provisional CO and place sts on second dpn. Using 3-Needle BO (see Special Techniques, page 159), join ends of Band.

## SLEEVES

With RS of Sleeve Cable Band facing, using dpns and beginning at seam, pick up and knit 30 (32, 34, 34, 34, 36, 38, 38, 42, 44) sts along edge of Sleeve Cable Band. Join for working in the rnd; pm for beginning of rnd. Begin St st (knit every rnd); work even until piece measures 3" (7.5 cm) from bottom of Sleeve Cable Band.

### Shape Sleeve

**Increase Rnd:** Increase 2 sts this rnd, then every 12 (12, 10, 10, 8, 10, 10, 8, 8, 6) rnds 4 (4, 5, 5, 6, 6, 6, 8, 8, 9) times, as follows: K1, M1-r, knit to last st, M1-l, k1—40 (42, 46, 46, 48, 50, 52, 56, 60, 64) sts. Work even until piece measures 17 ½ (17 ¾, 18, 18 ¼, 18 ½, 18 ¾, 19, 19, 19, 19 ½)" [44.5 (45, 45.5, 46.5, 47, 47.5, 48.5, 48.5, 48.5, 49.5) cm] from beginning of Sleeve Cable Band, ending 4 (4, 4, 4, 4, 6, 6, 6, 8, 10) sts before end of last rnd.

### Shape Cap

**Next Rnd:** BO 8 (8, 8, 8, 8, 12, 12, 12, 16, 20) sts, work to end—32 (34, 38, 38, 40, 38, 40, 44, 44, 44) sts remain. Working back and forth, work even for 1 row.

**Next Row (RS):** BO 0 (0, 2, 2, 2, 2, 2, 4, 6, 6) sts at beginning of next 2 rows, decrease 1 st each side every 6 rows 0 (0, 0, 1, 1, 1, 2, 3, 4, 4) time(s), every 4 rows 0 (1, 1, 0, 0, 1, 0, 1, 0, 1) time(s), then every other row 9 (9, 9, 9, 10, 8, 9, 3, 1, 0) time(s), then BO 1 (1, 1, 1, 1, 1, 1, 2, 2, 2) st(s) at beginning of next 4 rows. BO remaining 10 (10, 10, 10, 10, 10, 14, 14, 14) sts.

## FINISHING

Block pieces as desired. Sew shoulder seams. Set in Sleeves.

### Back Neckband

With RS facing, transfer sts on hold for Left Front to dpn. Rejoin yarn.

**Row 1 (RS):** Slip 1, work in Coin Cable as established to end.

**Row 2:** Work 11 sts, p2tog (last st together with 1 st picked up from neck edge).

Repeat Rows 1 and 2 until you reach center of Back neck. Cut yarn, leaving sts on needle.

With WS facing, transfer sts on hold for Right Front to dpn. Rejoin yarn.

**Row 1 (WS):** Slip 1, work in Coin Cable as established to end.

**Row 2:** Work 11 sts, k2tog (last st together with 1 st picked up from neck edge).

Repeat Rows 1 and 2 until you reach center of Back neck. Using 3-Needle BO, join ends of Neckband.

Sew button to Left Front, approximately 1" below beginning of neck shaping, just above cable cross row in pattern; cable cross row on Right Front will form a natural buttonhole.

### MODIFICATION IDEAS

This cardigan is an easy candidate for modification. A shorter length and plain hem will be especially flattering for bottom-heavy knitters, perhaps combined with shorter sleeves as well. Top-heavy knitters might consider narrowing the neckline or lengthening the cardigan to low-hip or even mid-thigh length. Curvier knitters can add waist shaping to the front panels of the cardigan for a closer fit.

# 5

# OTHER FIGURE FEATURES

No matter which of the main categories you fit into, you might have other figure characteristics you'd like to flatter with your sweaters. Do you have a substantial bust, or no bust at all? A fantastically curvy waist you'd like to highlight, or a thicker middle you'd like to minimize? Long legs and the short torso that usually goes with them, or the torso of a 6' woman and a 27" inseam? Then read on! This chapter is devoted to all of those little "extra" figure features we love... and love to hate.

## Larger Busts

While you might not appear particularly busty in a photo taken from the front, a photo taken from the side will reveal the truth. Most women with a large bust have a hard time finding a well-fitting buttoned shirt, and many knitters with a large bust shy away from sweaters due to memories of unfortunate fit problems in sweaters past. The reason most sweaters don't fit busty knitters is because they chose a sweater size that matched their full bust circumference, which led to a sweater that fit in the bust, but was way too big everywhere else. Remember, Ms. Average and all of her measurements assume that the wearer has a smaller bust, so if you choose a 42'' (106.5 cm) finished bust circumference, your sweater will result in shoulders that fit a woman with a 42'' (106.5 cm) *B-cup* bust—not the case for you, if you're reading this section!

Of course, if you choose a size based on your upper torso and work bust darts (see page 152), your sweater will fit you perfectly—but that isn't the end of the story! There are two main principles from Chapter 1 that you should keep in mind when choosing a sweater pattern that will flatter your bust:

- To lengthen the appearance of some portion of your body, cover that portion in a single block of color and texture.

- To shorten the appearance of some portion of your body, break up that portion into different blocks of color and texture.

Generally speaking, knitters with larger busts are flattered by sweaters with deeper necklines because the depth of the neckline breaks up the vertical distance of the bust and makes it appear shorter. (I've generally found that most women prefer their bust to appear shorter rather than longer.)

Depending on whether you are bottom-heavy, top-heavy, or proportional—and depending on what else is going on with the sweater—you might be most flattered by a wide, deep neckline or a narrow, deep neckline. (Remember, wide necklines broaden the shoulder/bust region, which is good for bottom-heavy shapes and proportional shapes if the sweater is also broadening to the hips; narrow necklines narrow the

The deep neckline of the Enrobed Wrap (page 138) is flattering to a large bust, and the tie nicely cinches a curvy waist.

shoulder/bust region, which is great for top-heavy shapes and proportional shapes if the hem is plain as well.)

A sufficiently deep neckline will also prevent the apparent relocation of the bust line from the neck/shoulder region down to the waist/hip region (otherwise known as the "waist boob").

Particularly flattering choices for busty knitters include the Dorica Hoodie (page 106), Dansez Pullover (page 118), and Enrobed Wrap (page 138); these sweaters feature deep necklines that break up the vertical length of the bust.

## Smaller Busts

Small-busted knitters also need to take extra care when choosing a sweater pattern. Many knitters with a small bust believe they can't wear deep necklines, lest the neckline point out some perceived lack in their anatomy. This isn't the case! The only situation in which a deep neckline is unflattering to a small-busted figure is when there is substantial positive ease in the fullest part of the bust, which causes the sweater to gap. As long as the sweater fits properly, a smaller-busted knitter is flattered by any neckline.

In fact, smaller-busted knitters are the only figure types who are truly flattered by high necklines and lots of patterning. The Minx Tank on page 124 is an especially flattering look for smaller-busted knitters since the gorgeous, wide cable isn't disrupted by the bustline.

## On the Straight

Though it may seem counterintuitive at first, straight shapes need waist shaping. Given the weight and stiffness of most of our hand-knits, the knitter's body tends not to be especially visible under our sweaters. In fact, we generally take on the sweater's shape, not the other way around! A straight torso in a boxy sweater will absolutely look like a box; a straight torso in a shaped sweater, on the other hand, will look more curvy than it actually is.

Straight knitters often struggle with traditional waist shaping, which is located near the side seams of the sweater's body. This removes fabric from the one place a straighter shape doesn't get smaller, while still leaving puddles of extra fabric in the middle of the front and back of the sweater. Fortunately, the vertical dart waist shaping used in the patterns in this book offers the perfect solution for straighter knitters who don't want to look boxy. The side seams are untouched, fabric is removed from the exact places the knitter loses volume, and (even better) the shaping on the front and back of the sweater doesn't have to match.

Note that if waist shaping is written into the pattern, it may need to be toned down. You may be most flattered by sweaters with shaping only on the sweater back—if you do only shape on the back, the location should coincide with your back curve. For details on this modification, see page 147.

In terms of a flattering style as well as a flattering fit, a straighter knitter has two fundamental choices:

- *Create* curves by overlaying them on the body— for example, by fastening a cardigan only in the middle, which tricks the eye into seeing an hourglass instead of the straighter shape.

- *Distract* from the lack of curves by choosing sweaters with other visual interest and/or vertical visual elements that distract from the wearer's lack of curves.

The Dorica Hoodie (see page 106), Delish Cardigan (see page 112), and Chimera Cardigan (see page 130) are all flattering to straighter knitters. The hoodie and cabled cardigans, particularly when fastened only in the middle, paint an hourglass on the wearer's body and simultaneously broaden both the shoulders and the hips of the wearer. These visual tricks make the waist look smaller and curvier by comparison. The open cardigan narrows the entire torso and distracts from the wearer's straighter waist through the long, vertical panel of the neckline.

Elora's curvy figure is accentuated by the lace detail at the cuffs of the Dansez Pullover (page 118), which draws attention to the waist. The deep scoop neck flatters her bust.

## Curves Ahead!

Women with very curvy waists need sweaters that match their figure. Working a large amount of waist shaping in a small vertical space can pose something of a modification challenge for curvy knitters, but it is a necessary mod to master to avoid looking thick in the waist.

Like all figures, curvy shapes require a bit of positive ease in the waist for comfort. However, to end up with positive ease of 2 to 3"/5 to 7.5 cm, curvy knitters often need to work additional waist shaping beyond what is specified in the pattern. Curvy knitters must also be very careful that the shaping in their sweaters matches their actual waist. For details, see page 147.

Beyond a proper fit, curvy figures are especially flattered by the following elements in a sweater:

- Sleeves that stop right where the waist curves, drawing the eye to the narrowest point of the waist.

- Sweaters that paint a horizontal line around the waist—e.g., belted sweaters, sweaters with ribbing around the waist, or a transition from one stitch pattern to another. (Just be sure they're located at the narrowest part of your waist!)

- Wide vertical panels of lace, cable, or other texture that highlight the narrow waist of a curvy figure.

The Dorica Hoodie (see page 106), Dansez Pullover (see page 118), and Enrobed Wrap (see page 138) are all flattering sweaters for curvy knitters since they provide visual pointers to this great figure feature.

## The Long and Short of It

Finally, some knitters might have especially long or short torsos compared to the length of their legs. Take a look at the photo you took of yourself from the front (see page 11) to see how your leg length and torso length compare. As you might expect, knitters with especially long or short torsos must pay a bit more attention to the length of their sweaters to ensure a flattering knit.

Women with a *longer* torso (and hence shorter legs) are best flattered by sweaters that end exactly at mid hip or higher, which gives the legs their maximum possible length. Further shorten the appearance of the torso by breaking it up into different sections.

- Sweaters that can be layered with shirts so that small bits of shirt show above the sweater neckline and below its hem.

- Deep necklines that keep each "zone" of the torso somewhat short in length.

- Sweaters where the prominent visual element makes a break with the hem treatment—e.g., a cabled front where the cable separates from a ribbed hem.

- Elbow- or three-quarter-length sleeves, which break the middle "zone" of the torso up into above-sleeve and below-sleeve sections.

Conversely, women with *shorter* torsos (and, hence, longer legs) are most flattered by sweaters that lengthen the torso. Some especially flattering features are:

- Mid-hip sweaters with more vertical elements than horizontal elements (since horizontal elements break up the length of the torso).

- Longer sweater lengths (past the hips, and even mid-thigh).

- Sweaters with higher necklines, providing one clean line of fabric from the high neck all the way to the sweater hem.

- Sweaters with a prominent vertical element, like a cable that stretches all the way down to the cast-on edge.

Any sweater in this book can be modified to flatter a long- or short-torsoed knitter by altering the length and visual elements of the sweater.

DeeDee's short torso is flattered by the length of the Delish Cardigan (page 112), which reaches past her hips.

The wide hood is balanced by deep lace ribbing at the hem.

The double-ended zipper allows the cardigan to be worn with negative ease in the bust without gapping.

Vertical lines of lace slim the torso and make the waist look small compared to the shoulders and hips.

Elora is wearing size 37–38" (94–96.5 cm) with an additional 1½" (4 cm) of bust darts and approximately 1" (2.5 cm) of positive ease in the upper torso.

# DORICA HOODIE

The elegant lace panels of this hoodie remind me of the clean lines of Doric columns found in classic Greek architecture. This sweater style can be flattering for both straight and curvy knitters, with waist shaping worked in the Stockinette stitch portions of the front and back. The double-ended zipper allows the cardigan to be worn several different ways.

. . . . . . . . . . . . . . . . . . . . . . . . .

## SIZES

To fit upper torso sizes 31–32 (33–34, 35–36, 37–38, 39–40, 40–41, 43–44, 47–48, 51–52, 55–56)" [78.5–81.5 (84–86.5, 89–91.5, 94–96.5, 99–101.5, 101.5–104, 109–112, 119.5–122, 129.5–132, 139.5–142) cm]

## FINISHED MEASUREMENTS

32½ (33½, 36½, 37½, 40½, 41½, 44½, 48½, 52½, 56½)" [82.5 (85, 92.5, 95.5, 103, 105.5, 113, 123, 133.5, 143.5) cm] chest

*Note: Sweater is intended to be worn with 1-2" (2.5-5 cm) positive ease in the upper torso.*

## YARN

Berroco Vintage [50% acrylic / 40% wool / 10% nylon; 217 yards (198 meters) / 100 grams]: 5 (5, 6, 6, 7, 7, 8, 8, 9, 10) hanks #5184 Sloe Berry

## NEEDLES

One pair straight needles size US 7 (4.5 mm)

One 36" (90 cm) long circular (circ) needle size US 7 (4.5 mm)

One pair double-pointed needles (dpn) size US 7 (4.5 mm)

Change needle size if necessary to obtain correct gauge.

## NOTIONS

Stitch markers; 18 (19, 19, 20, 20, 21, 21, 22, 23, 23)" [45.5 (48.5, 48.5, 51, 51, 53.5, 53.5, 56, 58.5, 58.5) cm] separating zipper

## GAUGE

20 sts and 26 rows = 4" (10 cm) in Stockinette stitch (St st)

## NOTES

Decreases should be worked to match the slant of the edge being shaped, as follows: For left-slanting edges: On RS rows, k1, ssk, work to end; on WS rows, work to last 3 sts, ssp, p1. For right-slanting edges: On RS rows, work to last 3 sts, k2tog,

k1; on WS rows, p1, p2tog, work to end. Increases should also be worked to match the slant of the edge being shaped, as follows: For right-slanting edges: On RS rows, work 1 st, M1-r, work to end; on WS rows, work to last st, M1-p, work 1 st. For left-slanting edges: On RS rows, work to last st, M1-l, work 1 st; on WS rows, work 1 st, M1-p-l, work to end.

## BACK

CO 77 (83, 87, 93, 97, 103, 107, 117, 127, 137) sts. Place markers 30 (33, 35, 38, 40, 43, 45, 50, 55, 60) sts in from each edge.

**Next Row (RS):** Work Mixed Lace Rib from Chart to first marker, beginning with st 1 (8, 6, 3, 1, 8, 6, 1, 6, 1), and ending with st 10, sm, work Simple Lace Rib from Chart to next marker, sm, work Mixed Lace Rib to end, beginning with st 8. *Note: You may not work a complete repeat at end of row.* Work even until piece measures 2 ½" (6.5 cm) from the beginning, ending with a WS row.

**Next Row (RS):** Work in St st to first marker, sm, continue in Simple Lace Rib to next marker, sm, work in St st to end. Work even until piece measures 3" (7.5 cm) from the beginning, ending with a RS row.

**Next Row (WS):** P26 (28, 29, 31, 32, 34, 36, 39, 42, 46), pm, p25 (27, 29, 31, 33, 35, 35, 39, 43, 45), pm, purl to end.

### Shape Waist

**Decrease Row (RS):** Decrease 2 sts this row, then every 6 rows 3 times, as follows: Knit to 2 sts before first marker, ssk, sm, work to last marker, sm, k2tog, knit to end—69 (75, 79, 85, 89, 95, 99, 109, 119, 129) sts remain. Work even until piece measures 7" (18 cm) from the beginning, ending with a WS row.

### Shape Bust

**Increase Row (RS):** Increase 2 sts this row, then every 8 rows 3 times, as follows: Knit to first marker, M1-r, sm, work to second marker, sm, M1-l, knit to end—77 (83, 87, 93, 97, 103, 107, 117, 127, 137) sts. Work even, removing shaping markers, until piece measures 12 ½ (12 ¾, 13, 13 ¼, 13 ½, 13 ¾, 14, 14 ½, 15, 15)" [32 (32.5, 33, 33.5, 34.5, 35, 35.5, 37, 38, 38) cm] from the beginning, ending with a WS row.

### Shape Armholes

**Next Row (RS):** BO 6 (6, 6, 6, 6, 6, 6, 8, 10, 12) sts at beginning of next 2 rows, 0 (2, 2, 2, 2, 2, 4, 6, 8, 8) sts at beginning of next 2 rows, then decrease 1 st each side every other row 3 (2, 4, 5, 5, 6, 5, 5, 5, 5) times—59 (63, 63, 67, 71, 75, 77, 79, 81, 87) sts remain. Work even until armhole measures 5 ½ (6, 6 ¼, 6 ½, 7, 7 ¼, 7 ½, 7 ¾, 8, 8 ½)" [14 (15, 16, 16.5, 18, 18.5, 19, 19.5, 20.5, 21.5) cm], ending with a WS row.

### Shape Neck

**Next Row (RS):** Work 18 (19, 19, 21, 22, 23, 23, 24, 24, 26) sts, join a second ball of yarn, BO center 23 (25, 25, 25, 27, 29, 31, 31, 33, 35) sts, work to end. Working both sides at the same time, work even for 1 row. Decrease 1 st at each neck edge every other row twice—16 (17, 17, 19, 20, 21, 21, 22, 22, 24) sts remain each side for shoulders. Work even until armhole measures 6 ½ (7, 7 ¼, 7 ½, 8, 8 ¼, 8 ½, 8 ¾, 9, 9 ½)" [16.5 (18, 18.5, 19, 20.5, 21, 21.5, 22, 23, 24) cm], ending with a WS row.

### Shape Shoulders

**Next Row (RS):** BO 8 (8, 8, 9, 10, 10, 10, 11, 11, 12) sts at each armhole edge once, then 8 (9, 9, 10, 10, 11, 11, 11, 11, 12) sts once.

## LEFT FRONT

CO 42 (42, 47, 47, 52, 52, 57, 62, 67, 72) sts.

**Next Row (RS):** Work Mixed Lace Rib to end, beginning with st 6 (6, 1, 1, 6, 6, 1, 6, 1, 6). Work even until piece measures 2 ½" (6.5 cm) from the beginning, ending with a WS row.

**Next Row (RS):** Work in St st to last 7 sts, pm, work in Mixed Lace Rib as established to end. Work even until piece measures 3" (7.5 cm) from the beginning, ending with a RS row.

**Next Row (WS):** Work 21 (21, 23, 23, 26, 26, 28, 31, 33, 36) sts, pm, purl to end.

Mixed Lace Rib

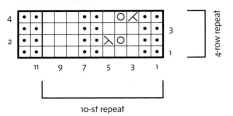

10-st repeat

Simple Lace Rib

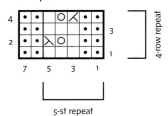

5-st repeat

### KEY

☐ Knit on RS, purl on WS.

· Purl on RS, knit on WS.

O Yo

⧄ K2tog

⧅ Ssk

MODIFICATION IDEAS

As written, Dorica is a perfectly flattering choice for proportional knitters with straight or curvy waists and any size bustline. Bottom-heavy knitters can minimize the visual impact of the hem of the sweater by shortening the ribbed section, or working a folded hem. Top-heavy knitters can minimize the visual impact of the hood by eliminating it altogether.

## Shape Waist

**Decrease Row (RS):** Decrease 1 st this row, then every 6 rows 3 times, as follows: Knit to 2 sts before first marker, ssk, sm, knit to end—38 (38, 43, 43, 48, 48, 53, 58, 63, 68) sts remain. Work even until piece measures 7" (18 cm) from the beginning, ending with a WS row.

## Shape Bust

**Increase Row (RS):** Increase 1 st this row, then every 8 rows 3 times, as follows: Knit to first marker, M1-r, sm, work to end—42 (42, 47, 47, 52, 52, 57, 62, 67, 72) sts. Work even until piece measures 12 ½ (12 ¾, 13, 13 ¼, 13 ½, 13 ¾, 14, 14 ½, 15, 15)" [32 (32.5, 33, 33.5, 34.5, 35, 35.5, 37, 38, 38) cm] from the beginning, ending with a WS row.

## Shape Armholes

**Next Row (RS):** BO 6 (6, 6, 6, 6, 6, 8, 10, 12) sts at armhole edge once, 0 (2, 2, 2, 2, 4, 6, 8, 8) sts once, then decrease 1 st at armhole edge every other row 3 (2, 4, 5, 5, 6, 5, 5, 5, 5) times—33 (32, 35, 34, 39, 38, 42, 43, 44, 47) sts remain. Work even until armhole measures 5 ½ (6, 6 ¼, 6 ½, 7, 7 ¼, 7 ½, 7 ¾, 8, 8 ½)" [14 (15, 16, 16.5, 18, 18.5, 19, 19.5, 20.5, 21.5) cm], ending with a RS row.

## Shape Neck

**Next Row (WS):** BO 13 (12, 14, 12, 15, 13, 16, 16, 17, 18)

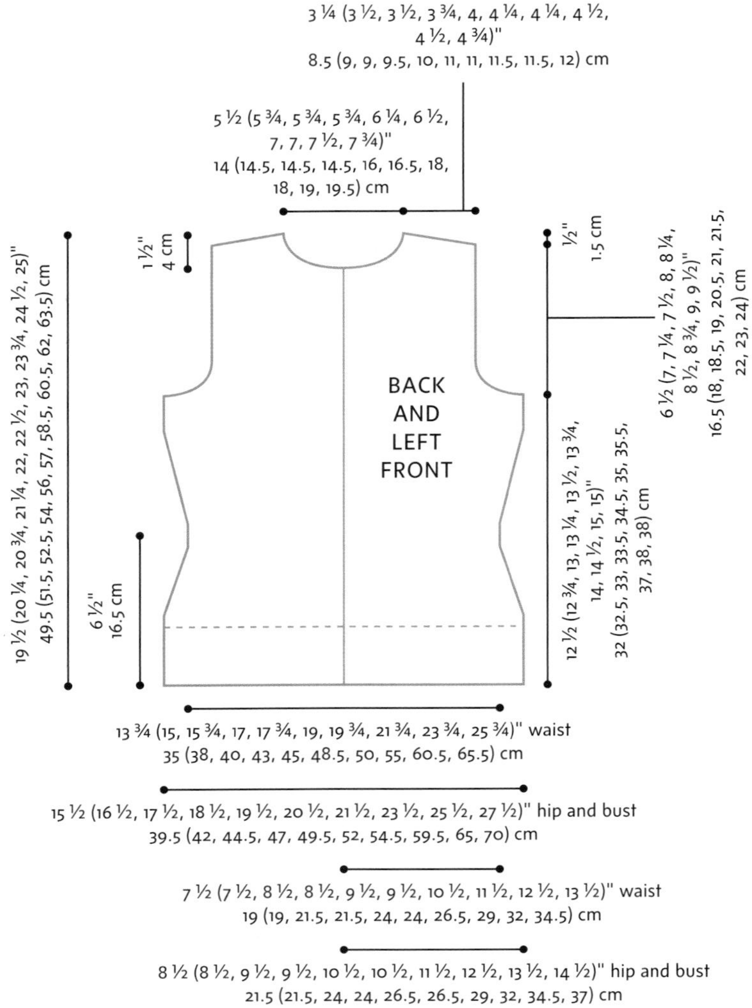
3 ¼ (3 ½, 3 ½, 3 ¾, 4, 4 ¼, 4 ¼, 4 ½, 4 ½, 4 ¾)"
8.5 (9, 9, 9.5, 10, 11, 11, 11.5, 11.5, 12) cm
5 ½ (5 ¾, 5 ¾, 5 ¾, 6 ¼, 6 ½, 7, 7, 7 ½, 7 ¾)"
14 (14.5, 14.5, 14.5, 16, 16.5, 18, 18, 19, 19.5) cm
19 ½ (20 ¼, 20 ¾, 21 ¼, 22, 22 ½, 23, 23 ¾, 24 ½, 25)"
49.5 (51.5, 52.5, 54, 56, 57, 58.5, 60.5, 62, 63.5) cm
1 ½"
4 cm
6 ½"
16.5 cm
BACK AND LEFT FRONT
½"
1.5 cm
6 ½ (7, 7 ¼, 7 ½, 8, 8 ¼, 8 ½, 8 ¾, 9, 9 ½)"
16.5 (18, 18.5, 19, 20.5, 21, 21.5, 22, 23, 24) cm
12 ½ (12 ¾, 13, 13 ¼, 13 ½, 13 ¾, 14, 14 ½, 15, 15)"
32 (32.5, 33, 33.5, 34.5, 35, 35.5, 37, 38, 38) cm
13 ¾ (15, 15 ¾, 17, 17 ¾, 19, 19 ¾, 21 ¾, 23 ¾, 25 ¾)" waist
35 (38, 40, 43, 45, 48.5, 50, 55, 60.5, 65.5) cm
15 ½ (16 ½, 17 ½, 18 ½, 19 ½, 20 ½, 21 ½, 23 ½, 25 ½, 27 ½)" hip and bust
39.5 (42, 44.5, 47, 49.5, 52, 54.5, 59.5, 65, 70) cm
7 ½ (7 ½, 8 ½, 8 ½, 9 ½, 9 ½, 10 ½, 11 ½, 12 ½, 13 ½)" waist
19 (19, 21.5, 21.5, 24, 24, 26.5, 29, 32, 34.5) cm
8 ½ (8 ½, 9 ½, 9 ½, 10 ½, 10 ½, 11 ½, 12 ½, 13 ½, 14 ½)" hip and bust
21.5 (21.5, 24, 24, 26.5, 26.5, 29, 32, 34.5, 37) cm

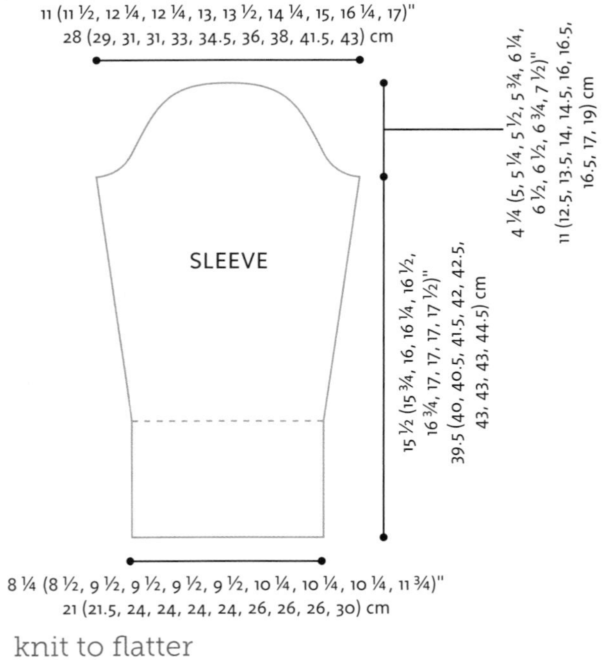
11 (11 ½, 12 ¼, 12 ¼, 13, 13 ½, 14 ¼, 15, 16 ¼, 17)"
28 (29, 31, 31, 33, 34.5, 36, 38, 41.5, 43) cm
SLEEVE
4 ¼ (5, 5 ¼, 5 ½, 5 ¾, 6 ¼, 6 ½, 6 ½, 6 ¾, 7 ½)"
11 (12.5, 13.5, 14, 14.5, 16, 16.5, 16.5, 17, 19) cm
15 ½ (15 ¾, 16, 16 ¼, 16 ½, 16 ¾, 17, 17, 17, 17 ½)"
39.5 (40, 40.5, 41.5, 42, 42.5, 43, 43, 43, 44.5) cm
8 ¼ (8 ½, 9 ½, 9 ½, 9 ½, 9 ½, 10 ¼, 10 ¼, 10 ¼, 11 ¾)"
21 (21.5, 24, 24, 24, 24, 26, 26, 26, 30) cm

sts at neck edge edge once, then decrease 1 st at neck edge every row 2 (2, 2, 2, 2, 2, 3, 3, 3, 3) times, then every other row 2 (1, 2, 1, 2, 2, 2, 2, 2, 2) time(s)—16 (17, 17, 19, 20, 21, 21, 22, 22, 24) sts remain. Work even until armhole measures 6 ½ (7, 7 ¼, 7 ½, 8, 8 ¼, 8 ½, 8 ¾, 9, 9 ½)" [16.5 (18, 18.5, 19, 20.5, 21, 21.5, 22, 23, 24) cm], ending with a WS row.

### Shape Shoulder

**Next Row (RS):** BO 8 (8, 8, 9, 10, 10, 10, 11, 11, 12) sts at armhole edge once, then 8 (9, 9, 10, 10, 11, 11, 11, 11, 12) sts once.

## RIGHT FRONT

CO 42 (42, 47, 47, 52, 52, 57, 62, 67, 72) sts.

**Next Row (RS):** Work Mixed Lace Rib to end, beginning with st 1. *Note: You may not work a complete repeat at end of row.* Work even until piece measures 2 ½" (6.5 cm) from the beginning, ending with a WS row.

Complete as for Left Front, reversing st pattern and all shaping.

## SLEEVES

CO 41 (43, 47, 47, 47, 47, 51, 51, 51, 59) sts. Place markers 18 (19, 21, 21, 21, 21, 23, 23, 23, 27) sts in from each edge.

**Next Row (RS):** P2 (0, 0, 0, 0, 0, 0, 0, 0, 1), work Mixed Lace Rib, beginning with st 6 (3, 1, 1, 1, 1, 9, 9, 9, 6), to last 2 (0, 0, 0, 0, 0, 0, 0, 0, 1) st(s), purl to end. *Note: You may not work a complete repeat at end of row.* Work even until piece measures 5" (12.5 cm) from the beginning, ending with a WS row.

**Next Row (RS):** Work in St st to marker, sm, work in Mixed Lace Rib to next marker, sm, work in St st to end. Work even for 1 row.

### Shape Sleeve

**Increase Row (RS):** Increase 1 st each side this row, then every 8 (8, 10, 10, 8, 6, 6, 4, 6) rows 6 (6, 6, 6, 8, 9, 9, 11, 14, 12) times—55 (57, 61, 61, 65, 67, 71, 75, 81, 85) sts. Work even until piece measures 15 ½ (15 ¾, 16, 16 ¼, 16 ½, 16 ¾, 17, 17, 17, 17 ½)" [39.5 (40, 40.5, 41.5, 42, 42.5, 43, 43, 43, 44.5) cm] from the beginning, ending with a WS row.

### Shape Cap

**Next Row (RS):** BO 6 (6, 6, 6, 6, 6, 8, 10, 12) sts at beginning of next 2 rows, 0 (2, 2, 2, 2, 2, 4, 6, 7, 7) sts at beginning of next 2 rows, decrease 1 st each side every 6 rows 0 (1, 1, 1, 0, 0, 1, 4, 5, 6) time(s), every 4 rows 1 (0, 0, 0, 1, 1, 1, 1, 0, 0) time(s), then every other row 9 (9, 10, 11, 13, 14, 12, 3, 3, 2) times, then BO 2 (2, 2, 2, 2, 2, 2, 3, 3, 3) sts at beginning of next 4 rows. BO remaining 15 (13, 15, 13, 13, 13, 15, 19, 19, 19) sts.

### FINISHING

Block pieces as desired. Sew shoulder seams. Set in Sleeves. Sew side and Sleeve seams.

### Hood

With RS facing, using circ needle, and beginning at Right Front neck edge, pick up and knit 19 (17, 20, 17, 21, 19, 23, 23, 24, 25) sts along Right Front neck edge, 38 (38, 40, 38, 42, 40, 46, 46, 48, 50) sts along Back neck edge, then 19 (17, 20, 17, 21, 19, 23, 23, 24, 25) sts along Left Front neck edge—76 (72, 80, 72, 84, 78, 92, 92, 96, 100) sts.

**Next Row (WS):** Work Simple Lace Rib across 7 sts, beginning with Row 2, pm, work in St st to last 7 sts, pm, work Simple Lace Rib to end, beginning with Row 2. Work even until piece measures 9 ½ (9 ½, 9 ½, 10, 10, 10, 10 ½, 10 ½, 11, 11)" [24 (24, 24, 25.5, 25.5, 25.5, 26.5, 26.5, 28, 28) cm], or desired length from pick-up row, ending with a WS row. Place markers either side of center 2 sts.

### Shape Hood

**Decrease Row (RS):** Decrease 2 sts this row, then every other row 5 times, as follows: Work to 2 sts before second marker, ssk, sm, k2, sm, k2tog, work to end—64 (60, 68, 60, 72, 66, 80, 80, 84, 88) sts remain. Divide sts evenly onto 2 needles, fold Hood in half with RSs together, and using Three-Needle BO (see Special Techniques, page 159), join halves together.

### I-Cord Front and Hood Band

With RS facing, using circ needle, and beginning at lower Right Front edge, pick up and knit 1 st per row along Right Front edge, Hood, and Left Front edge. Using dpns, CO 3 sts. *Do not turn; slide sts to opposite end of dpn. Using a second dpn and bringing yarn around behind dpn to right-hand side, k2, skp (1 st from I-Cord together with 1 st from circ needle). Repeat from * until all sts on circ needle have been worked. Thread tail through remaining sts, pull tight, and fasten off. Sew in zipper.

### BUST DARTS

The sample shown has bust darts added to each Front. The pattern calls for you to increase 1 stitch at the bust every 8 rows 4 times (see Increase Row under Shape Bust for Left and Right Fronts). In order to add bust darts to the sample, Increase Rows were worked at the bust every 6 rows instead of every 8, until a total of 7 bust Increase Rows were worked, instead of 4; this resulted in an extra 3 stitches at the bust. In order to get rid of those 3 extra stitches and end the neck shaping with the number of stitches required for the shoulders, those 3 stitches were added to the initial neck bind-off when working the first neck bind-off row (see Next Row under Shape Neck for Left and Right Fronts).

The narrow V neckline and plain hem balance each other.

The open front slims the torso.

The textured stitch pattern masks a thicker tummy.

DeeDee is wearing size 40-41" (101.5–104 cm) with zero ease in the upper torso.

# DELISH CARDIGAN

My love for soft, scrumptious yarn is well known by my friends, and this yarn is the mother of all deliciousness. This cardigan creates a perfectly flattering fit for straighter proportional figures, and waist shaping (located only on the back) adds an understated bit of curve to the wearer's figure.

. . . . . . . . . . . . . . . . . . . . . . . . . . . . . . . . . . .

## SIZES

To fit upper torso sizes 28–29 (30–31, 32–33, 34–35, 36–37, 38–39, 40–41, 44–45, 48–49, 52–53)" [71–73.5 (76–78.5, 81.5–84, 86.5–89, 91.5–94, 96.5–99, 101.5–104, 112–114.5, 122–124.5, 132–134.5) cm]

## FINISHED MEASUREMENTS

30 ½ (32, 34 ½, 36, 38 ½, 40, 42 ½, 46 ½, 50 ½, 54 ½)" [77.5 (81.5, 87.5, 91.5, 98, 101.5, 108, 118, 128.5, 138.5) cm] chest

*Note: Cardigan is intended to be worn with 1-2" (2.5-5 cm) positive ease in the upper torso.*

## YARN

HandMaiden Fine Yarns Lady Godiva [50% wool / 50% silk; 273 yards (250 meters) / 100 grams]: 4 (5, 5, 5, 6, 6, 6, 7, 8, 8) hanks Artichoke

## NEEDLES

One pair straight needles size US 8 (5 mm)

One pair straight needles size US 7 (4.5 mm)

One 36" (90 cm) long circular (circ) needle size US 8 (5 mm)

Change needle size if necessary to obtain correct gauge.

## NOTIONS

Stitch markers

## GAUGE

20 sts and 28 rows = 4" (10 cm) in Sand Stitch, using larger needles

## STITCH PATTERN

### Sand Stitch

(even number of sts; 4 row repeat)

**Rows 1 and 3 (RS):** Knit.

**Row 2:** *K1, p1; repeat from * to end.

**Row 4:** *P1, k1; repeat from * to end.

Repeat Rows 1-4 for Sand Stitch.

## NOTES

Unless otherwise specified, decreases should be worked to match the slant of the edge being shaped, as follows: For left-slanting edges: On RS rows, k1, ssk, work to end; on WS rows, work to last 3 sts, ssp, p1. For right-slanting edges: On RS rows, work to last 3 sts, k2tog, k1; on WS rows, p1, p2tog, work to end. Increases should also be worked to match the slant of the edge being shaped, as follows: For right-slanting edges: On RS rows, work 1 st, M1-r, work to end; on WS rows, work to last st, M1-p, work 1 st. For left-slanting edges: On RS rows, work to last st, M1-l, work 1 st; on WS rows, work 1 st, M1-p-l, work to end.

## BACK

Using smaller needles, CO 76 (80, 86, 90, 96, 100, 106, 116, 126, 136) sts. Begin St st; work even for 1 ½" (4 cm), ending with a RS row. Change to larger needles; knit 1 row (Turning Row).

**Next Row (RS):** Change to Sand Stitch; work even until piece measures approximately 3" (7.5 cm) from Turning Row, ending with Row 1 of Sand Stitch.

**Next Row (WS):** Continuing in Sand Stitch, work 21 (23, 25, 25, 27, 29, 31, 35, 39, 41) sts, pm, work 4 sts, pm, work 26 (26, 28, 32, 34, 34, 36, 38, 40, 46) sts, pm, work 4 sts, pm, work to end.

### Shape Waist

**Decrease Row (RS):** Decrease 2 sts this row, then every 6 rows 3 times, as follows: Work to 2 sts before first marker, work Waist Decreases Right Side from Chart, work to 2 sts before third marker, work Waist Decreases Left Side from Chart,

work to end—68 (72, 78, 82, 88, 92, 98, 108, 118, 128) sts remain. Work even until both Charts are complete, then work even in Sand Stitch for 6 rows.

### Shape Bust

**Increase Row (RS):** Increase 2 sts this row, then every 8 rows 3 times, as follows: Work to 2 sts before first marker, work Waist Increases Right Side from Chart, work to 2 sts before third marker, work Waist Increases Left Side from Chart, work to end—76 (80, 86, 90, 96, 100, 106, 116, 126, 136) sts. Work even until both Charts are complete, removing all markers on final row of Charts, then work even in Sand Stitch, until piece measures 13 (13 ¼, 13 ½, 13 ¾, 14, 14 ¼, 14 ½, 15, 15 ½, 15 ½)" [33 (33.5, 34.5, 35, 35.5, 36, 37, 38, 39.5, 39.5) cm] from Turning Row, ending with a WS row.

### Shape Armholes

**Next Row (RS):** BO 6 (6, 6, 6, 6, 6, 6, 8, 10, 12) sts at beginning of next 2 rows, 0 (2, 2, 2, 2, 2, 4, 6, 8, 8) sts at beginning of next 2 rows, then decrease 1 st each side every other row 3 (2, 3, 4, 4, 5, 5, 5, 5, 5) times—58 (60, 64, 66, 72, 74, 76, 78, 80, 86) sts

remain. Work even until armhole measures 5 ½ (6, 6 ¼, 6 ½, 7, 7 ¼, 7 ½, 7 ¾, 8, 8)" [14 (15, 16, 16.5, 18, 18.5, 19, 19.5, 20.5, 20.5) cm], ending with a WS row.

### Shape Neck

**Next Row (RS):** Work 18 (19, 20, 21, 22, 23, 23, 24, 24, 26) sts, join a second ball of yarn, BO center 22 (22, 24, 24, 28, 28, 30, 30, 32, 34) sts, work to end. Working both sides at the same time, work even for 1 row. Decrease 1 st at each neck edge every other row twice—16 (17, 18, 19, 20, 21, 21, 22, 22, 24) sts remain each side for shoulders. Work even until armhole measures 6 ½ (7, 7 ¼, 7 ½, 8, 8 ¼, 8 ½, 8 ¾, 9, 9)" [16.5 (18, 18.5, 19, 20.5, 21, 21.5, 22, 23, 23) cm], ending with a WS row.

### Shape Shoulders

**Next Row (RS):** BO 8 (9, 9, 10, 10, 11, 11, 11, 11, 12) sts at each armhole edge once, then 8 (8, 9, 9, 10, 10, 10, 11, 11, 12) sts once.

### LEFT FRONT

Using smaller needles, CO 38 (40, 44, 46, 48, 50, 54, 58, 64, 68) sts. Work even in St st for 1 ½" (4 cm), ending with a RS row. Change to larger needles; knit 1 row (Turning Row).

**Next Row (RS):** Change to Sand Stitch; work even until piece measures 13 (13 ¼, 13 ½, 13 ¾, 14, 14 ¼, 14 ½, 15, 15 ½, 15 ½)" [33 (33.5, 34.5, 35, 35.5, 36, 37, 38, 39.5, 39.5) cm] from Turning Row, ending with a WS row.

### Shape Armhole and Neck

*Note: Armhole and Neck shaping are worked at the same time; please read entire section through before beginning.*

**Next Row (RS):** BO 6 (6, 6, 6, 6, 6, 6, 8, 10, 12) sts at armhole edge once, then 0 (2, 2, 2, 2, 2, 4, 6, 8, 8) sts once, then decrease 1 st at armhole edge every other row 3 (2, 3, 4, 4, 5, 5, 5, 5, 5) times. AT THE SAME TIME, beginning on first decrease row, shape neck as follows:

## Waist Decreases Left Side

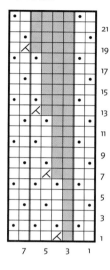

## Waist Decreases Right Side

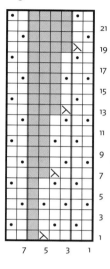

## Waist Increases Left Side

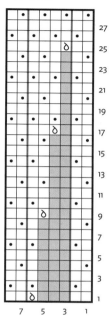

## Waist Increases Right Side

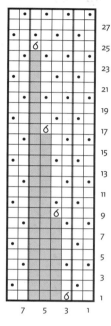

## KEY

| | |
|---|---|
| ☐ | Knit on RS, purl on WS. |
| ⊡ | Purl on RS, knit on WS. |
| ⌀ | M1-r |
| ⌀ | M1-l |
| ⧄ | K2tog |
| ⧅ | Ssk |
| │ | Marker position |

Note: At end of Decrease Charts and beginning of Increase Charts, you will have 2 markers together on each side with no sts between them. When working Increase Charts, work M1 increases on Row 1 in between markers.

3 ¼ (3 ½, 3 ½, 3 ¾, 4, 4 ¼, 4 ¼, 4 ½, 4 ½, 4 ¾)"
8.5 (9, 9, 9.5, 10, 11, 11, 11.5, 11.5, 12) cm
5 ¼ (5 ¼, 5 ½, 5 ½, 6 ½, 6 ½, 6 ¾, 6 ¾, 7 ¼, 7 ½)"
13.5 (13.5, 14, 14, 16.5, 16.5, 17, 17, 18.5, 19) cm
20 (20 ¾, 21 ¼, 21 ¾, 22 ½, 23, 23 ½, 24 ¼, 25, 25)"
51 (52.5, 54, 55, 57, 58.5, 59.5, 61.5, 63.5, 63.5) cm
1 ½"
4 cm
BACK
6 ½"
16.5 cm
turning row
½"
1.5 cm
6 ½ (7, 7 ¼, 7 ½, 8, 8 ¼, 8 ½, 8 ¾, 9, 9)"
16.5 (18, 18.5, 19, 20.5, 21, 21.5, 22, 23, 23) cm
13 (13 ¼, 13 ½, 13 ¾, 14, 14 ¼, 14 ½, 15, 15 ½, 15 ½)"
33 (33.5, 34.5, 35, 35.5, 36, 37, 38, 39.5, 39.5) cm
1 ½"
4 cm
13 ½ (14 ½, 15 ½, 16 ½, 17 ½, 18 ½, 19 ½, 21 ½, 23 ½, 25 ½)" waist
34.5 (37, 39.5, 42, 44.5, 47, 49.5, 54.5, 59.5, 65) cm
15 ¼ (16, 17 ¼, 18, 19 ¼, 20, 21 ¼, 23 ¼, 25 ¼, 27 ¼)" hip and bust
38.5 (40.5, 44, 45.5, 49, 51, 54, 59, 64, 69) cm
10 ¾ (11 ½, 12, 12 ½, 13 ¼, 13 ½, 14, 14 ¾, 16, 16 ¾)"
27.5 (29, 30.5, 32, 33.5, 34.5, 35.5, 37.5, 40.5, 42.5) cm
4 ¼ (4 ½, 5 ¼, 5 ½, 6, 6, 6 ½, 6 ¼, 6 ¾, 6 ¾)"
11 (11.5, 13.5, 14, 15, 15, 16.5, 16, 17, 17) cm
LEFT FRONT
SLEEVE
15 ½ (15 ¾, 16, 16 ¼, 16 ½, 16 ¾, 17, 17, 17, 17 ½)"
39.5 (40, 40.5, 41.5, 42, 42.5, 43, 43, 43, 44.5) cm
turning row
turning row
1 ½"
4 cm
7 ½ (8, 8 ¾, 9 ¼, 9 ½, 10, 10 ¾, 11 ½, 12 ¾, 13 ½)"
19 (20.5, 22, 23.5, 24, 25.5, 27.5, 29, 32.5, 34.5) cm
8 (8 ½, 8 ¾, 9 ¼, 9 ¼, 9 ½, 10, 10, 11 ¼, 11 ½)"
20.5 (21.5, 22, 23.5, 23.5, 24, 25.5, 25.5, 28.5, 29) cm

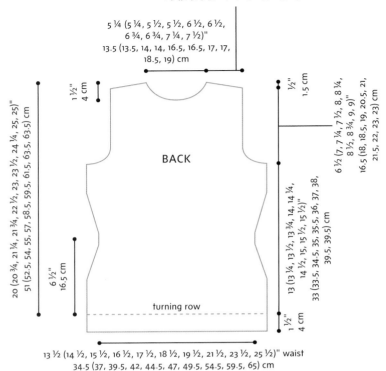

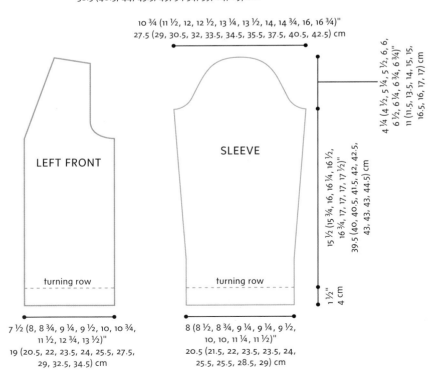

**Next Row (RS):** Decrease 1 st at neck edge this row, then every 3 rows 12 (12, 14, 14, 15, 15, 17, 16, 18, 18) times—16 (17, 18, 19, 20, 21, 21, 22, 22, 24) sts remain. Work even until armhole measures 6 ½ (7, 7 ¼, 7 ½, 8, 8 ¼, 8 ½, 8 ¾, 9, 9)" [16.5 (18, 18.5, 19, 20.5, 21, 21.5, 22, 23, 23) cm], ending with a WS row.

### Shape Shoulder

**Next Row (RS):** BO 8 (9, 9, 10, 10, 11, 11, 11, 12) sts at armhole edge once, then 8 (8, 9, 9, 10, 10, 10, 11, 11, 12) sts once.

### RIGHT FRONT

Work as for Left Front reversing all shaping.

### SLEEVES

Using smaller needles, CO 40 (42, 44, 46, 46, 48, 50, 50, 56, 58) sts. Begin St st; work even for 1 ½" (4 cm), ending with a RS row. Change to larger needles; knit 1 row (Turning Row).

**Next Row (RS):** Change to Rev St st; work even until piece measures 2" (5 cm) from Turning Row, ending with a WS row.

**Next Row (RS):** Change to Sand Stitch; work even until piece measures 2 ½" (6.5 cm) from Turning Row, ending with a WS row.

### Shape Sleeve

**Increase Row (RS):** Increase 1 st each side this row then every 10 (10, 10, 10, 8, 8, 8, 8, 8, 6) rows 6 (7, 7, 7, 9, 9, 9, 11, 11, 12) times, as follows: Work 1 st, M1-r, work to last st, M1-l, work 1 st—54 (58, 60, 62, 66, 68, 70, 74, 80, 84) sts. Work even until piece measures 15 ½ (15 ¾, 16, 16 ¼, 16 ½, 16 ¾, 17, 17, 17, 17 ½)" [39.5 (40, 40.5, 41.5, 42, 42.5, 43, 43, 43, 44.5) cm] from Turning Row, ending with a WS row.

### Shape Cap

**Next Row (RS):** BO 6 (6, 6, 6, 6, 6, 6, 8, 10, 12) sts at beginning of next 2 rows, 0 (2, 2, 2, 2, 2, 4, 6, 7, 7) sts at beginning of next 2 rows, decrease 1 st each

side every 6 rows 1 (1, 1, 1, 1, 2, 5, 6, 6) time(s), every 4 rows 0 (0, 1, 1, 1, 0, 1, 0, 0, 0) time(s), then every other row 9 (9, 9, 10, 12, 14, 11, 3, 2, 2) times, then BO 2 (2, 2, 2, 2, 2, 3, 3, 3) sts at beginning of next 4 rows. BO remaining 14 (14, 14, 14, 14, 14, 18, 18, 18) sts.

### FINISHING

Block pieces as desired. Sew shoulder seams. Set in Sleeves; sew side and Sleeve seams. Fold hems to WS at Turning Row and sew to WS, being careful not to let sts shown on RS.

### Front Bands/Collar

With RS facing, using larger needles, and beginning at Right Front hem, pick up and knit 68 (69, 70, 72, 73, 74, 75, 78, 80, 80) sts along Right Front to beginning of neck shaping, 32 (35, 36, 37, 40, 41, 43, 44, 46, 46) sts along Right Front neck edge, 38 (38, 40, 40, 44, 44, 46, 46, 48, 50) sts along Back neck edge, 32 (35, 36, 37, 40, 41, 43, 44, 46, 46) sts to beginning of Left Front neck shaping, then 68 (69, 70, 72, 73, 74, 75, 78, 80, 80) sts to Left Front hem—238 (246, 252, 258, 270, 274, 282, 290, 300, 302) sts total. Begin Rev St st; work even until piece measures 4" (10 cm) from pick-up row, ending with a RS row. BO all sts knitwise. *Note: Collar will roll to WS.*

The deep scoopneck of the pullover flatters a larger bust.

The width of the scoop neckline is balanced by an arched lace trim, which broadens the hips.

Lace detail on the sleeves calls attention to a curvy waist.

Elora is wearing size 38" (96.5 cm) with an additional 1½" (4 cm) of bust darts and approximately 1" (2.5 cm) of positive ease in the upper torso.

# DANSEZ PULLOVER

There's something about the easy, elegant scoop neckline of this sweater that reminds me of the sweatshirt my childhood ballet teacher would throw on at the end of every class. The waist shaping is located within the Stockinette stitch portion of the sweater, allowing for easy customization.

. . . . . . . . . . . . . . . . . . . . . . . . . . . . . . .

## SIZES

To fit upper torso sizes 30 (32, 34, 36, 38, 40, 42, 46, 50, 54)" [76 (81.5, 86.5, 91.5, 96.5, 101.5, 106.5, 117, 127, 137) cm]

## FINISHED MEASUREMENTS

30 ½ (32, 34, 36 ½, 38 ½, 40, 42, 46 ½, 50, 54 ½)" [77.5 (81.5, 86.5, 92.5, 98, 101.5, 106.5, 118, 127, 138.5) cm] chest

*Note: Sweater is intended to be worn with 0-1" (0-2.5 cm) positive ease in the upper torso.*

## YARN

Anzula Yarns Cricket [80% superwash merino / 10% cashmere / 10% nylon; 250 yards (228 meters) / 120 grams): 3 (3, 4, 4, 4, 4, 5, 5, 6, 6) hanks Root Beer

## NEEDLES

One pair straight needles size US 6 (4 mm)

One 24" (60 cm) long circular (circ) needle size US 6 (4 mm)

Change needle size if necessary to obtain correct gauge.

## NOTIONS

Stitch markers

## GAUGE

22 sts and 30 rows = 4" (10 cm) in Stockinette stitch (St st)

## NOTES

Unless otherwise specified, decreases should be worked to match the slant of the edge being shaped, as follows: For left-slanting edges: On RS rows, k1, ssk, work to end; on WS rows, work to last 3 sts, ssp, p1. For right-slanting edges: On RS rows, work to last 3 sts, k2tog, k1; on WS rows, p1, p2tog, work to end. Increases should also be worked to match the slant of the edge being shaped, as follows: For right-slanting edges: On RS rows, work 1 st, M1-r, work to end; on WS rows, work to last st, M1-p, work 1 st. For left-slanting edges: On RS rows, work to last st, M1-l, work 1 st; on WS rows, work 1 st, M1-p-l, work to end.

## STITCH PATTERN

**Oriel Lace Pattern (see Chart)**

(multiple of 12 sts + 1; 28-row repeat)

**Rows 1, 3, and 5 (RS):** *P1, ssk, k3, yo, p1, yo, k3, k2tog; repeat from * to last st, p1.

**Row 2 and all WS Rows:** Knit the knit sts and purl the purl sts as they face you; purl all yos.

**Row 7:** *P1, yo, k3, k2tog, p1, ssk, k3, yo; repeat from * to last st, p1.

**Row 9:** *P2, yo, k2, k2tog, p1, ssk, k2, yo, p1; repeat from * to last st, p1.

**Row 11:** *P3, yo, k1, k2tog, p1, ssk, k1, yo, p2; repeat from * to last st, p1.

**Row 13:** *P4, yo, k2tog, p1, ssk, yo, p3; repeat from * to last st, p1.

**Rows 15, 17, and 19:** *P1, yo, k3, k2tog, p1, ssk, k3, yo; repeat from * to last st, p1.

**Row 21:** *P1, ssk, k3, yo, k1, yo, k3, k2tog; repeat from * to last st, p1.

**Row 23:** *P1, ssk, k2, yo, k3, yo, k2, k2tog; repeat from * to last st, p1.

**Row 25:** *P1, ssk, k1, yo, k5, yo, k1, k2tog; repeat from * to last st, p1.

**Row 27:** *P1, ssk, yo, k7, yo, k2tog; repeat from * to last st, p1.

**Row 28:** Repeat Row 2.

Repeat Rows 1-28 for Oriel Lace Pattern.

## BACK

CO 85 (87, 97, 99, 109, 111, 113, 125, 137, 149) sts.

**Next Row (RS):** P0 (1, 0, 1, 0, 1, 2, 2, 2, 2), work Oriel Lace Pattern (from text or Chart) to last 0 (1, 0, 1, 0, 1, 2, 2, 2, 2) st(s), purl to end. Work even until Oriel Lace Pattern has been completed. Knit 1 row, decrease 1 (0, 3, 0, 3, 1, 0, 0, 0, 0) st(s) or increase 0 (1, 0, 1, 0, 0, 3, 3, 1, 1) st(s), working decrease or increase at beginning or end of row, rather than in center—84 (88, 94, 100, 106, 110, 116, 128, 138, 150) sts.

**Next Row (WS):** P28 (29, 31, 33, 35, 37, 39, 43, 46, 50) sts, pm, p28 (30, 32, 34, 36, 36, 38, 42, 46, 50) sts, pm, purl to end.

### Shape Waist

**Decrease Row (RS):** Continuing in St st, decrease 2 sts this row, then every 4 rows 4 times, as follows: Knit to 2 sts before first marker, ssk, sm, knit to next marker, sm, k2tog, knit to end—74 (78, 84, 90, 96, 100, 106, 118, 128, 140) sts remain. Work even until piece measures 7" (18 cm) from the beginning, ending with a WS row.

### Shape Bust

**Increase Row (RS):** Increase 2 sts this row, then every 8 rows 4 times, as follows: Work to first marker, M1-r, sm, work to next marker, sm, M1-l, work to end—84 (88, 94, 100, 106, 110, 116, 128, 138, 150) sts. Work even, removing markers on first row, until piece measures 13 (13 ¼, 13 ½, 13 ¾, 14, 14 ¼, 14 ½, 15, 15 ½, 15 ½)" [33 (33.5, 34.5, 35, 35.5, 36, 37, 38, 39.5, 39.5) cm] from the beginning, ending with a WS row.

### Shape Armholes

**Next Row (RS):** BO 6 (6, 6, 6, 6, 6, 6, 8, 10, 12) sts at beginning of next 2 rows, 2 (2, 2, 2, 2, 2, 4, 6, 8, 10) sts at beginning of next 2 rows, then decrease 1 st each side every other row 2 (3, 4, 6, 6, 7, 6, 7, 6, 6) times—64 (66, 70, 72, 78, 80, 84, 86, 90, 94) sts remain. Work even until armhole measures 5 ½ (6, 6 ¼, 6 ½, 7, 7 ¼, 7 ½, 7 ¾, 8, 8 ½)" [14 (15, 16, 16.5, 18, 18.5, 19, 19.5, 20.5, 21.5) cm], ending with a WS row.

Oriel Lace Pattern

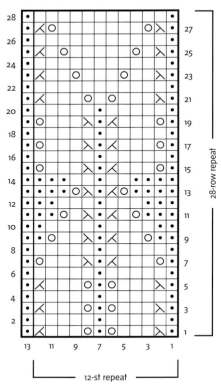

28-row repeat

12-st repeat

KEY

☐ Knit on RS, purl on WS.

⊡ Purl on RS, knit on WS.

Ⓞ Yo

◿ K2tog

◺ Ssk

### Shape Neck

**Next Row (RS):** K20 (21, 22, 22, 24, 24, 26, 26, 27, 28), join a second ball of yarn, BO center 24 (24, 26, 28, 30, 32, 32, 34, 36, 38) sts, knit to end. Working both sides at the same time, work even for 1 row. Decrease 1 st at each neck edge every other row twice—18 (19, 20, 20, 22, 22, 24, 24, 25, 26) sts remain each side for shoulders. Work even until armhole measures 6 ½ (7, 7 ¼, 7 ½, 8, 8 ¼, 8 ½, 8 ¾, 9, 9 ½)" [16.5 (18, 18.5, 19, 20.5, 21, 21.5, 22, 23, 24) cm], ending with a WS row.

### Shape Shoulders

**Next Row (RS):** BO 9 (10, 10, 10, 11, 11, 12, 12, 13, 13) sts at each armhole edge once, then 9 (9, 10, 10, 11, 11, 12, 12, 12, 13) sts once.

## FRONT

CO 85 (87, 97, 99, 109, 111, 113, 125, 137, 149) sts.

**Next Row (RS):** P0 (1, 0, 1, 0, 1, 2, 2, 2, 2), work Oriel Lace Pattern (from text or Chart) to last 0 (1, 0, 1, 0, 1, 2, 2, 2, 2) st(s), purl to end. Work even until Oriel Lace Pattern has been completed. Knit 1 row, decrease 1 (0, 3, 0, 3, 1, 0, 0, 0, 0) st(s) or increase 0 (1, 0, 1, 0, 0, 3, 3, 1, 1) st(s), working decrease or increase at beginning or end of row, rather than in center—84 (88, 94, 100, 106, 110, 116, 128, 138, 150) sts.

**Next Row (WS):** P21 (22, 24, 25, 27, 28, 29, 32, 35, 38) sts, pm, p42 (44, 46, 50, 52, 54, 58, 64, 68, 74) sts, pm, purl to end. Work as for Back to beginning of armhole shaping, ending with a WS row. Place marker between center 2 sts.

### Shape Armholes and Neck

*Note: Armhole and neck shaping are worked at the same time; please read entire section through before beginning.*

**Next Row (RS):** Shape armholes as for Back and, AT THE SAME TIME, knit to 5 (5, 5, 6, 6, 6,

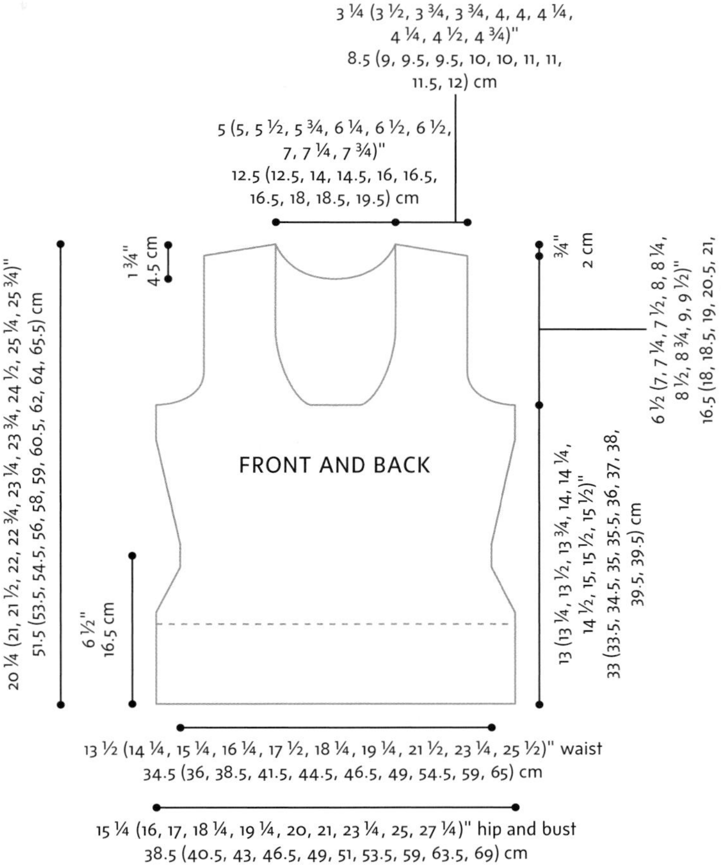
3 ¼ (3 ½, 3 ¾, 3 ¾, 4, 4, 4 ¼, 4 ¼, 4 ½, 4 ¾)"
8.5 (9, 9.5, 9.5, 10, 10, 11, 11, 11.5, 12) cm
5 (5, 5 ½, 5 ¾, 6 ¼, 6 ½, 6 ½, 7, 7 ¼, 7 ¾)"
12.5 (12.5, 14, 14.5, 16, 16.5, 16.5, 18, 18.5, 19.5) cm
20 ¼ (21, 21 ½, 22, 22 ¾, 23 ¼, 23 ¾, 24 ½, 25 ¼, 25 ¾)"
51.5 (53.5, 54.5, 56, 58, 59, 60.5, 62, 64, 65.5) cm
1 ¾"
4.5 cm
6 ½"
16.5 cm
FRONT AND BACK
¾"
2 cm
6 ½ (7, 7 ¼, 7 ½, 8, 8 ¼, 8 ½, 8 ¾, 9, 9 ½)"
16.5 (18, 18.5, 19, 20.5, 21, 21.5, 22, 23, 24) cm
13 (13 ¼, 13 ½, 13 ¾, 14, 14 ¼, 14 ½, 15, 15 ½, 15 ½)"
33 (33.5, 34.5, 35, 35.5, 36, 37, 38, 39.5, 39.5) cm
13 ½ (14 ¼, 15 ¼, 16 ¼, 17 ½, 18 ¼, 19 ¼, 21 ½, 23 ¼, 25 ½)" waist
34.5 (36, 38.5, 41.5, 44.5, 46.5, 49, 54.5, 59, 65) cm
15 ¼ (16, 17, 18 ¼, 19 ¼, 20, 21, 23 ¼, 25, 27 ¼)" hip and bust
38.5 (40.5, 43, 46.5, 49, 51, 53.5, 59, 63.5, 69) cm

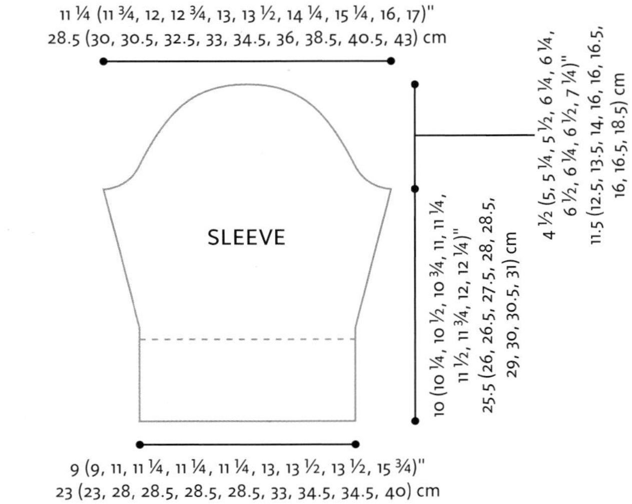
11 ¼ (11 ¾, 12, 12 ¾, 13, 13 ½, 14 ¼, 15 ¼, 16, 17)"
28.5 (30, 30.5, 32.5, 33, 34.5, 36, 38.5, 40.5, 43) cm
SLEEVE
4 ½ (5, 5 ¼, 5 ½, 6 ¼, 6 ¼, 6 ½, 6 ¼, 6 ½, 7 ¼)"
11.5 (12.5, 13.5, 14, 16, 16, 16.5, 16, 16.5, 18.5) cm
10 (10 ¼, 10 ½, 10 ¾, 11, 11 ¼, 11 ½, 11 ¾, 12, 12 ¼)"
25.5 (26, 26.5, 27.5, 28, 28.5, 29, 30, 30.5, 31) cm
9 (9, 11, 11 ¼, 11 ¼, 11 ¼, 13, 13 ½, 13 ½, 15 ¾)"
23 (23, 28, 28.5, 28.5, 28.5, 33, 34.5, 34.5, 40) cm

6, 7, 7, 7) sts before center marker, join a second ball of yarn, BO 10 (10, 10, 12, 12, 12, 12, 14, 14, 14) sts, knit to end. Working both sides at the same time, work even for 1 row. Decrease 1 st at each neck edge every row 4 (4, 4, 4, 5, 5, 5, 5, 6, 6) times, every other row 2 (2, 3, 3, 3, 4, 4, 4, 4, 4) times, then every 4 rows 3 (3, 3, 3, 3, 3, 3, 3, 3, 4) times—18 (19, 20, 20, 22, 22, 24, 24, 25, 26) sts remain when all shaping is complete. Work even until armhole measures same as for Back to shoulder shaping; shape shoulders as for Back.

### SLEEVES

CO 51 (51, 61, 63, 63, 63, 73, 75, 75, 87) sts.

**Next Row (RS):** P1 (1, 0, 1, 1, 1, 0, 1, 1, 1), work Oriel Lace Pattern to last 1 (1, 0, 1, 1, 1, 0, 1, 1, 1) st(s), purl to end. Work even until Oriel Lace Pattern has been completed.

**Next Row (RS):** K2tog, knit to end—50 (50, 60, 62, 62, 62, 72, 74, 74, 86) sts remain. Continuing in St st, work even until piece measures 4" (10 cm) from the beginning, ending with a WS row.

## BUST DARTS

The sample shown has bust darts added to the Front. The pattern calls for you to increase 2 stitches at the bust every 8 rows 5 times (see Increase Row under Shape Bust for Back). In order to add bust darts to this sample, Increase Rows were worked at the bust every 4 rows instead of every 8, until a total of 10 bust Increase Rows were worked, instead of 5; this resulted in an extra 10 stitches at the bust (5 stitches each side). In order to get rid of those 10 extra stitches, decreases were worked as follows: In Shape Armholes and Neck section for Front, 4 sts were added to the initial neck BO, and 1 additional decrease was added to each side of the neck in the every-row, every-other-row, and every-4-rows sections.

### Shape Sleeve

**Increase Row (RS):** Increase 1 st each side this row, then every 6 (6, 16, 12, 10, 8, 20, 12, 8, 16) rows 5 (6, 2, 3, 4, 5, 2, 4, 6, 3) times—62 (64, 66, 70, 72, 74, 78, 84, 88, 94) sts. Work even until piece measures 10 (10 ¼, 10 ½, 10 ¾, 11, 11 ¼, 11 ½, 11 ¾, 12, 12 ¼)" [25.5 (26, 26.5, 27.5, 28, 28.5, 29, 30, 30.5, 31) cm] from the beginning, ending with a WS row.

### Shape Cap

**Next Row (RS):** BO 6 (6, 6, 6, 6, 6, 6, 8, 10, 12) sts at beginning of next 2 rows, 2 (2, 2, 2, 2, 2, 4, 6, 8, 8) sts at beginning of next 2 rows, decrease 1 st each side every 6 rows 0 (1, 1, 0, 1, 0, 1, 4, 6, 7) time(s), every 4 rows 1 (0, 0, 1, 0, 1, 0, 1, 0, 0) time(s), then every other row 11 (12, 13, 15, 16, 17, 17, 5, 2, 2) times, then BO 2 (2, 2, 2, 2, 2, 4, 4, 4, 4) sts at beginning of next 4 rows. BO remaining 14 (14, 14, 14, 14, 14, 14, 20, 20, 20) sts.

### FINISHING

Block pieces as desired. Sew shoulder seams. Set in Sleeves; sew side and Sleeve seams.

### Neckband

With RS facing, using circ needle, and beginning at right shoulder seam, pick up and knit 40 (40, 42, 44, 46, 48, 48, 50, 52, 54) sts along Back neck edge, 34 (36, 38, 39, 42, 44, 45, 46, 48, 51) sts along left Front neck edge, 10 (10, 10, 12, 12, 12, 12, 14, 14, 14) sts from BO sts at center Front, then 34 (36, 38, 39, 42, 44, 45, 46, 48, 51) sts along right Front neck edge—118 (122, 128, 134, 142, 148, 150, 156, 162, 170) sts. Join for working in the rnd; pm for beginning of rnd. Begin St st (knit every rnd); work even for 7 rnds. BO all sts loosely, allowing neck edge to roll.

## MODIFICATION IDEAS

As written, Dansez is perfect for a proportional knitter with a curvy waist. Bust darts for bustier knitters like Elora can be worked using the instructions in the pattern as a template; straighter shapes might consider lengthening the sleeves to draw the eye away from the waist. Bottom-heavy knitters can easily widen the neckline; top-heavy knitters could narrow the neckline and/or lengthen the sleeves for maximum hip-broadening potential.

A high neckline and all-over cable pattern flatters a smaller-busted figure.

The cables stretch all the way to the hem of the sweater to add visual length to the torso.

Jenn is wearing size 32" (81.5 cm) with zero ease in the upper torso.

# MINX TANK

Sweaters with high necklines and allover texture tend to be most flattering on figures with smaller busts. This tank features both, combined with a lovely deep V in back.

· · · · · · · · · · · · · · · · · · · · · · · · · · · · · · · · ·

## SIZES

To fit upper torso sizes 28 (30, 32, 34, 36, 38, 40, 44, 48, 52)" [71 (76, 81.5, 86.5, 91.5, 96.5, 101.5, 112, 122, 132) cm]

## FINISHED MEASUREMENTS

30 (32, 34 ½, 36 ½, 38, 40, 42 ½, 46, 50 ½, 54)" [76 (81.5, 87.5, 92.5, 96.5, 101.5, 108, 117, 128.5, 137) cm] chest

*Note: Tank is intended to be worn with approximately 2" (5 cm) positive ease in the upper torso.*

## YARN

Sundara Yarn Fingering Silky Merino [50% silk / 50% merino wool; 500 yards (457 meters) / 150 grams]: 1 (1, 2, 2, 2, 2, 2, 2, 2) hank(s) Aged Oak Barrel

## NEEDLES

One pair straight needles size US 2 (2.75 mm)

One pair straight needles size US 1 (2.25 mm)

One 16" (40 cm) long circular (circ) needle size US 2 (2.75 mm)

Change needle size if necessary to obtain correct gauge.

## NOTIONS

Stitch markers (including 2 markers of different color); stitch holder

## GAUGE

26 sts and 36 rows = 4" (10 cm) in Stockinette stitch (St st), using larger needles

## NOTES

Unless otherwise specified, decreases should be worked to match the slant of the edge being shaped, as follows: For left-slanting edges: On RS rows, k1, ssk, work to end; on WS rows, work to last 3 sts, ssp, p1. For right-slanting edges: On RS rows, work to last 3 sts, k2tog, k1; on WS rows, p1, p2tog, work to end. Increases should also be worked to match the slant of the edge being shaped, as follows: For right-slanting edges: On RS rows, work 1 st, M1-r, work to end; on WS rows, work to last st, M1-p, work 1 st. For left-slanting edges: On RS rows, work to last st, M1-l, work 1 st; on WS rows, work 1 st, M1-p-l, work to end.

## BACK

Using smaller needles, CO 98 (104, 112, 118, 124, 130, 138, 150, 164, 176) sts. Begin St st; work even until piece measures 1 ½" (4 cm) from the beginning, ending with a RS row. Knit 1 row (Turning Row).

**Next Row (RS):** Change to larger needles; continuing in St st, work even until piece measures 3" (7.5) cm from Turning Row, ending with a RS row.

**Next Row (WS):** P33 (35, 37, 39, 41, 43, 46, 50, 55, 59), pm, P32 (34, 38, 40, 42, 44, 46, 50, 54, 58), pm, purl to end.

### Shape Waist

**Decrease Row (RS):** Decrease 2 sts this row, then every 4 rows 4 times, as follows: Knit to 2 sts before first marker, ssk, sm, knit to next marker, sm, k2tog, knit to end—88 (94, 102, 108, 114, 120, 128, 140, 154, 166) sts remain. Work even until piece measures 6 ½" (16.5 cm) from Turning Row, ending with a WS row.

### Shape Bust

**Increase Row (RS):** Increase 2 sts this row, then every 4 rows 4 times, as follows: Work to first marker, M1-r, sm, work to next marker, sm, M1-l, work to end—98 (104, 112, 118, 124, 130, 138, 150, 164, 176) sts. Work even, removing markers on first row, until piece measures 12 (12 ¾, 13, 13, 13 ¼, 13 ¼, 13 ½, 13 ½, 13 ¾, 13 ¾)" [30.5 (32.5, 33, 33, 33.5, 33.5, 34.5, 34.5, 35, 35) cm] from Turning Row, ending with a WS row.

## Shape Armholes

**Next Row (RS):** BO 8 (8, 8, 8, 8, 8, 8, 10, 12, 14) sts at beginning of next 2 rows, 0 (2, 2, 2, 2, 2, 4, 6, 8, 10) sts at beginning of next 2 rows, then decrease 1 st each side every other row 3 (3, 5, 6, 6, 7, 8, 8, 9, 8) times—76 (78, 82, 86, 92, 96, 98, 102, 106, 112) sts remain. Purl 1 row.

## Shape Neck

**Next Row (RS):** K38 (39, 41, 43, 46, 48, 49, 51, 53, 56), join a second ball of yarn, knit to end. Working both sides at the same time, purl 1 row.

**Decrease Row (RS):** Decrease 1 st at each neck edge this row, every row 9 (9, 9, 9, 11, 11, 11, 13, 13, 15) times, every other row 6 (7, 8, 9, 8, 9, 10, 8, 9, 9) times, then every 4 rows 6 (6, 6, 6, 7, 7, 7, 8, 8, 8) times—16 (16, 17, 18, 19, 20, 20, 21, 22, 23) sts remain each side for shoulders. Work even until armhole measures 7 (7 ½, 7 ¾, 8, 8 ¼, 8 ½, 9, 9 ¼, 9 ½, 9 ¾)" [18 (19, 19.5, 20.5, 21, 21.5, 23, 23.5, 24, 25) cm], ending with a WS row.

## Shape Shoulders

**Next Row (RS):** BO 8 (8, 9, 9, 10, 10, 10, 11, 11, 12) sts at each armhole edge once, then 8 (8, 8, 9, 9, 10, 10, 10, 11, 11) sts once.

## FRONT

Using smaller needles, CO 98 (104, 112, 118, 124, 130, 138, 150, 164, 176) sts. Begin St st; work even until piece measures 1 ½" (4 cm) from the beginning, ending with a RS row. Knit 1 row (Turning Row).

**Next Row (RS):** K19 (22, 26, 29, 32, 35, 39, 29, 36, 42), pm, [increase 3 sts evenly over next 12 sts, pm, k4, pm] 1 (1, 1, 1, 1, 1, 1, 2, 2, 2) time(s), increase 10 sts evenly over next 28 sts, pm, [k4, pm, increase 3 sts evenly over next 12 sts, pm] 1 (1, 1, 1, 1, 1, 1, 2, 2, 2) time(s), k19 (22, 26, 29, 32, 35, 39, 29, 36, 42)—114 (120, 128, 134, 140, 146, 154, 172, 186, 198) sts. Change to larger needles. Knit 1 row (Turning Row).

## Braided Cable

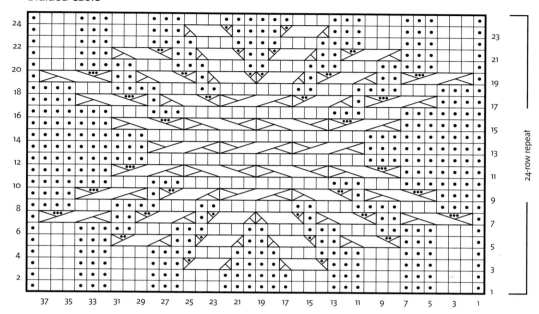

24-row repeat

## Open Cable

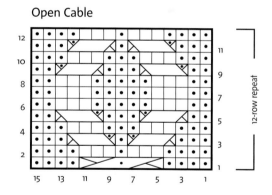

12-row repeat

## KEY

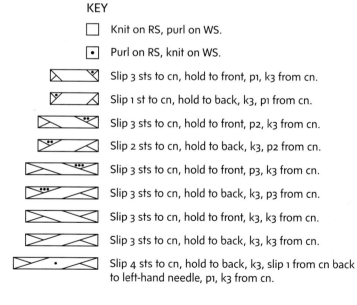

| | |
|---|---|
| ☐ | Knit on RS, purl on WS. |
| ⦁ | Purl on RS, knit on WS. |

Slip 3 sts to cn, hold to front, p1, k3 from cn.

Slip 1 st to cn, hold to back, k3, p1 from cn.

Slip 3 sts to cn, hold to front, p2, k3 from cn.

Slip 2 sts to cn, hold to back, k3, p2 from cn.

Slip 3 sts to cn, hold to front, p3, k3 from cn.

Slip 3 sts to cn, hold to back, k3, p3 from cn.

Slip 3 sts to cn, hold to front, k3, k3 from cn.

Slip 3 sts to cn, hold to back, k3, k3 from cn.

Slip 4 sts to cn, hold to back, k3, slip 1 from cn back to left-hand needle, p1, k3 from cn.

## MODIFICATION IDEAS

For the most flattering fit, make sure this tank ends at the right place on the hips. Proportional knitters should consider a spot just above their widest point, as we see on Jenn. Top-heavy knitters will want a slightly longer line on the tank to maximize their hip width. Bottom-heavy knitters should pair a shorter length with a slight widening of the neckline (this tank would look phenomenal with a boatneck). Bustier knitters could consider using the back neckline instructions for the front of this tank instead, working a deep V neckline (or possibly a scoop!) into the cable panel.

### SIZES 28-40 ONLY

**Next Row (RS):** Work in St st to first marker, sm, work Row 1 of Open Cable to next marker, sm, work in St st to next marker, sm, work Braided Cable to next marker, sm, work in St st to next marker, sm, work Open Cable to next marker, sm, work in St st to end.

### SIZES 44-52 ONLY

**Next Row (RS):** Work in St st to first marker, sm, work Row 7 of Open Cable to next marker, sm, work in St st to next marker, sm, work Row 1 of Open Cable to next marker, sm, work in St st to next marker, sm, work Braided Cable to next marker, sm, work in St st to next marker, sm, work Row 1 of Open Cable to next marker, sm, work in St st to next marker, sm, work Row 7 of Open Cable to next marker, sm, work in St st to end.

### ALL SIZES

Work even until piece measures 3" (7.5) cm from Turning Row, ending with a WS row. Place marker of different color 18 (21, 25, 28, 31, 34, 38, 28, 35, 41) sts in from each side for waist shaping.

#### Shape Waist

**Decrease Row (RS):** Decrease 2 sts this row, then every 4 rows 4 times, as follows: Knit to 2 sts before first waist marker, ssk, sm, work to next waist marker, sm, k2tog, knit to end—104 (110, 118, 124, 130, 136, 144, 162, 176, 188) sts remain. Work even until piece measures 6 ½" (16.5 cm) from Turning Row, ending with a WS row.

#### Shape Bust

**Increase Row (RS):** Increase 2 sts this row, then every 4 rows 4 times, as follows: Knit to first waist marker, M1-r, sm, work to next waist marker, sm, M1-l, knit to end—114 (120, 128, 134, 140, 146, 154, 172, 186, 198) sts. Work even, removing shaping markers on first row, until piece measures 12 (12 ¾, 13, 13, 13 ¼, 13 ¼, 13 ½, 13 ½, 13 ¾, 13 ¾)" [30.5 (32.5, 33, 33, 33.5, 33.5, 34.5, 34.5, 35, 35) cm] from Turning Row, ending with a WS row.

#### Shape Armholes

**Next Row (RS):** Shape armholes as for Back—92 (94, 98, 102, 108, 112, 114, 124, 128, 134) sts remain. Work even until armhole measures 4 (4 ½, 4 ¾, 5, 5 ¼, 5 ½, 6, 6 ¼, 6 ½, 6 ¾)" [10 (11.5, 12, 12.5, 13.5, 14, 15, 16, 16.5, 17) cm], ending with a WS row.

#### Shape Neck

**Next Row (RS):** Work 36 (36, 37, 38, 39, 40, 40, 41, 42, 43) sts, join a second ball of yarn, BO center 20 (22, 24, 26, 30, 32, 34, 42, 44, 48) sts, work to end.

Working both sides at the same time, decrease 1 st each neck edge every row 20 times—16 (16, 17, 18, 19, 20, 20, 21, 22, 23) sts remain each side. Work even until armhole measures same as for Back to beginning of shoulder shaping; shape shoulders as for Back.

### FINISHING

Sew shoulder seams. Sew side seams. Block piece as desired.

#### Armhole Edging

With RS facing, using circ needle, and beginning at center underarm, pick up and knit 8 (10, 10, 10, 10, 10, 12, 16, 20, 24) sts from BO sts, 45 (48, 50, 52, 53, 55, 58, 60, 61, 63) sts to shoulder seam, 45 (48, 50, 52, 53, 55, 58, 60, 61, 63) sts to BO underarm sts, then 8 (10, 10, 10, 10, 10, 12, 16, 20, 24) sts from BO sts—106 (116, 120, 124, 126, 130, 140, 152, 162, 174) sts. Join for working in the rnd; pm for beginning of rnd. Knit 4 rnds. BO all sts knitwise.

#### Neckband

With RS facing, using circ needle, and beginning at right shoulder seam, pick up and knit 47 (51, 50, 51, 53, 54, 56, 58, 58, 62) sts along right Back neck edge, 47 (51, 50, 51, 53, 54, 56, 58, 58, 62) sts along left Back neck edge, then 60 (62, 62, 64, 68, 70, 70, 72, 74, 78) sts along Front neck—154 (164, 162, 166, 174, 178, 182, 188, 190, 202) sts. Join for working in the rnd; pm for beginning of rnd. Knit 4 rnds. BO all sts loosely.

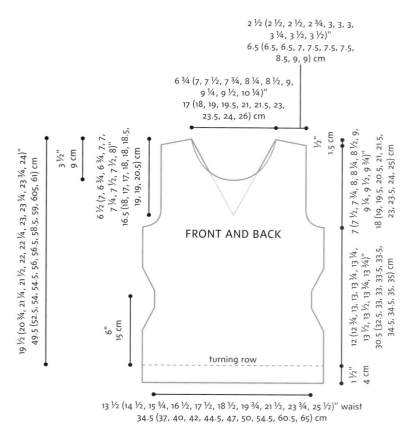

2 ½ (2 ½, 2 ½, 2 ¾, 3, 3, 3, 3 ¼, 3 ½, 3 ½)"
6.5 (6.5, 6.5, 7, 7.5, 7.5, 7.5, 8.5, 9, 9) cm

6 ¾ (7, 7 ½, 7 ¾, 8 ¼, 8 ½, 9, 9 ¼, 9 ½, 10 ¼)"
17 (18, 19, 19.5, 21, 21.5, 23, 23.5, 24, 26) cm

½"
1.5 cm

3 ½"
9 cm

6 ½ (7, 6 ¾, 6 ¾, 7, 7, 7 ¼, 7 ½, 7 ½, 8)"
16.5 (18, 17, 17, 18, 18, 18.5, 19, 19, 20.5) cm

19 ½ (20 ¾, 21 ¼, 21 ½, 22, 22 ¼, 23, 23 ¼, 23 ¾, 24)"
49.5 (52.5, 54, 54.5, 56, 56.5, 58.5, 59, 60.5, 61) cm

FRONT AND BACK

7 (7 ½, 7 ¾, 8, 8 ¼, 8 ½, 9, 9 ¼, 9 ½, 9 ¾)"
18 (19, 19.5, 20.5, 21, 21.5, 23, 23.5, 24, 25) cm

12 (12 ¾, 13, 13, 13 ¼, 13 ¼, 13 ½, 13 ½, 13 ¾, 13 ¾)"
30.5 (32.5, 33, 33, 33.5, 33.5, 34.5, 34.5, 35, 35) cm

6"
15 cm

1 ½"
4 cm

turning row

13 ½ (14 ½, 15 ¾, 16 ½, 17 ½, 18 ½, 19 ¾, 21 ½, 23 ¾, 25 ½)" waist
34.5 (37, 40, 42, 44.5, 47, 50, 54.5, 60.5, 65) cm

15 (16, 17 ¼, 18 ¼, 19, 20, 21 ¼, 23, 25 ¼, 27)" hip and bust
38 (40.5, 44, 46.5, 48.5, 51, 54, 58.5, 64, 68.5) cm

Cable panels travel
the torso to create an
hourglass waist.

Elora is wearing size
37–38" (94–96.5 cm) with
approximately 1" (2.5 cm)
of ease in the upper torso.

# CHIMERA CARDIGAN

This cardigan is offered with two sleeve lengths: long (shown at left) and short (shown on page 137). The cable panels travel over the wearer's curves, which are accentuated by waist shaping.

. . . . . . . . . . . . . . . . . . . . . . . . . . . . . . . . . .

## SIZES

To fit upper torso sizes 29–30 (31–32, 33–34, 35–36, 37–38, 39–40, 41–42, 45–46, 49–50, 53–54)" [73.5–76 (78.5–81.5, 84–86.5, 89–91.5, 94–96.5, 99–101.5, 104–106.5, 114.5–117, 124.5–127, 134.5–137) cm]

## FINISHED MEASUREMENTS

31 (33, 35, 37, 39, 41, 43, 47, 51, 55)" [78.5 (84, 89, 94, 99, 104, 109, 119.5, 129.5, 139.5) cm] chest

*Note: Cardigan is intended to be worn with 1-2" (2.5-5 cm) positive ease in the upper torso.*

## YARN

Quince and Company Chickadee [100% American wool; 181 yards (166 meters) / 50 grams]: **Short-Sleeve Version:** 5 (5, 5, 6, 6, 7, 7, 8, 9, 10) hanks Twig; **Long-Sleeve Version:** 6 (7, 7, 8, 8, 9, 10, 10, 11, 12) hanks Pomegranate

## NEEDLES

One pair straight needles size US 5 (3.75 mm)

One 24" (60 cm) long circular (circ) needle size US 5 (3.75 mm)

Change needle size if necessary to obtain correct gauge.

## NOTIONS

Stitch markers; cable needle; 9 (10, 10, 10, 11, 11, 12, 12, 13, 13) ½" (13 mm) buttons

## GAUGE

24 sts and 32 rows = 4" (10 cm) in Stockinette stitch (St st)

## ABBREVIATIONS

**C6B:** Slip 3 sts to cn, hold to back, k3, k3 from cn.

**C6F:** Slip 3 sts to cn, hold to front, k3, k3 from cn.

**T4B-p:** Slip 1 st to cn, hold to back, k3, p1 from cn.

**T4F-p:** Slip 3 sts to cn, hold to front, p1, k3 from cn.

**T5B-p:** Slip 2 sts to cn, hold to back, k3, p2 from cn.

**T5F-p:** Slip 3 sts to cn, hold to front, p2, k3 from cn.

## STITCH PATTERNS

### Twisted Rib

(even number of sts, 2-row repeat)

**Row 1 (WS):** *K1, p1-tbl; repeat from * to end.

**Row 2:** *K1-tbl, p1; repeat from * to end.

Repeat Rows 1 and 2 for Twisted Rib.

### Looping Wave (see Chart)

(panel of 23 sts; 24-row repeat)

**Row 1 (WS):** K3, p3, k6, p6, k5.

**Row 2:** P5, C6B, p6, T4F-p, p2.

**Row 3 and all WS Rows:** Knit the knit sts and purl the purl sts as they face you.

**Rows 4 and 6:** Repeat Row 3.

**Row 8:** P5, C6B, p6, T4B-p, p2.

**Row 10:** P4, T4B-p, T5F-p, p3, T4B-p, p3.

**Row 12:** P3, T4B-p, p3, T5F-p, T4B-p, p4.

**Row 14:** P2, T4B-p, p6, C6F, p5.

**Rows 16 and 18:** Repeat Row 3.

**Row 20:** P2, T4F-p, p6, C6F, p5.

**Row 22:** P3, T4F-p, p3, T5B-p, T4F-p, p4.

**Row 24:** P4, T4F-p, T5B-p, p3, T4F-p, p3.

Repeat Rows 1-24 for Looping Wave.

## NOTES

Instructions are given for both Short-Sleeve and Long-Sleeve versions.

Unless otherwise specified, decreases should be worked to match the slant of the edge being shaped, as follows: For left-slanting edges: On RS rows, k1, ssk, work to end; on WS rows, work to last 3 sts, ssp, p1. For right-slanting edges:

On RS rows, work to last 3 sts, k2tog, k1; on WS rows, p1, p2tog, work to end. Increases should also be worked to match the slant of the edge being shaped, as follows: For right-slanting edges: On RS rows, work 1 st, M1-r, work to end; on WS rows, work to last st, M1-p, work 1 st. For left-slanting edges: On RS rows, work to last st, M1-l, work 1 st; on WS rows, work 1 st, M1-p-l, work to end.

## BACK

CO 103 (109, 115, 121, 127, 133, 139, 151, 163, 175) sts.

**Next Row (WS):** P1 (1, 1, 0, 0, 0, 0, 1, 1, 0), work Twisted Rib across 10 (12, 14, 18, 20, 22, 24, 28, 34, 40) sts, pm, work Looping Wave across 23 sts, beginning with Row 1, pm, p1-tbl, work Twisted Rib across 34 (36, 38, 38, 40, 42, 44, 46, 46, 48) sts, pm, work Looping Wave across 23 sts, beginning with Row 13, pm, work Twisted Rib, beginning with p1-tbl,

to last 1 (1, 1, 0, 0, 0, 0, 1, 1, 0) st(s), p1 (1, 1, 0, 0, 0, 0, 1, 1, 0). Work even until piece measures 1½" (4 cm) from the beginning, ending with a WS row.

**Next Row (RS):** K1 (1, 1, 0, 0, 0, 0, 1, 1, 0), [k1, slip 1] 5 (6, 7, 9, 10, 11, 12, 14, 17, 20) times, sm, work to next marker, sm, slip 1, [k1, slip 1] 17 (18, 19, 19, 20, 21, 22, 23, 23, 24) times, sm, work to next marker, sm, [slip 1, k1] 5 (6, 7, 9, 10, 11, 12, 14, 17, 20) times, k1 (1, 1, 0, 0, 0, 0, 1, 1, 0). Work even, working Looping Wave panels as established, and working all other sts in St st, until piece measures 2" (5 cm), ending with a WS row.

### Shape Waist

**Decrease Row (RS):** Decrease 2 sts this row, then every 8 rows 4 times, as follows: Work to second marker, sm, k1, ssk, knit to 3 sts before next marker, k2tog, k1, sm, work to end—93 (99, 105, 111, 117, 123,

## Looping Wave

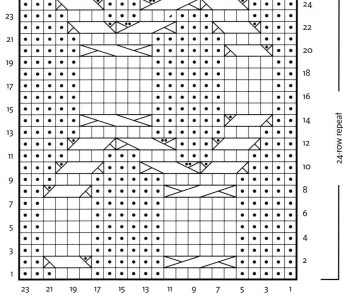

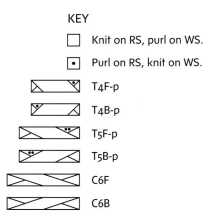

KEY

| | |
|---|---|
| □ | Knit on RS, purl on WS. |
| • | Purl on RS, knit on WS. |
| ⟋⟍ | T4F-p |
| ⟍⟋ | T4B-p |
| ⟋⟍ | T5F-p |
| ⟍⟋ | T5B-p |
| ⟋⟍ | C6F |
| ⟍⟋ | C6B |

Note: Chart begins with a WS row; work first row from left to right.

129, 141, 153, 165) sts remain. Work even until piece measures 7" (18 cm) from the beginning, ending with a WS row.

### Shape Bust

**Increase Row (RS):** Increase 2 sts this row, then every 8 rows 4 times, as follows: Work to second marker, sm, k1, M1-r, knit to 1 st before next marker, M1-l, k1, sm, work to end—103 (109, 115, 121, 127, 133, 139, 151, 163, 175) sts. Work even until piece measures 12 ½ (12 ¾, 13, 13 ¼, 13 ½, 13 ¾, 14, 14 ½, 15, 15)" [32 (32.5, 33, 33.5, 34.5, 35, 35.5, 37, 38, 38) cm] from the beginning, ending with a WS row.

### Shape Armholes

**Next Row (RS):** BO 6 (6, 6, 6, 6, 6, 8, 10, 12, 14) sts at beginning of next 2 rows, 2 (2, 2, 2, 2, 4, 4, 6, 8, 10) sts at beginning of next 2 rows, then decrease 1 st each side every other row 2 (4, 5, 7, 7, 6, 6, 6, 7, 6) times—83 (85, 89, 91, 97, 101, 103, 107, 109, 115) sts remain. Work even until armhole measures 5 ½ (6, 6 ¼, 6 ½, 7, 7 ¼, 7 ½, 7 ¾, 8, 8 ½)" [14 (15, 16, 16.5, 18, 18.5, 19, 19.5, 20.5, 21.5) cm], ending with a WS row.

### Shape Neck

**Next Row (RS):** Work 28 (28, 29, 30, 32, 33, 33, 34, 35, 37) sts, join a second ball of yarn, BO center 27 (29, 31, 31, 33, 35, 37, 39, 39, 41) sts, work to end. Working both sides at the same time, work even for 1 row. Decrease 1 st at each neck edge every other row twice—26 (26, 27, 28, 30, 31, 31, 32, 33, 35) sts remain each side for shoulders. Work even until armhole measures 6 ½ (7, 7 ¼, 7 ½, 8, 8 ¼, 8 ½, 8 ¾, 9, 9 ½)" [16.5 (18, 18.5, 19, 20.5, 21, 21.5, 22, 23, 24) cm], ending with a WS row.

### Shape Shoulders

**Next Row (RS):** BO 13 (13, 13, 14, 15, 15, 15, 16, 16, 17) sts at each armhole edge once, then 13 (13, 14, 14, 15, 16, 16, 16, 17, 18) sts once.

**LEFT FRONT**

CO 52 (54, 58, 60, 64, 66, 70, 76, 82, 88) sts.

**Next Row (WS):** P0 (0, 0, 1, 1, 1, 1, 0, 0, 1), work Twisted Rib across 18 (18, 20, 18, 20, 20, 22, 24, 24, 24) sts, pm, work Looping Wave across 23 sts, beginning with Row 13, pm, work Twisted Rib, beginning with p1-tbl, across 10 (12, 14, 18, 20, 22, 24, 28, 34, 40) sts, p1 (1, 1, 0, 0, 0, 0, 1, 1, 0). Work even until piece measures 1 ½" (4 cm) from the beginning, ending with a WS row.

**Next Row (RS):** K1 (1, 1, 0, 0, 0, 0, 1, 1, 0), [k1, slip 1] 5 (6, 7, 9, 10, 11, 12, 14, 17, 20) times, sm, work to next marker, sm, [slip 1, k1] 9 (9, 10, 9, 10, 10, 11, 12, 12, 12) times, k0 (0, 0, 1, 1, 1, 1, 0, 0, 1). Work even, working Looping Wave panel as established, and working all other sts in St st, until piece measures 2" (5 cm) from the beginning, ending with a WS row.

### Shape Waist

**Decrease Row (RS):** Decrease 1 st this row, then every 8 rows 4 times, as follows: Work to second marker, sm, k1, ssk, work to end—47 (49, 53, 55, 59, 61, 65, 71, 77, 83) sts remain. Work even until piece measures 7" (18 cm) from the beginning, ending with a WS row.

### Shape Bust

**Increase Row (RS):** Increase 1 st this row, then every 8 rows 4 times, as follows: Work to second marker, sm, k1, M1-r, work to end—52 (54, 58, 60, 64, 66, 70, 76, 82, 88) sts. Work even until piece measures 12 ½ (12 ¾, 13, 13 ¼, 13 ½, 13 ¾, 14, 14 ½, 15, 15)" [32 (32.5, 33, 33.5, 34.5, 35, 35.5, 37, 38, 38) cm] from the beginning, ending with a WS row.

### Shape Armhole

**Next Row (RS):** BO 6 (6, 6, 6, 6, 6, 8, 10, 12, 14) sts at armhole edge once, 2 (2, 2, 2, 2, 4, 4, 6, 8, 10) sts once, then decrease 1 st at armhole edge every other row 2 (4, 5, 7, 7, 6, 6, 6, 7, 6) times—42 (42, 45, 45, 49, 50, 52, 54, 55, 58) sts remain. Work even until armhole measures 3 (3 ½, 3 ¾, 4, 4 ½, 4 ¾, 5, 5 ¼, 5 ½, 6)" [7.5 (9, 9.5, 10, 11.5, 12, 12.5, 13.5, 14, 15) cm], ending with a RS row.

### Shape Neck

**Next Row (WS):** BO 8 (8, 9, 8, 9, 9, 10, 11, 11, 11) sts at neck edge once, decrease 1 st at neck edge every row 5 (5, 6, 6, 6, 6, 7, 7, 7, 8) times, then every other row 3 (3, 3, 3, 4, 4, 4, 4, 4, 4) times—26 (26, 27, 28, 30, 31, 31, 32, 33, 35) sts remain. Work even until armhole measures 6 ½ (7, 7 ¼, 7 ½, 8, 8 ¼, 8 ½, 8 ¾, 9, 9 ½)" [16.5 (18, 18.5, 19, 20.5, 21, 21.5, 22, 23, 24) cm], ending with a WS row.

### Shape Shoulder

**Next Row (RS):** BO 13 (13, 13, 14, 15, 15, 15, 16, 16, 17) sts

at armhole edge once, then 13 (13, 14, 14, 15, 16, 16, 17, 18) sts once.

### RIGHT FRONT

CO 52 (54, 58, 60, 64, 66, 70, 76, 82, 88) sts.

**Next Row (WS):** P1 (1, 1, 0, 0, 0, 0, 1, 1, 0), work Twisted Rib across 10 (12, 14, 18, 20, 22, 24, 28, 34, 40) sts, pm, work Looping Wave across 23 sts, beginning with Row 1, pm, work Twisted Rib, beginning with p1-tbl, across 18 (18, 20, 18, 20, 20, 22, 24, 24, 24) sts, p0 (0, 0, 1, 1, 1, 1, 0, 0, 1). Work even until piece measures 1 ½" (4 cm) from the beginning, ending with a WS row.

**Next Row (RS):** K0 (0, 0, 1, 1, 1, 1, 0, 0, 1), [k1, slip 1] 9 (9, 10, 9, 10, 10, 11, 12, 12, 12) times, sm, work to next marker, sm, [slip 1, k1] 5 (6, 7, 9, 10, 11, 12, 14, 17, 20) times, k1 (1, 1, 0, 0, 0, 0, 1, 1, 0). Work even, working Looping Wave panel as established, and working all other sts in St st, until piece measures 2" (5 cm) from the beginning, ending with a WS row.

Complete as for Left Front, reversing st pattern and all shaping.

### SHORT SLEEVES

CO 66 (70, 72, 76, 78, 82, 84, 90, 96, 102) sts. Begin Twisted Rib; work even until piece measures 1/2" (1.5 cm) from the beginning, ending with a WS row.

**Next Row (RS):** *Slip 1, k1; repeat from * to end. Continuing in St st across all sts, work even until piece measures 1 ½ (1 ¾, 2, 2 ¼, 2 ½, 2 ¾, 3, 3 ¼, 3 ½, 4)" [4 (4.5, 5, 5.5, 6.5, 7, 7.5, 8.5, 9, 10) cm] from the beginning, ending with a WS row.

### Shape Cap

**Next Row (RS):** BO 6 (6, 6, 6, 6, 6, 8, 10, 12, 14) sts at beginning of next 2 rows, 2 (2, 2, 2, 2, 4, 4, 6, 8, 9) sts at beginning of next 2 rows, decrease 1 st each side every 6 rows 1 (1, 1, 0, 1, 1, 2, 5, 6, 8) time(s), every 4 rows 0 (0, 0, 1, 0, 1, 1, 1, 1, 0) time(s), then every other row 10 (12, 13, 15, 16, 15, 13, 4, 2, 1) time(s),

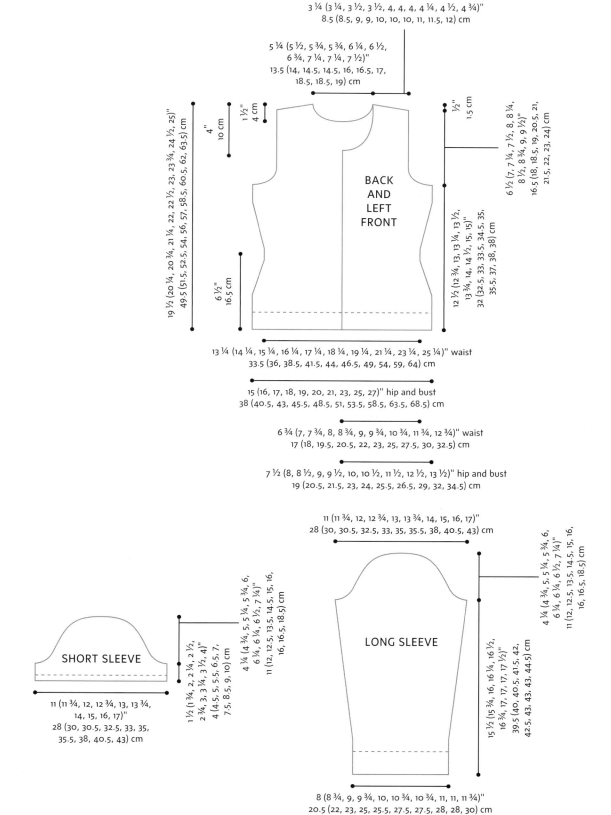

3 ¼ (3 ¼, 3 ½, 3 ½, 4, 4, 4, 4 ¼, 4 ½, 4 ¾)"
8.5 (8.5, 9, 9, 10, 10, 10, 11, 11.5, 12) cm

5 ¼ (5 ½, 5 ¾, 5 ¾, 6 ¼, 6 ½,
6 ¾, 7 ¼, 7 ¼, 7 ½)"
13.5 (14, 14.5, 14.5, 16, 16.5, 17,
18.5, 18.5, 19) cm

1 ½"
4 cm

4"
10 cm

½"
1.5 cm

6 ½ (7, 7 ¼, 7 ½, 8, 8 ¼,
8 ½, 8 ¾, 9, 9 ½)"
16.5 (18, 18.5, 19, 20.5, 21,
21.5, 22, 23, 24) cm

19 ½ (20 ¼, 20 ¾, 21 ¼, 22, 22 ½, 23, 23 ¾, 24 ½, 25)"
49.5 (51.5, 52.5, 54, 56, 57, 58.5, 60.5, 62, 63.5) cm

6 ½"
16.5 cm

BACK
AND
LEFT
FRONT

12 ½ (12 ¾, 13, 13 ¼, 13 ½,
13 ¾, 14, 14 ½, 15, 15)"
32 (32.5, 33, 33.5, 34.5, 35,
35.5, 37, 38, 38) cm

13 ¼ (14 ¼, 15 ¼, 16 ¼, 17 ¼, 18 ¼, 19 ¼, 21 ¼, 23 ¼, 25 ¼)" waist
33.5 (36, 38.5, 41.5, 44, 46.5, 49, 54, 59, 64) cm

15 (16, 17, 18, 19, 20, 21, 23, 25, 27)" hip and bust
38 (40.5, 43, 45.5, 48.5, 51, 53.5, 58.5, 63.5, 68.5) cm

6 ¾ (7, 7 ¾, 8, 8 ¾, 9, 9 ¾, 10 ¾, 11 ¾, 12 ¾)" waist
17 (18, 19.5, 20.5, 22, 23, 25, 27.5, 30, 32.5) cm

7 ½ (8, 8 ½, 9, 9 ½, 10, 10 ½, 11 ½, 12 ½, 13 ½)" hip and bust
19 (20.5, 21.5, 23, 24, 25.5, 26.5, 29, 32, 34.5) cm

11 (11 ¾, 12, 12 ¾, 13, 13 ¾, 14, 15, 16, 17)"
28 (30, 30.5, 32.5, 33, 35, 35.5, 38, 40.5, 43) cm

4 ¼ (4 ¾, 5, 5 ¼, 5 ¾, 6,
6 ¼, 6 ½, 6 ½, 7 ¼)"
11 (12, 12.5, 13.5, 14.5, 15, 16,
16, 16.5, 18.5) cm

LONG SLEEVE

4 ¼ (4 ¾, 5, 5 ¼, 5 ¾, 6,
6 ¼, 6 ¼, 6 ½, 7 ¼)"
11 (12, 12.5, 13.5, 14.5, 15, 16,
16, 16.5, 18.5) cm

SHORT SLEEVE

1 ½ (1 ¾, 2, 2 ¼, 2 ½,
2 ¾, 3, 3 ¼, 3 ½, 4)"
4 (4.5, 5, 5.5, 6.5, 7,
7.5, 8.5, 9, 10) cm

11 (11 ¾, 12, 12 ¾, 13, 13 ¾,
14, 15, 16, 17)"
28 (30, 30.5, 32.5, 33, 35,
35.5, 38, 40.5, 43) cm

15 ½ (15 ¾, 16, 16 ¼, 16 ½,
16 ¾, 17, 17, 17 ½)"
39.5 (40, 40.5, 41.5, 42,
42.5, 43, 43, 44.5) cm

8 (8 ¾, 9, 9 ¾, 10, 10 ¾, 10 ¾, 11, 11, 11 ¾)"
20.5 (22, 23, 25, 25.5, 27.5, 27.5, 28, 28, 30) cm

then BO 3 (3, 3, 3, 3, 3, 4, 4, 4) sts at beginning of next 4 rows. BO remaining 16 (16, 16, 16, 16, 16, 22, 22, 22) sts.

### LONG SLEEVES

CO 48 (52, 54, 58, 60, 64, 64, 66, 66, 70) sts. Begin Twisted Rib; work even until piece measures 2 ½" (6.5 cm) from the beginning, ending with a WS row.

**Next Row (RS):** *Slip 1, k1; repeat from * to end. Continuing in St st across all sts, work even until piece measures 3" (7.5 cm) from the beginning, ending with a WS row.

### Shape Sleeve

**Increase Row (RS):** Increase 1 st each side this row, then every 10 (10, 10, 10, 10, 10, 10, 8, 6, 6) rows 8 (8, 8, 8, 8, 8, 9, 11, 14, 15) more times—66 (70, 72, 76, 78, 82, 84, 90, 96, 102) sts. Work even until piece measures 15 ½ (15 ¾, 16, 16 ¼, 16 ½, 16 ¾, 17, 17, 17, 17 ½)"

## BUST DARTS

The long-sleeved sample shown has bust darts added to each Front. The pattern calls for you to increase 1 stitch at the bust every 8 rows 5 times (see Increase Row under Shape Bust for Left and Right Fronts). In order to add bust darts to this sample, Increase Rows were worked at the bust every 4 rows instead of every 8, until a total of 9 bust Increase Rows were worked, instead of 5; this resulted in an extra 4 stitches at the bust. In order to avoid altering the movement of the cable panel, the additional bust Increase Rows were worked outside the cable panel (between the the cable panel and the armhole) rather than inside (between the cable panel and the neck) where the existing increases are located. In order to get rid of those 4 extra stitches without disturbing the cable placement, decreases were worked as follows: In the Shape Neck section of the Left and Right Fronts, the first right-side row of neck shaping included a bust dart decrease located in the Stockinette stitch section between the cable panel and the armhole edge, slanting toward the cable panel. These decreases were worked every other right-side row until 4 decrease rows were worked.

[39.5 (40, 40.5, 41.5, 42, 42.5, 43, 43, 43, 44.5) cm] from the beginning, ending with a WS row. Shape Cap as for Short Sleeves.

### FINISHING

Block pieces as desired. Sew shoulder seams. Set in Sleeves; sew side and Sleeve seams.

### Neckband

Using circ needle, and beginning at Right Front neck edge, pick up and knit 30 (30, 31, 30, 32, 32, 33, 34, 34, 35) sts along Right Front neck edge, 47 (49, 51, 51, 53, 55, 57, 59, 59, 61) sts along Back neck edge, then 30 (30, 31, 30, 32, 32, 33, 34, 34, 35) sts along Left Front neck edge—107 (109, 113, 111, 117, 119, 123, 127, 127, 131) sts. Begin Twisted Rib, beginning with p1-tbl; work even until piece measures ½" (1.5 cm) from pick-up row, ending with a RS row. BO all sts in pattern.

### Button Band

Using circ needle, and beginning at Left Front neck edge, pick up and knit 93 (99, 101, 105, 109, 111, 115, 119, 123, 127) sts along Left Front edge. Begin Twisted Rib, beginning with p1-tbl; work even for 9 rows. BO all sts in pattern.

### Buttonhole Band

Using circ needle, and beginning at lower Right Front edge, pick up and knit 93 (99, 101, 105, 109, 115, 119, 123, 127) sts along Right Front edge. Work as for Button Band for 3 rows. Place markers for 9 (10, 10, 10, 11, 11, 12, 12, 13, 13) buttons, the first ¾" (2 cm) below neck edge, the last ¾" (2 cm) from bottom edge, and the remaining buttons evenly spaced between.

**Buttonhole Row (RS):** Work to first marker, *yo, work 2 sts together (k2tog-tbl if next st to be worked is a purl st, p2tog if next st to be worked is a knit st); repeat from * through last marker, work to end. Complete as for Button Band.

Sew buttons opposite buttonholes.

Jess is wearing size
35–36" (89–91.5 cm)
with zero ease in the
upper torso.

Diagonal lines accentuate curves.

Tie the wrap in a pretty bow to draw attention to the waist.

Jenn is wearing size 33" (84 cm) with 3" (7.5 cm) of bust darts added and approximately 1" (2.5 cm) of positive ease in the upper torso.

# ENROBED WRAP

Worked entirely in Garter stitch and Stockinette stitch, this cozy wrap sweater is easy to modify and looks great on a variety of figures. Knitters with curves can cinch the waist with an eye-catching bow, while straighter shapes can tie a simple overhand knot, letting the wrap's diagonal lines create the illusion of curves.

. . . . . . . . . . . . . . . . . . . . . . . . . . . . . . . . . . . . .

## SIZES

To fit upper torso sizes 29 (31, 33, 35, 37, 39, 41, 45, 49, 53)" [73.5 (78.5, 84, 89, 94, 99, 104, 114.5, 124.5, 134.5) cm]

## FINISHED MEASUREMENTS

30 (32, 34 ½, 36 ½, 38, 40, 42 ½, 46, 50 ½, 54)" [76 (81.5, 87.5, 92.5, 96.5, 101.5, 108, 117, 128.5, 137) cm] chest

*Note: Wrap is intended to be worn with approximately 1" (2.5 cm) positive ease in the upper torso.*

## YARN

Brooklyn Tweed Shelter [100% Targhee-Columbia wool; 140 yards (128 meters) / 50 grams]: 6 (7, 8, 8, 9, 10, 10, 11, 12, 13) hanks #026 Tent or #07 Thistle.

## NEEDLES

One pair straight needles size US 8 (5 mm)

One 36" (90 cm) long circular (circ) needle size US 8 (5 mm)

Change needle size if necessary to obtain correct gauge.

## NOTIONS

Stitch markers; 1 ½ yards (1.5 meters) 1" (2.5 cm) wide grosgrain ribbon (optional)

## GAUGE

18 sts and 26 rows = 4" (10 cm) in Stockinette stitch (St st)

## NOTES

Unless otherwise specified, decreases should be worked to match the slant of the edge being shaped, as follows: For left-slanting edges: On RS rows, k1, ssk, work to end; on WS rows, work to last 3 sts, ssp, p1. For right-slanting edges: On RS rows, work to last 3 sts, k2tog, k1; on WS rows, p1, p2tog, work to end. Increases should also be worked to match the slant of the edge being shaped, as follows: For right-slanting edges: On RS rows, work 1 st, M1-r, work to end; on WS rows, work to last st, M1-p, work 1 st. For left-slanting edges: On RS rows, work to last st, M1-l, work 1 st; on WS rows, work 1 st, M1-p-l, work to end.

## BACK

CO 68 (72, 78, 82, 86, 90, 96, 104, 114, 122) sts. Begin Garter st (knit every row); work even until piece measures 1 ½" (4 cm) from the beginning, ending with a WS row.

**Next Row (RS):** Change to St st; work even until piece measures 3" (7.5 cm) from the beginning, ending with a RS row.

**Next Row (WS):** P23 (24, 26, 27, 29, 30, 32, 35, 38, 41), pm, p22 (24, 26, 28, 28, 30, 32, 34, 38, 40), pm, purl to end.

### Shape Waist

**Decrease Row (RS):** Decrease 2 sts this row, then every 6 rows 3 times, as follows: Knit to 2 sts before first marker, ssk, sm, knit to next marker, sm, k2tog, knit to end—60 (64, 70, 74, 78, 82, 88, 96, 106, 114) sts remain. Work even until piece measures 7" (18 cm) from the beginning, ending with a WS row.

### Shape Bust

**Increase Row (RS):** Increase 2 sts this row, then every 8 rows 3 times, as follows: Knit to first marker, M1-r, sm, knit to next marker, sm, M1-l, knit to end—68 (72, 78, 82, 86, 90, 96, 104, 114, 122) sts. Work even until piece measures 13 ½ (14 ¼, 14 ½, 14 ½, 14 ¾, 14 ¾, 15, 15, 15 ¼, 15 ½)" [34.5 (36, 37, 37, 37.5, 37.5, 38, 38, 38.5, 39.5) cm] from the beginning, ending with a WS row.

### Shape Armholes

**Next Row (RS):** BO 6 (6, 6, 6, 6, 6, 8, 8, 10) sts at beginning of next 2 rows, 0 (0, 2, 2, 2, 2, 4, 6, 6) sts at beginning of next 2 rows, then decrease 1 st each side every other row 2 (3, 2, 3, 3, 4, 6, 5, 6, 6) times, as follows—52 (54, 58, 60, 64, 66,

68, 70, 74, 78) sts remain. Work even until armhole measures 5 ½ (6, 6 ¼, 6 ½, 7, 8 ¼, 8 ¼, 8 ½, 8 ½, 8 ½)" [14 (15, 16, 16.5, 18, 21, 21, 21.5, 21.5, 21.5) cm], ending with a WS row.

## Shape Neck and Shoulders

*Note: Neck and shoulder shaping are worked at the same time; please read entire section through before beginning.*

**Next Row (RS):** K16 (16, 17, 17, 18, 19, 19, 20, 21, 22), join a second ball of yarn, BO center 20 (22, 24, 26, 28, 28, 30, 30, 32, 34) sts, knit to end. Working both sides at the same time, work even for 1 row. Decrease 1 st at each neck edge every other row twice. AT THE SAME TIME, when armhole measures 6 ½ (7, 7 ¼, 7 ½, 8, 9 ¼, 9 ¼, 9 ½, 9 ½, 9 ½)" [16.5 (18, 18.5, 19, 20.5, 23.5, 23.5, 24, 24, 24) cm], ending with a WS row, shape shoulders as follows:

**Next Row (RS):** BO 7 (7, 8, 8, 8, 9, 9, 9, 10, 10) sts at armhole edge once, then 7 (7, 7, 7, 8, 8, 8, 9, 9, 10) sts once.

## LEFT FRONT

CO 60 (66, 70, 76, 78, 84, 88, 96, 106, 114) sts. Begin Garter st; work even until piece measures 1 ½" (4 cm) from the beginning, ending with a WS row.

**Next Row (RS):** Change to St st; work even until piece measures 3" (7.5 cm) from the beginning, ending with a RS row.

**Next Row (WS):** P17 (18, 20, 21, 22, 23, 24, 26, 29, 31), pm, p34 (36, 38, 40, 42, 44, 48, 52, 56, 60), pm, purl to end.

## Shape Waist

**Decrease Row (RS):** Decrease 2 sts this row, then every 6 rows 3 times, as follows: Knit to 2 sts before first marker, ssk, sm, knit to next marker, sm, k2tog, knit to end—52 (58, 62, 68, 70, 76, 80, 88, 98, 106) sts remain. Work even until piece measures 6 ½" (16.5 cm) from the beginning, removing marker closest to neck edge on first row, and ending with a WS row.

## Shape Neck Edge and Bust

*Note: Neck edge and bust shaping are worked at the same time; please read entire section through before beginning. Neck edge shaping will not be completed until approximately 1 ½" (4 cm) before the beginning of the shoulder shaping.*

**Decrease Row (RS):** Decrease 1 st at neck edge this row, every row 0 (0, 0, 0, 0, 0, 0, 5, 17, 25) times, every other row 28 (34, 36, 45, 45, 49, 52, 51, 45, 42) times, then every 4 rows 5 (4, 4, 0, 1, 1, 0, 0, 0, 0) time(s). AT THE SAME TIME, when piece measures 7" (18 cm) from the beginning, ending with a WS row, shape bust as follows:

**Increase Row (RS):** Continuing with neck edge shaping, increase 1 st this row, then every 8 rows 3 times, as follows: Work to marker, M1-r, sm, work to end. AT THE SAME TIME, Continuing with neck edge shaping, work even until piece measures 13 ½ (14 ¼, 14 ½, 14 ½, 14 ¾, 14 ¾, 15, 15, 15 ¼, 15 ½)" [34.5 (36, 37, 37, 37.5, 37.5, 38, 38, 38.5, 39.5) cm] from the beginning, ending with a WS row. *Note: If your row gauge matches the given gauge, and you have worked to the exact measurements given, you should have 33 (37, 40, 46, 47, 53, 56, 64, 65, 68) sts remaining. However, due to differences in gauge and measuring, you may find that you have a few sts more or less than these st counts; this will not be a problem because the shaping was written with 1 ½" (4 cm) of work-even space between the end of the neck edge shaping and the end of the shoulders, to accommodate differences in row gauge.*

## Shape Neck Edge and Armhole

*Note: Neck edge and armhole shaping are worked at the same time; please read entire section through before beginning.*

**Next Row (RS):** Continuing with neck edge shaping, BO 6 (6, 6, 6, 6, 6, 8, 8, 10) sts at armhole edge once, 0 (0, 2, 2, 2, 2, 2, 4, 6, 6) sts once, then decrease 1 st at armhole edge every other row 2 (3, 2, 3, 3, 4, 6, 5, 6, 6) times—14 (14, 15, 15, 16, 17, 17, 18, 19,

20) sts remain when neck edge shaping is complete. Work even until armhole measures 6 ½ (7, 7 ¼, 7 ½, 8, 9 ¼, 9 ¼, 9 ½, 9 ½, 9 ½)" [16.5 (18, 18.5, 19, 20.5, 23.5, 23.5, 24, 24, 24) cm], ending with a WS row.

### Shape Shoulder

**Next Row (RS):** BO 7 (7, 8, 8, 8, 9, 9, 9, 10, 10) sts at armhole edge once, then 7 (7, 7, 7, 8, 8, 8, 9, 9, 10) sts once.

## RIGHT FRONT

Work as for Left Front until piece measures 3" (7.5 cm) from the beginning, ending with a RS row.

**Next Row (WS):** K9 (12, 12, 15, 14, 17, 16, 18, 21, 23), pm, k34 (36, 38, 40, 42, 44, 48, 52, 56, 60), pm, knit to end.

Complete as for Left Front, reversing all shaping.

## SLEEVES

CO 42 (44, 46, 48, 50, 52, 54, 60, 64, 68) sts. Begin Garter st; work even until piece measures 1 ½" (4 cm) from the beginning.

### Work Cuff Pattern and Shape Sleeve

*Note: Cuff pattern and Sleeve shaping are worked at the same time; please read entire section through before beginning.*

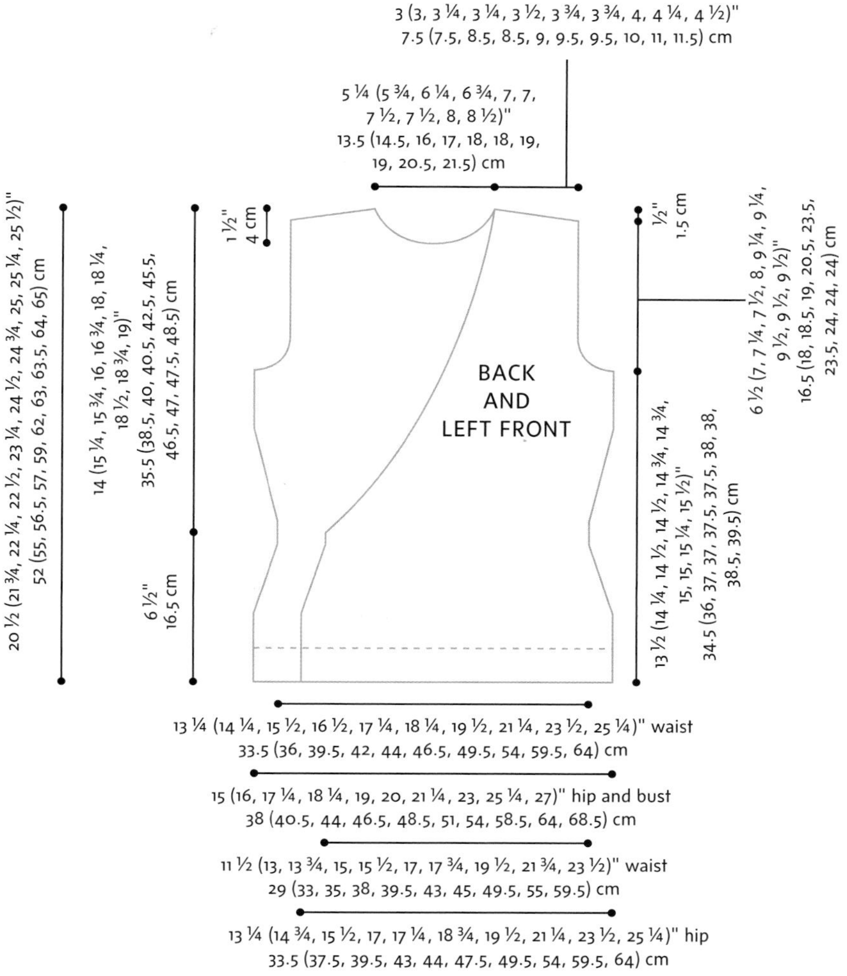
3 (3, 3 ¼, 3 ¼, 3 ½, 3 ¾, 3 ¾, 4, 4 ¼, 4 ½)"
7.5 (7.5, 8.5, 8.5, 9, 9.5, 9.5, 10, 11, 11.5) cm
5 ¼ (5 ¾, 6 ¼, 6 ¾, 7, 7, 7 ½, 7 ½, 8, 8 ½)"
13.5 (14.5, 16, 17, 18, 18, 19, 19, 20.5, 21.5) cm
20 ½ (21 ¾, 22 ¼, 22 ½, 23 ¼, 24 ½, 24 ¾, 25, 25 ¼, 25 ½)"
52 (55, 56.5, 57, 59, 62, 63, 63.5, 64, 65) cm
14 (15 ¼, 15 ¾, 16, 16 ¾, 18, 18 ¼, 18 ½, 18 ¾, 19)"
35.5 (38.5, 40, 40.5, 42.5, 45.5, 46.5, 47, 47.5, 48.5) cm
6 ½"
16.5 cm
1 ½"
4 cm
BACK AND LEFT FRONT
½"
1.5 cm
6 ½ (7, 7 ¼, 7 ½, 8, 9 ¼, 9 ¼, 9 ½, 9 ½, 9 ½)"
16.5 (18, 18.5, 19, 20.5, 23.5, 23.5, 24, 24, 24) cm
13 ½ (14 ¼, 14 ½, 14 ½, 14 ¾, 14 ¾, 15, 15, 15 ¼, 15 ½)"
34.5 (36, 37, 37, 37.5, 37.5, 38, 38, 38.5, 39.5) cm
13 ¼ (14 ¼, 15 ½, 16 ½, 17 ¼, 18 ¼, 19 ½, 21 ¼, 23 ½, 25 ¼)" waist
33.5 (36, 39.5, 42, 44, 46.5, 49.5, 54, 59.5, 64) cm
15 (16, 17 ¼, 18 ¼, 19, 20, 21 ¼, 23, 25 ¼, 27)" hip and bust
38 (40.5, 44, 46.5, 48.5, 51, 54, 58.5, 64, 68.5) cm
11 ½ (13, 13 ¾, 15, 15 ½, 17, 17 ¾, 19 ½, 21 ¾, 23 ½)" waist
29 (33, 35, 38, 39.5, 43, 45, 49.5, 55, 59.5) cm
13 ¼ (14 ¾, 15 ½, 17, 17 ¼, 18 ¾, 19 ½, 21 ¼, 23 ½, 25 ¼)" hip
33.5 (37.5, 39.5, 43, 44, 47.5, 49.5, 54, 59.5, 64) cm

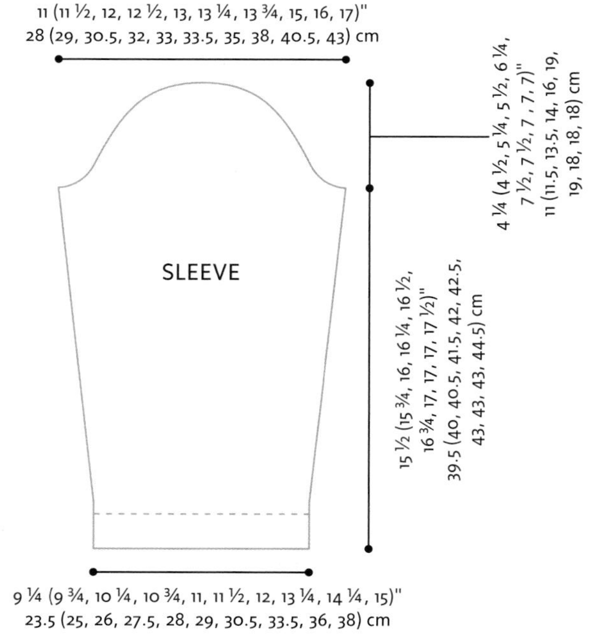
11 (11 ½, 12, 12 ½, 13, 13 ¼, 13 ¾, 15, 16, 17)"
28 (29, 30.5, 32, 33, 33.5, 35, 38, 40.5, 43) cm
4 ¼ (4 ½, 5 ¼, 5 ½, 6 ¼, 7 ½, 7 ½, 7, 7, 7)"
11 (11.5, 13.5, 14, 16, 19, 19, 18, 18, 18) cm
SLEEVE
15 ½ (15 ¾, 16, 16 ¼, 16 ½, 16 ¾, 17, 17, 17, 17 ½)"
39.5 (40, 40.5, 41.5, 42, 42.5, 43, 43, 43, 44.5) cm
9 ¼ (9 ¾, 10 ¼, 10 ¾, 11, 11 ½, 12, 13 ¼, 14 ¼, 15)"
23.5 (25, 26, 27.5, 28, 29, 30.5, 33.5, 36, 38) cm

## BUST DARTS

The samples shown on pages 138 and 143 have bust darts added to each Front. The pattern calls for you to increase 1 stitch at the bust every 8 rows 4 times (see Increase Row under Shape Neck Edge and Bust for Left and Right Fronts). In order to add bust darts to the sample, Increase Rows were worked at the bust every other row instead of every 8, until a total of 10 bust Increase Rows were worked, instead of 4; this resulted in an extra 6 stitches at the bust. In order to get rid of those 6 extra stitches and end the neck shaping with the number of stitches required for the shoulders, the extra stitches were decreased along the neck edge, by working 4 additional right-side Decrease Rows than what the pattern called for, and 2 wrong-side Decrease Rows (see Decrease Row under Shape Neck Edge and Bust for Left and Right Fronts), evenly distributed among the right-side Decrease Rows. Note that if the neck shaping for your size has you work 1 or more every-4-row decreases, then you can work that many additional right-side Decrease Rows, then work the additional Decrease Rows needed to get rid of the extra 6 stitches as wrong-side row decreases; if your size has you work only every-row or every-other-row decreases, then you will need to work the 6 additional Decrease Rows as wrong-side Decrease Rows. Depending on the neck shaping instructions for your size, you may need to work additional every-other-row or every-row decreases to get rid of the extra 6 stitches.

**Next Row (WS):** P1, knit to last st, p1. Work even for 1 row.

**Next Row (WS):** P2, knit to last 2 sts, p2. Work even for 1 row.

Continue in this manner, purling 1 more st at beginning and end of every WS row, until you have purled across the entire WS row and are now working in St st. AT THE SAME TIME, when piece measures 2" (5 cm) from the beginning, work Sleeve shaping as follows:

**Increase Row (RS):** Continuing with cuff pattern, increase 1 st each side this row, then every 18 (20, 20, 20, 20, 20, 22, 22, 22, 22) rows 3 times, as follows: Work 1 st, M1-r, work to last st, M1-l, work 1 st—50

(52, 54, 56, 58, 60, 62, 68, 72, 76) sts. Work even until piece measures 15 ½ (15 ¾, 16, 16 ¼, 16 ½, 16 ¾, 17, 17, 17, 17 ½)" [39.5 (40, 40.5, 41.5, 42, 42.5, 43, 43, 43, 44.5) cm] from the beginning, ending with a WS row.

### Shape Cap

**Next Row (RS):** BO 6 (6, 6, 6, 6, 6, 6, 8, 8, 10) sts at beginning of next 2 rows, 0 (0, 2, 2, 2, 2, 2, 4, 6, 6) sts at beginning of next 2 rows, decrease 1 st each side every 6 rows 1 (1, 2, 2, 2, 4, 3, 5, 5, 5) time(s), every 4 rows 0 (0, 0, 0, 1, 0, 1, 1, 1, 1) time(s), then every other row 8 (9, 7, 8, 8, 8, 9, 2, 2, 2) times, then BO 2 (2, 2, 2, 2, 2, 2, 3, 3, 3) sts at beginning of next 4 rows. BO remaining 12 (12, 12, 12, 12, 12, 12, 16, 16, 16) sts.

### FINISHING

Block pieces as desired. Sew shoulder seams. Set in Sleeves; sew Sleeve seams. Sew side seams, leaving 1" (2.5 cm) hole in left side seam at your natural waist, for Tie.

### Neckband/Ties

CO 126 (130, 136, 140, 144, 148, 154, 162, 172, 180) sts, with RS facing, beginning at base of Right Front neck edge (opposite hole in left side seam), pick up and knit 73 (79, 82, 86, 89, 92, 94, 99, 103, 108) sts along Right Front neck edge, 34 (36, 38, 40, 42, 42, 44, 44, 46, 48) sts along Back neck, 73 (79, 82, 86, 89, 92, 94, 99, 103, 108) sts along Left Front neck edge, CO 58 sts—364 (382, 396, 410, 422, 432, 444, 462, 482, 502) sts. *Note: The total number of sts does not have to be exact.* Begin Garter st; work even for 1" (2.5 cm). BO all sts.

Cut 2 lengths of ribbon (optional), one to match length of each Tie. Sew to WS of Tie, being careful not to let sts show on WS.

Morgan is wearing size 39" (99 cm) with 3" (7.5 cm) of bust darts added and zero ease in the upper torso.

## MODIFICATION IDEAS

The neckline for this wrap sweater is easy to widen or narrow to suit bottom-heavy and top-heavy knitters; as written, the neckline and long sleeves are nicely balanced, suiting a proportional figure. All knitters should make sure that the tie falls at the narrowest part of the waist.

**6**

# MODIFICATIONS

Once you've chosen a sweater pattern, picked a base size, and examined the pattern schematic, all you have left to do (besides knit) is figure out what modifications you need to make in order to get the sweater of your dreams. If you're confused by modification math or unsure how to implement changes to a pattern, this chapter is for you!

## Where to Make Modifications

Regardless of construction, all sweaters are essentially composed of three tubes: one for the torso and two for the arms. They're joined together at the top—usually in a complicated way, because we ourselves are joined together at the top in a complicated way. My first rule for simplifying modifications is to ensure that the top of the sweater fits the shoulders. Trying to fiddle with complex sleeve cap math is much more challenging than making three or four easy modifications elsewhere.

My second rule is to stack the deck in your favor by choosing a size based on your upper torso. This is a departure from the typical recommendation to knit to bust size. My reasoning: If you choose a size to fit your shoulders properly, most modifications you need to make will be easy.

My third rule is to make modifications that don't affect a seam so the modifications don't interfere when you sew the sweater pieces together. The illustration at right shows the pieces of a seamed sweater, with the seams highlighted in blue and orange. The orange seam is for the set-in sleeve, and you shouldn't need to modify this if you've chosen the right base size. We'll skip those modifications in this chapter and focus instead on modifications that either don't affect seams at all or that affect only the blue seams (shoulders, sides, and sleeves). For each modification, I briefly describe the basic approach

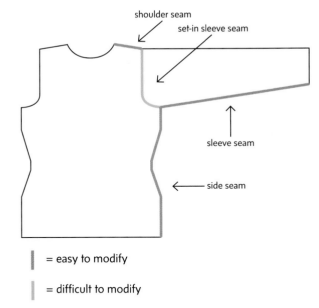

shoulder seam

set-in sleeve seam

sleeve seam

side seam

| = easy to modify

| = difficult to modify

and For each modification, I briefly descibe the basic approach and then outline the arithmetic required to execute it. The chart below includes all of the possible modifications you can make to a sweater and the difficulty level of each. You will probably only need to implement a few of these modifications. And since you will need to make the same modifications to nearly every sweater you knit for yourself, you'll become comfortable with them over time.

| MODIFICATION | LEVEL OF DIFFICULTY | OTHER PIECES AFFECTED |
|---|---|---|
| Waist shaping (page 147) | Easy | None |
| Body length (page 148) | Easy | Front and back |
| Sleeve length (page 148) | Easy | None |
| Neck depth/shape (page 150) | Easy | None |
| Neck width (page 151) | Medium | Front and back |
| Bust shaping (page 152) | Medium | None |
| Bicep circumference | Challenging | All |
| Sleeve cap/armhole | Challenging | All |

# Waist Shaping

The sweaters in this book all feature waist shaping executed in the middle of the knitted piece, as this produces the most flexible and flattering fit. For sweater patterns from other sources that don't have waist shaping or have shaping near the side seams (and that have a stitch pattern simple enough to allow for manipulating stitch counts, like Stockinette stitch or Garter stitch), you can add waist shaping where there was none, or relocate shaping from the side seams to the middle of the piece by placing markers at the ⅓ / ⅓ / ⅓ intervals of the back stitches, and at the ¼ / ½ / ¼ intervals of the front stitches. Work decrease rows with decreases slanting into the markers, and increase rows with the increases slanting out from the markers, like so:

**Decrease Row (RS):** Knit to 2 stitches before marker, ssk, slip marker, knit to next marker, slip marker, k2tog, knit to end.

**Increase Row (RS):** Knit to marker, M1-r, slip marker, knit to next marker, slip marker, M1-l, knit to end.

For the sweaters in this book, if you desire more or less shaping than the amount written in the pattern, or if you need to change the vertical length of the shaping (the number of rows over which the shaping takes place) to match your body, you'll need to calculate a new rate of shaping (that is, the number of rows to be worked even—without shaping—between shaping rows).

*For example, I want to add shaping to a sweater pattern with a gauge of 4 stitches and 6 rows = 1" (2.5 cm). I've chosen a smaller base size for my upper torso, but would like to accommodate my larger hips. So I'll cast on extra stitches at the hem and then remove them before reaching the correct number of waist stitches for my base size.*

Here's how to do the general calculation for a rate of shaping, with numbers for this example in italics:

1. Look at your own body measurements to determine the number of inches you have in which to work the shaping. (If you are working the garment with negative ease, you should add some length to accommodate the stretch factor as described on page 16.) *My hem-to-waist distance is 6" (15 cm).*

   *I'd like to knit the sweater with positive ease, and work 2" of seed stitch at the bottom of the sweater. Thus, I have 4" (10 cm) over which to work the waist decreases.*

2. Multiply the number of inches available for shaping by the row gauge to get the total number of rows you have to complete the shaping. *My sweater has a row gauge of 6 rows = 1" (2.5 cm), so I have 6 x 4 = 24 rows over which to perform my shaping.*

3. Determine the total number of shaping rows you'll need to work. This may be the same number of shaping rows as is written in the pattern, or it may be more (if you desire more shaping) or fewer (if you desire less shaping). *In my example, I know by subtracting the stitch counts that I need to work 6 shaping rows to get to the proper number of waist stitches.*

4. Divide the total number of rows by the number of shaping rows, rounding down. This will give you the number of rows from one shaping row to the next. I personally like to round down to the nearest even number, to ensure my shaping rows occur on right-side rows only. *My calculation is 24 rows divided by 6 shaping rows, or one shaping row every 4 rows.*

5. Subtract one to get the number of rows to work even after each shaping row. *I work 3 rows even between shaping rows.*

You can use this calculation independently for the waist decreases and increases on the front, back, or both pieces of the sweater since locating the waist shaping in the center of the piece leaves the side seams unaffected. Note that, typically, around 1" (2.5 cm) is worked even at the narrowest part of the waist before beginning bust increases.

## Body Length

Changing the length of a sweater is a super-easy modification that has enormous impact on where key elements, such as waist shaping or the hem, fall on your figure. In many cases, the amount to be shortened or lengthened is so small that you can simply modify by knitting a shorter or longer distance in portions of the body that are worked even (see those sections in the illustration below).

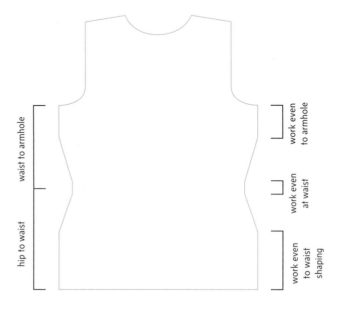

To do this, first look at the pattern's schematic. Compare the distance from the hem to the narrowest point of the waist to your own "hip-to-waist" measurement (check your worksheet from page 19). The difference between these numbers is the change in length you must work. Next, compare the pattern's schematic measurement from waist to armhole shaping to your own "waist-to-armhole" measurement; again, the difference in these measurements tells you how much length you must add or subtract from that portion of the sweater body.

If you are adding length, simply do so in the appropriate place on the sweater body (e.g., either in the hip-to-waist section or the waist-to-armhole section), recalculating the shaping as described in the previous section if necessary.

If you are subtracting length, there are two possible scenarios: You might be subtracting so little length that it does not affect

any waist shaping in the garment. If this is the case, simply subtract the length from the appropriate section or sections of the sweater body. But if subtracting the length does alter the waist shaping, use the calculation on page 147 to determine your new rate of increase/decrease.

If you are satisfied with the length and amount of each type of waist shaping (decreases and increases), but the shaping is simply located in the wrong place for your body (i.e., too low or too high), change the length of the straight portions on the body of the sweater (before waist decreases, between the decreases and increases, and after the increases) to match your figure as appropriate.

## Sleeve Length

Changing sleeve length is one of the easiest modifications you can make to a sweater. Compare your desired sleeve length with the length noted in the pattern schematic, and determine the difference. In many cases, the difference will be small enough that you can add or subtract the length from the portions of the sleeve that are worked even (in the illustration below, in the cuff and just below the cap).

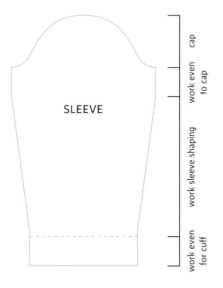

SLEEVE

If you must change the rate of sleeve increases (for example, because you're shortening or lengthening a sleeve by large amounts), perform the following calculation: *For this example, let's assume that I'm turning short sleeves into long sleeves. The gauge for this project is 4 stitches and 6 rows = 1" (2.5 cm); the pattern calls for 48 bicep stitches. My wrist measures 7" (18 cm).*

1   Determine the number of inches (centimeters) in the increase portion of the sleeve from your body measurement and the sleeve's shape: Subtract the inches (centimeters) worked even after the cast-on row (e.g., for ribbing), along with an additional 2" (5 cm) for safety, from your desired sleeve length to cap shaping. *My sleeve will have a 2" (5 cm) cuff at the hem, and my desired sleeve length measurement is 17" (43 cm). This gives me 17 − 4 = 13" (43 − 10 = 33 cm) of sleeve in which to work my shaping.*

2   Multiply the number of inches (centimeters) available for shaping by the row gauge to get the total number of rows in which you must complete the shaping. *For my sleeves, 13 x 6 = 78 rows [(33÷2.5 = 13.2) x 6 = 79.2 rows].*

3   Determine the total number of increase rows to be worked during this length. This may be the same number of increase rows as written in the pattern, or it may be fewer (e.g., if you are changing long sleeves to elbow-length sleeves, since you will start by casting on more stitches). *My wrist stitch count, including desired ease, is 36. My final stitch count is 48, giving a difference of 12 stitches. Since there are 2 stitches increased on each row, that's 6 increase rows.*

4   Divide the total number of rows by the number of increase rows, rounding down to an even number. This will give you the number of rows from one increase to the next. *One option, if I didn't mind increasing on wrong side rows, would be to work an increase row every 13 rows. However, I'd prefer to work them every 12 rows for simplicity, and to keep all my increases on right-side rows.*

5   Subtract one to get the number of rows to work even after each increase row. *I'll work 11 rows even in between each of my increase rows.*

Note that in this example, we changed the length of the sleeve to such an extent that we had to rework the number of increase rows entirely. This is fine! The only thing that shouldn't change from the pattern as written is the number of stitches in the sleeve before beginning the cap shaping. (The maximum sleeve width is an important number for determining the shape of the sleeve cap—and that's math we're avoiding in this book.)

The Chimera Cardigan (page 130) with short sleeves.

The Chimera Cardigan (page 130) with long sleeves.

V-neck

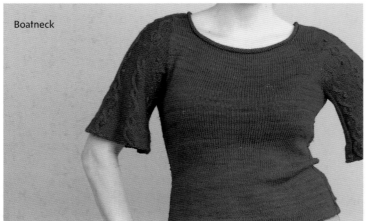

Boatneck

Square neckline

Round neckline

## Neck Depth and/or Shape

Changing the *depth* of a neckline without changing its width or shape is a simple modification. Instead of working the neck shaping as written in the pattern at the specified neck depth, just work the same shaping sooner (to lower a neckline) or later (to raise a neckline) based on your preferred neck depth, remembering to make any necessary adjustments for neck trim added in finishing. Here's an example: *I'd like to lower a sweater's crew neckline, written with a depth of 3"/7.5 cm, to a deeper scoop neck to better flatter my large bust. I know from the measurements I took as described on page 19 that my preferred neckline depth is 8"/20 cm. The sweater measures 22"/56 cm from hem to shoulder, so I'll work the neck shaping exactly as written when my sweater front measures 22 − 8 = 14"/35.5 cm from the hem.*

To change the *shape* of a neck without altering the width, you need one magic number: The total number of stitches you must remove in the neck in order to end up with the correct number of shoulder stitches. Calculate it by subtracting twice the number of shoulder stitches from the number of stitches after all armhole shaping is completed. (Hint: This number will be the same on the front and back of the sweater, in order to ensure that the shoulders line up appropriately, and may be easier to determine from the instructions for the back.)

There are too many possible necklines to cover detailed descriptions for shaping them all in this short section. Instead, following are some rules of thumb for the most common neckline shapes. For each, you'll need the neck depth (see above), turned into a number of rows via your row gauge, and the total number of stitches to remove. I encourage you to be confident here! You're not affecting any seam, after all, and this portion of a sweater is a cinch to rip out if you don't like how it looks.

- **V-NECKS** typically decrease the neck stitches evenly over the entire depth of the neck, minus an inch of wiggle room at the top. To determine the rate of decrease: Calculate the number of rows in the neck by multiplying the neck depth by your row gauge. Divide by half the number of total stitches in the neckline, and round down. Call this number A. Decrease one stitch every A rows to ensure a smooth V-neck. To see examples of how V-necks are worked, see the Draper Vest/Cardigan (page 25), Coin Cable Cardigan (page 95), and Delish Cardigan (page 113).

- BOATNECKS are typically bound off all at once, either at the shoulder line or up to 1" (2.5 cm) below it. At most, you should aim to decrease ½" (1.5 cm) of the stitches on each side of the boat- neck after the first bind-off row. To see an example of how a boatneck is worked, see the Flutter Pullover (page 57).

- SQUARE NECKS bind off the entire width of the neck in a single row, at the desired depth, then work straight to the shoulder. If you want to keep the edges on a square neck from rolling, work a non-roll edging. To see an example of how a square neckline is worked, see the Squared Cardigan (page 89).

- ROUND NECKS, like the traditional crewneck or a deeper scoopneck, involve an initial bind-off followed by a section of curved decreases, followed by (perhaps a small amount of) even knitting to the shoulders. A good rule of thumb is to bind off 50% of the total neck stitches at the bottom of the scoop- or crewneck, decrease another 25% in increments of 1 stitch every row, and then decrease the remaining 25% of stitches one at a time every RS row. You should consult your own measurements for desired neck depth, but defaults typically start crewneck shaping 2 to 2 ½" (5 to 6.5 cm) below shoulder shaping, round necklines 2 ½ to 3 ½" (6.5 to 9 cm) below shoulder shaping, and deep scoopnecks more than 4" (10 cm) below shoulder shaping. To see examples of how a round neckline is worked, see the Cypress Cardigan (page 31), Classic Pullover (page 77), and Chimera Cardigan (page 131).

When in doubt, or if you desire a more complicated neckline, draw the new neckline on a piece of knitter's graph paper. (It's important to use knitter's graph paper for this, rather than plain graph paper, because it shows the correct ratio between stitch width and row height—and that means you'll get an accurate representation of the neckline on your page.) You can then chart the exact stitches closest to your drawn line, and translate those directly into your instructions.

## Neck Width

If you would like to change the width of your neckline as well as the depth and/or shape, begin by calculating the number of stitches in your desired neckline (and the number of shoulder stitches left in the pattern). Here's an example, with my calculations in italics: *Suppose that I'd like to widen the neckline of my sweater from 5" (12.5 cm) to 7" (18 cm) to suit a bottom-heavy frame. We'll stick with the same 4 stitches and 6 rows = 1" (2.5 cm) gauge.*

1. Multiply the desired width in inches (centimeters) by your stitch gauge, and round to the nearest even number. Call this number A. *I'd like to remove 7" x 4 = 28 stitches [(18 cm ÷ 2.5) x 4 = 28.8, rounded down] in my neckline, rather than the pattern's original 20.*

2. Subtract A from the total number of cross-chest stitches, and divide by 2. This is the number of stitches in each shoulder. Call this number B. *My sweater has a cross-chest measurement of 11 ½" (29 cm), and a total of 46 stitches. My shoulder stitch total is now 9 instead of the original 13.*

Your first step is to recalculate your shoulder instructions. The easiest shoulder bind-off instructions involve binding off roughly half the shoulder stitches on each of 2 rows. If you know you want your shoulders to slope more gradually or steeply, multiply the desired depth of shoulder shaping by your row gauge (rounding to an even number), divide that by 2 (since you bind off every other row for each shoulder), and then divide the resulting number by the number of stitches in the shoulder. You may have to round that number up or down for each bind-off row. *In my case, I'm happy with a nearly even split of my bind-offs. I'll begin by binding off 5 stitches, then bind off 4 on the final row.*

Your second step is to rework the neck shaping on both the front and back of your sweater. Back neck shaping can be easily accomplished by binding off all but 1" (2.5 cm) of stitches approximately 1" (2.5 cm) below the start of shoulder shaping, and then decreasing the additional stitches every RS row. Front neck shaping can be calculated following the instructions above for your desired neck shape. *In my case, I'll bind off 24 stitches on my first bind-off row, then work two neck decrease rows per side to create a sloped boatneck shape.*

## Bust Shaping

Bust darts can seem like a scary thing, but fear not! The principle is very simple: You're adding extra fabric over a part of your body that needs it. True, the sweater front won't lie flat on a table, but hey—you're not shaped like a table if you need bust darts! The great news about bust darts is that they don't affect a single seam.

There are two basic ways to add extra fabric over the bust: extra *width* via vertical darts, or extra *length* via short rows. The former is easier to work, but only possible if the stitch pattern allows for stitches to be easily added in and taken away (e.g., Stockinette or Garter stitch). The latter is sometimes the only option, and is definitely handy to know, so we'll cover both. Since the patterns in this book are written with vertical darts for waist and bust shaping already, you should adjust the existing darts for additional shaping when knitting the sweaters in this book.

If you still have negative ease in the fullest part of the bust, even after adding substantial width via vertical darts, then both vertical darts and short rows will be needed. This should happen only in the rarest of cases! You can sometimes avoid it by working multiple vertical darts at once. If you need to add more than a couple of inches of bust shaping, or if your waist is so high you need to work the shaping over only a few inches and want to work multiple vertical darts, I highly recommend Sandi Wiseheart's excellent bust tutorial series, which can be found here: http://sandiwiseheart.wordpress.com/tutorials/.

Vertical darts are my preferred choice for bust shaping whenever possible. They offer several advantages: They are easy to adapt to existing waist shaping, and they add the width you need for your bust to the front of the sweater, exactly where you need it. This keeps the sweater from gapping and distorting over the bust, and is the method used for all the patterns in this book. You calculated how many inches (centimeters) of vertical bust dart you need on page 19; all that's left is to translate that into stitches, and figure out where to place them. You ideally want your vertical darts to end a couple of inches (several centimeters) below the widest point of your bust; that way, all of the visible shaping involved won't be distracting.

Here is an example of how to add vertical darts, with my calculations in italics. *I've decided to knit a sweater at the gauge of 4 stitches and 6 rows = 1" (2.5 cm). I'm including vertical darts for my bust, and I'd like to add 2 ½" (6.5 cm) to the front. Let's assume the pattern already has 4 rows of bust shaping, to which I must add my darts.*

1  Determine how many bust dart rows you must add to achieve your desired number of bust dart stitches: Multiply your needed width by your stitch gauge, rounding to the nearest even number. Divide by 2 since you will increase 2 stitches per dart row. Call this number A. *I'd like to add 2.5" x 4 = 10 stitches [(6.5 cm ÷ 2.5) x 4 = 10.4 stitches, rounded down] of dart; dividing by 2 results in an additional 5 increase rows on the front of my sweater for the darts.*

2  Determine the vertical distance that both the bust darts *and any existing bust shaping* must fall within: Calculate the distance between your waist and the fullest part of your bust (the beginning of the armhole) and subtract 2" (5 cm). Multiply that number by your row gauge, rounding up. Call the resulting number B. *Let's assume the hem-to-waist height is 6" (15 cm), and the hem-to-armhole height is 12 ½" (32 cm). This gives us a vertical distance of 4 ½" (11.5 cm). Multiplied by my row gauge, I have 27 rows in which to work all shaping.*

3   Determine the total number of increase rows you must work by adding A to the number of bust shaping rows that the pattern already calls for. Call this number C. In my case, *I'm adding 5 shaping rows to the existing 4 rows of the pattern, resulting in 9 total increase rows.*

4   Determine the number of rows you work even between increase rows: Divide B by C, rounding down. Subtract 1 for the increase row itself. (If this number is less than zero, you will need multiple vertical darts! Please see Sandi Wiseheart's exhaustive tutorial series for placement, referenced on page 152.) Call this number D. *In my case, 27 divided by 9 = working a dart every third row. This will cause some increases to be on wrong-side rows. I'm okay with increasing on the wrong side, so that's what I'll do. If I'd prefer to work only on right-side rows, I have two choices: I could work a shorter, more pronounced dart by working my increase rows every other row. Or, I could alternate every-other-row increases with every-four-rows increases, to keep all my increases on right-side rows, yet still work within my desired dart length.*

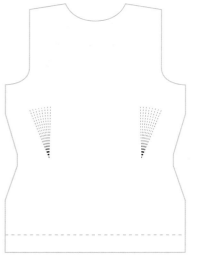

Placement of Vertical Dart Bust Shaping

Vertical bust darts should always be located below the widest point of your bust.

You are now ready to work your vertical bust darts. The default placement for single vertical darts is to add stitches at markers between 25% / 50% / 25% of the stitches in the front of your sweater. When you reach the narrowest point of your waist when knitting the front of your sweater, work an increase row followed by D even rows; repeat until you have worked A increase rows.

Now knit the new, larger number of stitches to the armhole shaping as specified. Shape the armholes exactly as specified in the pattern, too! Otherwise, you'll be changing the sleeve cap math—which we're trying to avoid.

*"So what do I do with those extra stitches?"* I hear you asking. Once you have reached the fullest part of the bust, you must begin to decrease the extra stitches increased in the dart, since

I added 1½" (4 cm) of vertical bust darts to the Squared Cardigan (page 89).

you want to end with the correct number of shoulder stitches. You have two fundamental choices.

The best choice, when it's possible, is to remove those extra stitches in your neckline shaping. Remember the neckline shaping instructions on page 151? You can just plug in your new number of neckline stitches into the guidelines in that list, or (if you're feeling adventurous) evenly sprinkle them throughout the different kinds of neck decreases written into your pattern already. (Remember: No seam is being affected here, so you can feel free to be a little more adventurous about your knitting.)

*My example pattern is a V-neck, so I want to evenly distribute those decreases along with the neck decreases already given in the pattern. Let's suppose the pattern already specifies 10 decrease rows over the entire 7" (18 cm) neck depth. The instructions indicate working a decrease row every 4 rows. My new, modified instructions will require working 15 decrease rows over the same vertical distance. The neck depth of 7" (18 cm) includes 42 rows. Divide 42 by 15 and round down; this tells me that I'll need to work a decrease row every other row to ensure the decreases are completed by the beginning of the shoulder shaping. Once I've worked all of my decreases, I'll work even on the shoulder stitches until I've reached the correct length.*

There are some cases when this approach won't work. For example, when adding the darts to the long-sleeved sample for the Chimera Cardigan (see page 130), I knew I didn't want the extra dart stitches to fall between the cable panels since that would exaggerate the hourglass shape made by the existing waist shaping. So I worked the dart entirely outside the cable panels, and needed to remove the extra stitches on the shoulder side of those cable panels (rather than in the neckline), too.

In this case, I decreased my stitches slanting into the cable panels. When removing stitches from directly under where your shoulder seam would be, slant them in whichever direction works best (typically toward a cable or lace panel, but toward the shoulder seam in an allover textured stitch). You'll need to be extra careful when blocking your pieces to ensure your armhole remains the proper depth for the set-in sleeve seaming.

## SHORT ROWS

It can be challenging to incorporate vertical darts into sweaters with allover stitch patterns. In those cases, you must use short rows for bust shaping. Short row darts add length under the fullest part of the bust and can be helpful to add shaping to other non-bust areas, too (see page 157). To calculate how many short rows you need, take the short row measurement from your sheet on page 19, multiply it by your row gauge, and round down to the nearest even number (since they come in pairs). You want the shortest short row to be about 2" (5 cm) wider than the distance from nipple to nipple; the longest can go to roughly ½" (1.5 cm) from the side seam of the garment. They should be placed so the final row falls about 1 to 2" (2.5 to 5 cm) below the widest point of your bust. Since a good rule of thumb is that the armhole shaping begins at the widest point of your bust, it follows that your short rows should be completed by 1 to 2" (2.5 to 5 cm) before the armhole shaping. The illustration at right shows where the finished short row shaping dart will appear on the front of a sweater.

Here is an example of the calculations, with my numbers in italics. *My gauge is 4 stitches and 6 rows = 1" (2.5 cm).*

1 Determine how many short rows you need: Multiply your personal measurement by your row gauge, and round down to the nearest even number. Divide by 2 (because short rows come in pairs). Call this number A. *I'd like to add 1 ½"* *(4 cm) of short rows, which turns into 9 rows, rounded down to 8. So my value for A is 4.*

2 Determine placement: In most cases, subtract 2" (5 cm) from the total hem-to-armhole length given in the pattern. This should be approximately 2" (5 cm) below the fullest part of your bust. If the fullest part of your bust is lower, subtract additional distance—you don't want the short row shaping over the fullest part of your bust! Call this length B. *In our example, my sweater is 12 ½" (32 cm) from hem to armhole, so I'll start working my short-row shaping when the sweater measures 10 ½" (26.5 cm) from the cast-on edge.*

Determine the number of stitches that will be "left alone" in between the shortest of the short rows:

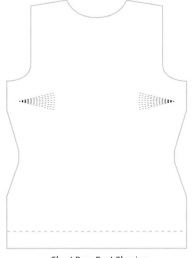

Short Row Bust Shaping

Short row bust shaping should always be located under the fullest part of the bust, where it won't be as visible.

## Swatching Short Rows

Before tackling short-row darts in a sweater, I strongly suggest you make a swatch to get comfortable with the method. With smooth, worsted weight yarn and a pair of needles of the appropriate size, CO 36 sts and work even in St st for 1" / 2.5 cm, ending with a WS row.

**Next row (RS):** Knit to last 5 sts, wrap and turn (see Special Techniques, page 159), leaving last 4 sts on left-hand needle.

**Next row (WS):** Purl to last 5 sts, wrap and turn, leaving last 4 sts on left-hand needle.

**Next row (RS):** Knit to 3 sts before the last wrapped stitch, wrap and turn.

**Next row (WS):** Purl to 3 sts before the last wrapped stitch, wrap and turn.

Repeat the last two rows twice more. You have worked 4 short row wraps per side, adding 8 rows total to the center 8 sts.

**Next row (RS):** Knit to end, working the wrapped sts with their wraps.

**Next row (WS):** Purl to end, working the wrapped sts with their wraps.

Continue in St st for an additional 1" / 2.5 cm, then BO all sts.

Your short row dart should make a very visible bump in your swatch when laying flat on a table, and if you look closely you should be able to see the trapezoidal shape of the dart as pictured on page 156. (For extra visibility, consider working the dart stitches in a contrasting color yarn!)

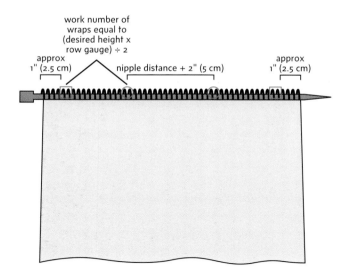

work number of
wraps equal to
(desired height x
row gauge) ÷ 2

approx
1" (2.5 cm)     nipple distance + 2" (5 cm)     approx
1" (2.5 cm)

This will be the placement of the stitches on the needle when working short rows. The distance between ☐ and ☐ is the longest short row you will work. The distance between ◯ and ◯ is the shortest short row you will work.

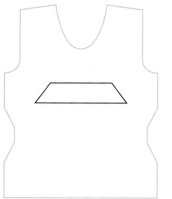

This will be the shape of the short-row dart, when completed.

3  Measure from nipple to nipple, add 2", and multiply by your stitch gauge. This is the number of stitches that will not be involved in the short row shaping in the middle of your sweater. Call this number C. *Let's say my nipple-to-nipple distance is 8" (20.5 cm). So we're leaving 40 stitches alone in my example.*

4  Determine the number of stitches on each side of the sweater that will be left alone: Take your stitch gauge and round up if necessary. Call this number D. *My stitch gauge is 4—no rounding up necessary!*

5  Calculate the number of stitches between short row wraps: Multiply D x 2 and add this to C, then subtract the resulting number from the total number of stitches in the front of the sweater. Divide this by 2; this is the total number of stitches over which you will work the short rows on each side (these are the stitches between ☐ and ◯ in the illustration at left). Divide that number by (A-1), and round down. This is the number of stitches you will work even before the short row wraps. Call this number E. *Okay, here's how this translates to my example: The total number of stitches on the front of my sweater is 72. I now subtract the stitches left alone on the sides (4 on each side—8 total) and the stitches left alone in the middle (40) from that total—giving me 24 stitches over which to work the short rows in total, 12 stitches on each side. I now divide that number by 3 (my value A from Step 1 minus 1). (The "minus 1" is for the stitch that is wrapped at the end of each short row. I will work 3 stitches before I wrap the next stitch.). The number of stitches in each short-row segment is 4; 3 stitches worked and 1 stitch wrapped.*

You are now ready to work your short rows. Work until your sweater measures B from the hem, ending with a WS row. On the next row, work until (D+1) stitches remain, wrap and turn. On the following row, work until (D+1) stitches remain, wrap and turn. Then, work until E stitches before the last wrapped stitch, wrap and turn. Continue in this manner until all of your

## Other Areas for Short Rows

The process for adding short rows to accommodate rounded shoulders, a perky backside, or a larger lower stomach is similar to the process for adding short rows to your bust. (These illustrations show you where to place the short rows in three scenarios).

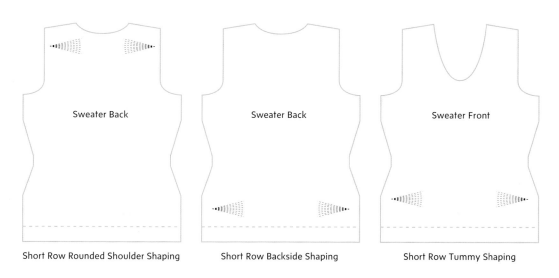

Short Row Rounded Shoulder Shaping          Short Row Backside Shaping          Short Row Tummy Shaping

short rows have been worked. Finally, work even across the full length of the next two rows, working your wraps together with the wrapped stitches to avoid any gaps.

*Here we go! I work my sweater until it measures 10 ½" (26.5 cm) from my cast-on edge, ending with a WS row. Here are the instructions for my short rows:*

*Short Row 1 (RS): Knit until 5 stitches remain, then wrap and turn.*

*Short Row 2: Purl until 5 stitches remain, then wrap and turn. I've worked 1 of my 4 short-row pairs.*

*Short Row 3: Knit until 4 stitches before the last wrapped stitch, wrap and turn.*

*Short Row 4: Purl until 4 stitches before the last wrapped stitch, wrap and turn.*

*Repeat Short Rows 3 and 4 twice—40 stitches remain unworked in the middle, and we've completed the short-row dart.*

*Next Row (RS): Knit to the end of the row, working the wraps together with their wrapped stitches.*

*Final Dart Row (WS): Purl to the end of the row, working the wraps together with their wrapped stitches.*

Voilà! You now have extra length on the front of your garment to accommodate your bust.

# ABBREVIATIONS

**BO** Bind off

**Circ** Circular

**Cn** Cable needle

**CO** Cast on

**Dpn** Double-pointed needle(s)

**K1-tbl** Knit 1 stitch through the back loop.

**K2tog** Knit 2 stitches together.

**K** Knit

**M1 or M1-l (make 1-left slanting)**
With the tip of the left-hand needle inserted from front to back, lift the strand between the 2 needles onto the left-hand needle; knit the strand through the back loop to increase 1 stitch.

**M1-p (make 1 purlwise-right slanting)**
With the tip of the left-hand needle inserted from back to front, lift the strand between the 2 needles onto the left-hand needle; purl the strand through the front loop to increase 1 stitch.

**M1-p-l (make 1 purlwise-left slanting)** With the tip of the left-hand needle inserted from front to back, lift the strand between the 2 needles onto the left-hand needle; purl the strand through the back loop to increase 1 stitch.

**M1-r (make 1-right slanting)**
With the tip of the left-hand needle inserted from back to front, lift the strand between the 2 needles onto the left-hand needle; knit the strand through the front loop to increase 1 stitch.

**P2tog** Purl 2 stitches together.

**Pm** Place marker

**P** Purl

**Psso (pass slipped stitch over)**
Pass the slipped stitch on the right-hand needle over the stitch(es) indicated in the instructions, as in binding off.

**Rnd(s)** Round(s)

**RS** Right side

**S2kp2** Slip the next 2 stitches together to the right-hand needle as if to knit 2 together, k1, pass the 2 slipped stitches over the Knit Stitch.

**Skp (slip, knit, pass)**
Slip the next stitch knitwise to the right-hand needle, k1, pass the slipped stitch over the knit stitch.

**Sk2p (double decrease)**
Slip the next stitch knitwise to the right-hand needle, k2tog, pass the slipped stitch over the stitch from the k2tog.

**Sm** Slip marker

**Ssk (slip, slip, knit)**
Slip the next 2 stitches to the right-hand needle one at a time as if to knit; return them to the left-hand needle one at a time in their new orientation; knit them together through the back loops.

**Ssp (slip, slip, purl)**
Slip the next 2 stitches to the right-hand needle one at a time as if to knit; return them to the left-hand needle one at a time in their new orientation; purl them together through the back loops.

**St(s)** Stitch(es)

**Tbl** Through the back loop

**Tog** Together

**WS** Wrong side

**Wrp-t** Wrap and turn (see Special Techniques—Short Row Shaping)

**Wyif** With yarn in front

**Yo** Yarnover

# SPECIAL TECHNIQUES

## Backward Loop CO

Make a loop (using a slip knot) with the working yarn and place it on the right-hand needle (first st CO), *wind yarn around thumb clockwise, insert right-hand needle into the front of the loop on thumb, remove thumb and tighten st on needle; repeat from * for remaining sts to be CO, or for casting on at the end of a row in progress.

## Cable CO

Make a loop (using a slip knot) with the working yarn and place it on the left-hand needle (first st CO), knit into slip knot, draw up a loop but do not drop st from left-hand needle; place new loop on left-hand needle; *insert the tip of the right-hand needle into the space between the last 2 sts on the left-hand needle and draw up a loop; place the loop on the left-hand needle. Repeat from * for remaining sts to be CO, or for casting on at the end of a row in progress.

## Provisional (Crochet Chain) CO

Using a crochet hook and smooth yarn (crochet cotton or ravel cord used for machine knitting), work a crochet chain with a few more chains than the number of sts needed; fasten off. If desired, tie a knot on the fastened-off end to mark the end that you will be unraveling from later. Turn the chain over; with a needle one size smaller than required for piece and working yarn, starting a few chains in from the beginning of the chain, pick up and knit 1 st in each bump at the back of the chain, leaving any extra chains at the end unworked.

Change to needle size required for project on first row.

When ready to work the live sts, unravel the chain by loosening the fastened-off end and 'unzipping' the chain, placing the live sts on a spare needle

## Short Row Shaping

Work the number of sts specified in the instructions, wrap and turn (wrp-t) as follows:

To wrap a knit st, bring yarn to the front (purl position), slip the next st purlwise to the right-hand needle, bring yarn to the back of work, return the slipped st on the right-hand needle to the left-hand needle purlwise; turn, ready to work the next row, leaving the remaining sts unworked. To wrap a purl stitch, work as for wrapping a knit st, but bring yarn to the back (knit position) before slipping the st, and to the front after slipping the st.

When short rows are completed, or when working progressively longer short rows, work the wrap together with the wrapped st as you come to it as follows:

If st is to be worked as a knit st, insert the right-hand needle into the wrap from be-low, then into the wrapped st; k2tog; if st is to be worked as a purl st, insert needle into the wrapped st, then down into the wrap; p2tog. (Wrap may be lifted onto the left-hand needle, then worked together with the wrapped st if this is easier.)

## Three-Needle BO

Place the sts to be joined onto two same-size needles; hold the pieces to be joined with the right sides facing each other and the needles parallel, both pointing to the right. Holding both needles in your left hand, using working yarn and a third needle the same size or one size larger, insert third needle into first st on front needle, then into first st on back needle; knit these 2 sts together; *knit next st from each needle together (2 sts on right-hand needle); pass first st over second st to BO 1 st. Repeat from * until 1 st remains on third needle; cut yarn and fasten off.

## Tubular CO

Using waste yarn and Backward Loop CO, CO half the number of sts required. Cut waste yarn. Using working yarn, [purl one row, knit one row] twice. With the right-hand needle, pick up the first half st in working yarn at the very beginning of the row and place it on the left-hand needle; k1-tbl. *P1; using the tip of the left-hand needle, pick up the next purl bump from the first row in working yarn and k1-tbl; repeat from * to the last st, p1. Carefully unpick waste yarn.

# ACKNOWLEDGMENTS

This book is dedicated to my mother. She taught me to knit, to persevere, to be thoughtful, and to believe that I can do anything.

A tremendous amount of work went into creating the book you have in your hands, and I've been very lucky to have had the best of help. First and foremost, thank you to my husband, Jonathan, and my sons Jacob and Daniel, who accepted the insanity of my writing a book while working full-time with complete aplomb. Jonathan made dinners and handled a tremendous amount of childcare, and all three shared my enthusiasm and never once told me that normal people don't knit at the breakfast table (and the dinner table, and in the restaurant, and at the movies, and at the museum). You guys are wonderful.

Thanks, too, to the amazing team at STC Craft: Liana Allday, my supremely patient editor; Karen Schaupeter, our incredibly creative stylist; Karen Pearson, who put everyone at ease and captured these beautiful photographs; our models—Ann, Jackie, Morgan, Ali, Jessica, Tessa, Jenn, Elora, and DeeDee—who made the room come alive with their loveliness; Sue McCain, the best tech editor ever; Caro Sheridan, Kirsten Kapur, and Elinor Brown, who contributed such wonderful designs; and Deb Barnhill, whose perfect stitches saved the day when the samples got overwhelming.

A "Who's Who" of yarn companies donated the materials for the incredible samples in this book. Thanks to Malabrigo, Quince and Company, Swans Island, Blue Sky Alpacas, Valley Yarns, SweetGeorgia Yarn, Louet, Lorna's Laces, Fibre Company, Lion Brand, Bijou Basin Ranch, The Plucky Knitter, Blue Moon Fiber Arts, Hand-Maiden Fine Yarns, Berroco, Brooklyn Tweed, Anzula, and Sundara Yarn.

A special thanks must go out to those who set me on the journey of sharing my experiences and thoughts on favorite sweaters. Thanks to Marlena Clark for encouraging me to take up knitting again when I was looking for a hobby; thanks to Caro Sheridan and Debbie Brisson for bringing me into the publishing world by getting me involved with their awesome book *Knitting It Old School*; thanks to Danielle Dugan and Diana Loren for (somewhat forcefully) suggesting that I write the Fit to Flatter tutorials; thanks to Beth Russell, Jackie Pawlowski, Kellee Middlebrooks, Caro, Debbie, and Marlena (again) for being a fantastic and patient sounding board for my ideas; thanks to Linda Roghaar, whose encouragement helped me present my idea in the best possible way. Thanks to the wonderful, amazing women who have read the Fit to Flatter tutorials, taken my class, and supported one another in the Ravelry group. You have been such a fantastic audience.

Finally, thanks to the Knitnighters, who helped me create the Fit to Flatter tutorials, modeled for endless photo shoots, improved my ideas, and are collectively the most incredible group of friends anyone could have. This book would not exist without you.